# Initial English Language
# Teacher Education

Also available from Bloomsbury

*Teacher Cognition and Language Education*, Simon Borg
*Teaching Teachers*, Angi Malderez
*Understanding Language Classroom Contexts*,
Martin Wedell and Angi Malderez

# Initial English Language Teacher Education

*International Perspectives on Research, Curriculum and Practice*

Edited by Darío Luis Banegas

Bloomsbury Academic
An imprint of Bloomsbury Publishing Plc

# B L O O M S B U R Y
LONDON · OXFORD · NEW YORK · NEW DELHI · SYDNEY

**Bloomsbury Academic**

An imprint of Bloomsbury Publishing Plc

50 Bedford Square          1385 Broadway
London                     New York
WC1B 3DP                   NY 10018
UK                         USA

**www.bloomsbury.com**

**BLOOMSBURY and the Diana logo are trademarks of Bloomsbury Publishing Plc**

First published 2017

**British Library Cataloguing-in-Publication Data**
A catalogue record for this book is available from the British Library.

ISBN: HB: 978-1-4742-9440-9
ePDF: 978-1-4742-9442-3
ePub: 978-1-4742-9441-6

**Library of Congress Cataloging-in-Publication Data**
A catalog record for this book is available from the Library of Congress.

Typeset by Deanta Global Publishing Services, Chennai, India
Printed and bound in Great Britain.

# Contents

# List of Figures

# List of Tables

# Notes on Contributors

**Mariel Amez** has been lecturer at the Second Language Teacher Education programme at the Institute of Higher Education 'Olga Cossettini', Rosario, Argentina, for twenty-five years. She has also coordinated and taught postgraduate programmes for EFL teachers, and is secretary to the Rosario Teacher Association (APrIR), Argentina. Her research interests include teacher education, literature, and online learning, on which she has published articles and given presentations both in Argentina and abroad.

**Carl Edlund Anderson** is professor in the Department of Foreign Languages and Cultures at the Universidad de La Sabana, Colombia. Currently editor-in-chief of the *Latin American Journal of Content and Language Integrated Learning* (LACLIL), his research interests include CLIL, rhetorical communication, indigenous languages, world Englishes and comparative philology.

**Darío Luis Banegas** is a curriculum developer and teacher educator with the Ministry of Education of Chubut, Argentina, and Associate Fellow at the University of Warwick, UK. He coordinates an IELTE programme in Esquel and facilitates professional development courses. He is also an online tutor at an online IELTE programme in Argentina. Darío is the founding editor of the *Argentinian Journal of Applied Linguistics*. His main interests are content and language integrated learning, IELTE and action research.

**Fernanda Coelho Liberali** is professor and researcher at the Post-Graduation Program in Applied Linguistics and Language Studies, at the Post-Graduation Program in Education: Teacher Education and in the English Department at the Pontific Catholic University of São Paulo (PUC–SP), Brazil. She holds a PhD in Applied Linguistics from the Postgraduate Program of Applied Linguistics, PUC-SP, Brazil.

**Liliana Cuesta Medina** is professor at the Department of Foreign Languages and Cultures, Universidad de La Sabana, Colombia, where she is also the

Academic Coordinator of the master's in language teaching – autonomous learning environments programme. She holds a PhD in English Philology from the Universidad Nacional de Educación a Distancia, UNED-Madrid, Spain. Her research areas include CALL, CLIL, academic writing, cyberbullying and self-regulation in blended/virtual learning environments, on which topics she has published in a number of indexed journals.

**Gabriel Diaz Maggioli** is the general coordinator of the Linguistic Policy Strategic Line at the National Administration of Public Education, Uruguay. He has been a teacher educator at the undergraduate and graduate level in Uruguay, Belize, Panama, the United States and Ecuador. He has also developed and participated in teacher education projects for the World Bank, the British Council, UNESCO and the US Department of State. He has been involved in professional development projects in the Americas, East Asia, Europe and the Middle East.

**Elsa Dobboletta** has been a teacher educator for fifteen years at I. E. S. Olga Cossettini in Rosario, Argentina, where she currently lectures on action research and English for Specific Purposes. She also works at Universidad Tecnológica Nacional, Argentina, teaching English in engineering courses. Her research interests include praxis and education, language and culture.

**Linda M. Hanington** is a language teacher and teacher educator with extensive experience in Europe and Southeast Asia. She is currently working at the National Institute of Education, Nanyang Technological University, Singapore. A focus of her current research is blended learning, both in the sense of blending online and face-to-face teaching and blending the development of teachers' personal language skills with an appreciation of methodology.

**Alice Kiai** is senior lecturer at the Catholic University of Eastern Africa, in Nairobi, Kenya, where she teaches and supervises Bachelor of Education (English) and Master of Arts (Applied Linguistics) students. She holds a BEd. (Linguistics and literature) and an MA (Linguistics) from the University of Nairobi, Kenya. Her doctorate is in English Language Teaching and Applied Linguistics from the University of Warwick, UK. Her research interests include second language acquisition, materials development and critical discourse analysis.

**Angelina Nduku Kioko** is professor of English and linguistics at the United States International University – Africa, Kenya. She holds a Bachelor of Education (English and literature), Master of Arts (linguistics) from the University of Nairobi, Kenya, and a PhD in Linguistics from Monash University, Australia. She has had close to thirty years' experience teaching English and Linguistics at university, and supervising postgraduate research. Her publications are in morpho-syntax, morpho-phonology, sociolinguistics and language learning materials. Her current research interests are in the field of language and education in multilingual contexts.

**Donna Lim** is lecturer with the National Institute of Education, Nanyang Technological University, Singapore. Her area of expertise is in developing literacy in primary schools and she currently teaches primary EL methodology courses. She holds a PhD in Learning Environments (particularly in the primary English classroom) from Curtin University, Perth, Australia. She has considerable teaching experience with young EL learners and enjoys working with primary schools to improve EL teaching and learning.

**Georgina Ma** has extensive international language teaching, language teacher training and educational management experience. She currently works for UniServices Limited, the commercial research, knowledge transfer and custom education company for the University of Auckland, New Zealand. She is completing her doctor of philosophy through the University of the Witwatersrand, South Africa.

**Graciela I. Manzur** is an ELT teacher and teacher educator. She has worked at teacher education programmes at Universidad Nacional de San Juan and Flacso, Argentina. She holds an MA in Teaching English as a Foreign Language from FUNIBER, and postgraduate studies on Education and New Technologies from Flacso. Her main areas of interests are online education, ICT, discourse analysis, narrative, systemic functional linguistics and appraisal theory.

**Jermaine S. McDougald** is director of the master's programs in English language teaching at the Department of Foreign Languages and Cultures, Universidad de La Sabana, Colombia. He is currently the managing editor of the *Latin American Journal of Content and Language Integrated Learning* (LACLIL), and his research interests include CLIL, young learners, teacher training and international education.

**Willy A. Renandya** is senior lecturer in the English Language and Literature department at the National Institute of Education, Nanyang Technological University, Singapore, where he currently teaches applied linguistics. He has extensive teaching experience in Asia and has published numerous articles and books. He is the co-editor of *Methodology in Language Teaching: An Anthology of Current Practice* (with Jack C. Richards, 2002, 2008) and author of *Motivation in the Language Classroom* (2014). He actively manages an online teacher professional development programme called Teacher Voices (http://www.facebook.com/groups/teachervoices/).

**Agustin Reyes Torres** is associate professor in the language and literature education department at the Universitat de València, Spain. His line of research focuses on the education and training of pre-service teachers of English, more specifically the implementation of reflective teaching, twenty-first century literacy and the use of children's literature in the foreign language class.

**Claudia Saraceni** is principal lecturer in Applied Linguistics at the University of Bedfordshire, UK, and has taught for more than twenty years at higher education level in the UK. She has gained extensive experience and expertise in the following fields: language teaching and learning, language acquisition, applied linguistics, L2 materials development, language teaching methodology and stylistic text analysis. She has been professionally recognized as a fellow by the Higher Education Academy. Claudia is also a member of MATSDA, the Materials Development Association, and of ALA, the Association for Language Awareness.

**Luis S. Villacañas de Castro** is assistant professor in the Language and Literature Education Department, Universitat de València, Spain. His research interests lie where critical pedagogy and ELT intersect. Apart from developing identity texts with university EFL student-teachers, he is taking part in several CAR projects with in-service EFL teachers working in primary schools of his region.

**Chunmei Yan** is associate professor at the School of Foreign Languages at Central China Normal University, China. As the director of the Language

Teacher Education Research Centre affiliated to the School, she has been leading various initiatives to improve the school's masters of education programme. She has been widely publishing her research in international journals in a variety of professional areas, such as TESOL methodology, cross-cultural communication, pre-service teacher education, in-service teacher education and school change.

**Cecilia A. Zemborain** is an ELT teacher, teacher educator and curriculum developer. She is also an online tutor for Lenguas Vivas for Grammar, Phonetics and the Pre-service Teacher Practicum modules. She is co-founder of a school project based on active learning and innovative pedagogical approaches and has recently completed a postgraduate course on education and ICT. Her main areas of interest are professional and ongoing teacher development, innovative teaching and autonomous learning.

# List of Abbreviations and Acronyms

BANA      *Britain, Australia and North America*

CELTA      *Certificate in English language teaching to adults*

CHAT      *Cultural Historical Activity Theory*

CPD      *Continuous professional development*

CPR      *Cardiopulmonary resuscitation*

CS      *Curriculum studies*

EFL      *English as a foreign language*

EL      *English language*

ELT      *English language teaching*

ELTE      *English language teacher education*

ESL      *English as a  second language*

IELTE      *Initial English language teacher education*

IES      Instituto de Educación Superior *(Institute of Higher Education)*

IMO      *In my opinion*

ITE      *Initial teacher education*

KNBS      *Kenya National Bureau of Statistics*

L1      *Language 1*

L2      *Language 2*

LACE      Linguagem em Atividades do Contexto Escolar

LEA      *Language experience approach*

LMS      *Learning management system*

LT      *Language teaching*

MKOS      *More knowledgeable others*

MLEA      *Modified Language Experience Approach*

MOE      *Ministry of Education*

MOOC      *Massive online open course*

| MT | *Mother tongue* |
|---|---|
| NIE | *National Institute of Education* |
| PPP | *Presentation-practice-production* |
| PSLE | *Primary school leaving examination* |
| SBA | *Shared book approach* |
| SCT | *Sociocultural theory* |
| SD | *Standard deviation* |
| SES | *Socio-economic status* |
| SLA | *Second language acquisition* |
| SLTE | *Second language teacher education* |
| SRL | *Self-regulated learning* |
| ST | *Student-teacher* |
| STELLAR | *Strategies for English language learning and reading* |
| TE | *Teacher education* |
| TEFL | *Teaching English as a foreign language* |
| TEP | *Teacher education programme* |
| TESOL | *Teaching English to speakers of other languages* |
| TOTS | *Teacher of teachers* |
| TP | *Teaching practice* |
| ZPD | *Zone of proximal development* |

# Introduction

Darío Luis Banegas

Not long ago, I had the following conversation with my ten-year-old niece, Lourdes:

> Lourdes: 'Uncle, I want to be a teacher when I grow up.'
> Darío: 'Sounds fantastic. But what kind of teacher? A school teacher? An Art teacher?'
> Lourdes: 'I'd like to be a primary school teacher. But I think I will be a teacher of English. I like English at school.'
> Darío: 'A teacher like me? You'll inherit my books. Why a teacher of English?'
> Lourdes: 'I want to travel the world, like you do.'

The motivations to become a teacher of English seem clear to my niece. Becoming a teacher of English or any other language can take you to different territories, both metaphorically and literally. Following the unoriginal metaphor of travelling, we can envisage language teacher education as a journey through which we develop continually in different directions. Although such a journey is far from linear, it has a beginning. Where does our journey begin? Do we need a passport? Stamps? Like Lourdes, and for all of us, this journey began at school when we were primary school learners or even earlier. And there are other learners who go through non-institutional and informal language practices. In one way or another, we have all been learners, and our teaching trajectories and biographies inscribed in the *specificities* of our contexts start there: a classroom in kinder or primary school. People can spend around fifteen years as learners before entering a higher education institution to start, for example, formal initial English language teacher education (IELTE).

The aim of this edited collection is to understand some of the processes and experiences that teacher educators and teacher learners undergo in their initial teacher education journey in less researched settings. In this journey, we wish to concentrate on the voices of teacher educators and teacher learners. Thus, the book adopts a bottom-up approach and democratic stance as we seek to examine what they think, feel and do in the different spheres that initial teacher education entails. The contributors come to share how IELTE is approached in less represented settings internationally. My colleagues come from Argentina, Brazil, China, Colombia, Kenya, Singapore, South Africa, Spain, the UK and Uruguay.

## Initial English language teacher education

Second language teacher education (SLTE) can be broadly configured into two vaguely temporalized territories: (1) pre-service/initial teacher education and (2) in-service teacher education (Edge and Mann 2013). The literature offers recent edited collections that attest to the growing, yet limited, interest in the field in both territories worldwide and the complex, sometimes tense, transitions between them (Burns and Richards 2009; Farrell 2015c; Johnson and Golombek 2011; Wright and Beaumont 2015).

In an extensive review of SLTE in BANA countries (Britain, Australia and North America), Wright (2010) refers to those programmes and activities that occur before we gain our first experiences as teachers. In this edited book, IELTE is used to refer to those programmes with different lengths and curricula offered by the state and private higher education sectors to produce qualified teachers of English primarily for state-run educational systems. I personally avoid the use of *pre-service*, as in my experience as a teacher educator in Argentina IELTE programmes are taken by people who have recently graduated from secondary school as well as others who have other (teaching) degrees, for example in Biology, or have taught English in formal education for some time without a teaching qualification (see also Dick 2013).

IELTE encompasses a wide range of undergraduate programmes at both tertiary and university institutions. In terms of time we can find, at one end, those that last a few weeks such as Cambridge CELTA or Trinity CertTESOL (see Anderson 2015) and, at the other end, those that usually last between three and four years (see Banegas 2014; Barahona 2016; Debreli 2012). In terms of delivery mode, face-to-face seems to be the norm; nevertheless, online distance and blended programmes can also be found worldwide as illustrated in Banegas and Manzur Busleimán (2014) or England (2012).

IELTE actors receive a wide range of names. Those who teach future teachers are called teacher trainers, lecturers, teachers of teachers (ToTs) and teacher educators among other terms. Conversely, those who are in the process of becoming teachers are usually referred to as trainees, teacher trainees, teacher-learners, future teachers and student-teachers, to name a few. Regarding terminology and underpinning concepts, Richards (3002015: 697–8) makes a helpful distinction between *teacher training* and *teacher development*. The former 'involves providing novice teachers with the practical skills and knowledge needed to prepare them for their initial teaching experience', while the latter 'serves a longer-term goal and seeks to facilitate growth of the teacher's general understanding of teaching'. Burns and Richards (2009) have suggested that SLTE has shifted from teacher training to teacher development as the theorization of context-situated practice. It is the aim of this edited book to show that shift and encourage institutions to move from training to development in the quest for sustainability and vision in teacher education.

## Theoretical perspectives in IELTE

As mentioned above, IELTE is materialized through concrete preparation programmes. The delineation of an IELTE programme and curriculum entails agreement on the theoretical foundations and resulting knowledge base, which guides the decisions and shapes that each particular programme features. At a theoretical level, the current IELTE territory is characterized by three broad interrelated perspectives: sociocultural theory (SCT), cognitivism and criticality. The chapters in this book are mostly based on the first perspective given the current interest in the social turn in language education. However, readers will find traces of the other two views discussed to a lesser extent.

Based on a Vygotskian view of SCT, different authors adhere to the spread of this perspective in language education (Lantolf and Poehner 2014), IELTE (Burns and Richards 2009; Johnson 2009; Johnson and Golombek 2011, 1782016) and beyond. Although SCT is widely discussed in the literature, it still captivates researchers and educators in general. According to Swain, Kinnear and Steinman (2015), SCT is both new and old, and they define it as a theory 'about how humans think through the creation and use of mediating tools'. To these authors, Vygotskian SCT, essentially a theory of mind with connections between internal and external processes, has been enriched by the work of scholars who explore pedagogical contexts as ecosystems, that is, an ecological approach to language learning and teaching (Kramsch 2008).

Furthermore, Swain, Kinnear and Steinman (2015) observe that SCT is undergoing a narrative turn in education as teachers keep track of their stories and lived experiences through journals and participation in focus group interviews. In this regard, the authors add

> SCT seeks to understand mental development and learning by considering not only the contextual specifics but also the process over time, rather than focusing only on a particular moment of spoken or written production.

Thus, there is an interest within SCT in IELTE in the power of narrative inquiry to understand the transformation and development of the identities of future teachers as well as novice teachers (Sarasa 2013). In addition, it is observed that we should examine the teaching-learning relationships that unfold in practice and the practicum, and the mediation and interactions explored by teacher educators in supporting teaching (Diaz Maggioli 2013, 2014; Golombek and Klager 2015; Johnson 2015; Johnson and Golombek 2011). It is because of this narrative turn in SCT and the opportunities it affords that we endorse SCT in this book.

Linked to SCT, cognitivism finds its way in IELTE through teacher cognition, defined as what teachers think, know and believe (Borg 2006b). Those under a teacher cognition perspective suggest that IELTE programmes should be further informed by teacher cognition research of teacher-learners. It is believed that a higher presence of teacher cognition findings can help understand teacher-learners' biographies and how they conceptualize and enact their teaching practices. In this line, Kubanyiova and Feryok (2015) propose that teachers' inner lives and ecologies of practice be studied through the concept of intentionality without disregarding the context in which SLTE occurs. In a similar vein, Golombek (2015) embraces SCT but believes that SLTE should also scrutinize language teacher educators' emotions, cognitions and activity. Through self-inquiry and journal writing, the author reveals how cognitions are examined between a teacher educator and a group of teacher-learners. The author (Golombek 2015: 481) concludes by saying that 'it is not just consistency between our rhetoric and practice as teacher educators which can promote teacher learner professional development, but what we do in response to inconsistencies in our rhetoric and practice as well'.

Last, following Hawkins and Norton (2009), criticality in IELTE aims to challenge dominant ideologies and the perpetuation of inequality. In this respect, critical IELTE takes a Freiran stance and seeks to empower teacher educators and future teachers as agents of change by promoting pedagogies that respond to their local contexts and cultures (Banegas and Velázquez 2014; Rixon 2015). The ultimate aim of such pedagogies is educational and social change. Through liberatory education, people will be in a position to transform their reality and challenge oppression. Under this perspective, we can include the presence of interculturality, inclusive education and action research in IELTE programmes (Amez 2015; Coady, Harper and De Jong 2015; Mugford 2015; Porto 2010; Villacañas de Castro 2014a, 2015) as they are deeply rooted in context and aim at creating spaces for reflection underpinned by autonomy, social justice (see Esau 2013) and equality.

## The knowledge base and main themes

Coherent with a sociocultural perspective, Johnson (2009) proposes a revised knowledge base of IELTE consisting of three broad interrelated areas:

1. What L2 teachers need to know in terms of the content of L2 teacher education.
2. The pedagogies that are taught in IELTE programmes.
3. The practices enacted by teacher educators to deliver areas 1 and 2 above.

As a response for change in the knowledge base, Zhang and Zhan (2014: 569) define it as 'the repertoire of knowledge, expertise, skills and understanding that teachers need to possess in order to become effective in their profession'. The authors propose six categories: content knowledge, pedagogical knowledge, pedagogical content knowledge, contextual knowledge, continuity with past experiences and support knowledge. Such categories may remind us of Shulman's (1987) seminal work, but they show a sociocultural angle that includes student-teachers' biographies conceptualized as *continuity with past experiences* and the need to mentor them, termed as *support knowledge*, as they move into teaching as novice teachers (see also Mann and Tang 2012).

The second and third areas listed above reveal two major concerns. On the one hand, there is a need to engage in congruent practices in IELTE so that theory and practice are experienced as a complex unit by teacher-learners. In other words, those pedagogies, approaches and methods, such as communicative language teaching or task-based learning (Richards 2015), that are taught in programmes to be then transpolated to learners need to be experienced by future teachers in IELTE classrooms. On the other hand, this calls for IELTE programmes that are not solely based on knowledge from other disciplines or authors located in dominant markets. It is high time that IELTE programmes drew on what teachers do and observe, theorized practices, teacher cognitions, action research and reflective teaching as it happens in IELTE and language teaching contexts with all kinds of learners.

A look at teacher educators' practices in IELTE could be systematized through research paradigms that help us investigate how teacher educators enact and engage in those approaches that are hoped to be found in classrooms populated by children, teenagers and adults. With this opportunity to analyse, reflect and act upon practices in IELTE, special attention should be given to action research in pre-service teacher education. Following Güngör (2016), action research can help bridge the gap between 'theoretical considerations and classroom realities' (p. 137) and 'reveal more insights from local teaching contexts to learn from divergent experiences and to embrace contextual differences more gently in various language teacher education programmes' (p. 149).

I shall refer to three recent studies in particular, hoping that they can help us see the role of action/teacher research in the formal initial education of future teachers. Action research in IELTE can promote reflections and collaboration mediated by technology. For example, in an action research project carried out with pre-service teachers in Poland and Romania, Wach (2015) concludes that collaborative learning, reflection on EFL teaching and learning can be attained through action research projects across universities. The author highlights that

> the main didactic implication derived from this study is that involving students
> in cross-cultural collaboration online, and not only in EFL didactics courses,
> appears to be a relevant teaching procedure. (p. 42)

In a study carried out with pre-service teachers at an elementary education programme in the United States, Crawford-Garrett et al. (2015) examined the process behind an action research project carried out by three pre-service teachers as part of the capstone assignment for the programme. Based on the positive outcome of the experience and data analysis, the authors assert that action research allowed the pre-service teachers to draw on their lived experiences. Furthermore, they (Crawford-Garrett et al. 2015: 493) state that

> the action research process fostered a deep engagement with certain ideas
> and allowed the pre-service teachers a space to develop these ideas fully and
> test nascent theories about teaching and learning. Moreover, these in-depth

explorations positioned the pre-service teachers as knowledgeable practitioners and agentive actors able to design and reflect on specific practices and justify their use in various contexts.

In a similar vein, Ulvik and Riese (2016) investigated the impact of doing action research with a group of pre-service teachers in Norway. According to the results obtained through focus groups, interviews and questionnaires (op. cit.: 450),

> the experience offered a possibility to challenge themselves and to try something out that expanded their horizon and made them reflect in depth and become more critical. They broadened their knowledge regarding specific problems, and they learned about themselves.

It was not only student-teachers who assessed the experience as positive; their teacher educators too noted that doing action research was seen as a professional development opportunity, a chance to take risks and a possibility to initiate collaboration between them and their student-teachers (see also Castro Garcés and Martínez Granada 2016).

Nonetheless, the authors discuss the limitations and threats of introducing action research in pre-service teacher education. They suggest that there should be enough time built into the programme to facilitate reflection and discussion of the links between theory and practice in teaching. They also assert that inquiry should be integrated as a 'natural part of teacher education'. In other words, research should become part of the knowledge base itself and be linked to the context of those who engage with it.

Such a call for a revitalized and contextualized knowledge base in IELTE, which is also research-informed, goes hand in hand with an interest in issues such as change, process, context and interculturality in SLTE (Wright and Beaumont 2015). However, other themes are also important in the current IELTE territory. I particularly refer to teacher-learners' beliefs, novice teaching transition, identity, motivation and curriculum innovation.

Several studies focus on teacher-learners' beliefs in language teaching and learning prior and after exposure to courses on ELT methodologies and the practicum during their IELTE programmes (Borg et al. 2015; Çapan 2014; Debreli 2012; Lee 2015). Studies concur that future teachers' beliefs are shaped by their biographies as learners and, to a lesser extent, by IELTE programmes, but these enter a conflicting zone when they compare the pedagogies taught in the programme with lessons observed at schools. This tension remains after they graduate, and therefore the passage from teacher-learners to novice teachers has received attention by authors who suggest that the practicum and the institutions should offer novice teachers support during their first teaching experiences (Farrell 2012).

Notions around novice teaching and the perceived disjuncture between IELTE preparation and practice in real classrooms are firmly tied to the practicum in IELTE and the motivational dynamics that illuminate teachers' trajectories and *under-construction* identities. In this regard, IELTE programmes need to offer additional spaces to discuss and reflect on teacher motivation and identity with the aim of helping teacher-learners create a sustainable teacher vision of themselves (Kubanyiova 2014; Kumazawa 2013).

Last, more recent publications such as Edge and Mann (2013) and Johnson (2013) examine in-context innovation in IELTE and encourage the development of revised teacher educator practices that help build congruence within IELTE programmes. Along these lines, the incorporation of online platforms and applications (Bonadeo 2013; Massi et al. 2012), the updatedness and localization of reading materials (Banegas 2015) and the revision of IELTE curricula from a critical perspective (Gimenez et al. 2016) to support teacher learning are envisaged as innovative undertakings. However, we should remind ourselves that innovation is context-bound and it requires systematization, reflection and evaluation.

As I have concluded elsewhere (Banegas 2016),

> Innovation and change in teacher education curriculum development are vital, dynamic, and necessary processes. These, it seems, need to occur progressively and with the full endorsement of all actors involved. Participation and ongoing programme evaluation are necessary to examine the extent to which such changes are implemented, challenged, created and re-created in practice depending on a whole array of contextual factors.

## Structure of the book

Drawing on other perspectives such as criticality, but primarily on SCT, the twelve chapters in this book address the following issues through the eyes of future teachers and teacher educators: future teachers' beliefs, the practicum and the tensions between theory and practice, the role of feedback, teacher development and identity, critical pedagogies, online teacher education and intercultural awareness. Such topics are discussed through research, changes in curriculum development and, above all, practice.

In Chapter 1, Amez and Doboletta discuss to what extent the perceptions, beliefs and priorities of a group of pre-service and novice English language teachers in Argentina are aligned with discussions regarding curricular reform at the time of writing (2016). They highlight that participants' observations, made from an experiential and holistic perspective, stress the importance of a dialectical relationship between the institutional ILTE curriculum and primary and secondary schools' social and cultural context.

In Chapter 2, Yan examines how student-teachers' engagement with learning of coursework can be enhanced through an action research project in an EFL pre-service course offered by a pre-service teacher education programme based in a national teacher education university in China. Yan's study highlights the necessity of teacher educators strategically scaffolding learning platforms to enhance student-teachers' engagement with their academic learning.

In Chapter 3, Lim, Hanington and Renandya examine IELTE provision for those preparing to teach in lower primary schools in the light of recent developments in Singapore. They particularly focus on the 2010 English Language Syllabus and the implementation of the Strategies for English Language Learning and Reading (STELLAR) programme.

Chapter 4, authored by Kiai and Kioko, captures the voices of six English language student-teachers and six English language teacher educators from two Kenyan universities with the aim of examining the alignment of university teacher education programmes to the secondary school curriculum, discussing English language teacher education in Kenyan universities within the framework of SCT, and highlighting issues that Kenyan university English language teacher educators need to address in their research and curriculum innovation.

Chapter 5 comes from South Africa. Ma reports on a research project done as a small-scale, context-specific needs analysis aimed to provide a 'snap-shot' of the macro aspects of practices in post-observation feedback. Taking stock of the state of post-observation feedback on a pre-service English as a Foreign Language teacher education course is a useful way to better understand the discourse and provide some empirical basis on areas of post-observation feedback that could be improved and developed in the future.

In Chapter 6, Diaz Maggioli from Uruguay outlines a potential framework for the development of online courses that blend conceptual understanding with experiential learning in IELTE. The chapter lays out the theoretical background, which includes the role of technology in initial teacher education; the nature of technology-mediated teacher learning; pathways for the construction of technology-mediated learning opportunities; the incorporation of experiential learning through the use of technology; and the assessment of teacher learning.

Chapter 7, authored by Manzur and Zemborain, focuses on the trajectories of three IELTE student-teachers and their practicum in the south of Argentina. The qualitative data reveal that the student-teachers' online learning experiences merge with their past histories as students of face-to-face education. The authors conclude that such experiences shape their L2 student-teachers' views of teaching and learning and, in turn, the way they live and interpret their teaching practices.

In Chapter 8, Cuesta Medina, Anderson and McDougald discuss preliminary findings from a study of teacher educators of Colombian student-teachers of English with regard to characteristics and habits regarding self-regulated learning. They conclude that teacher education should be revitalized through specific changes to existing paradigms, practices and the language curricula, especially during initial teacher and graduate education, as well as in the early years of teaching.

From Colombia we travel to Spain through Chapter 9 in which Reyes Torres analyses his teacher education practices. He believes that for heterogeneous and multilingual groups of students to work together and learn, reflection is the common ground. The chapter illustrates the development of pre-service teachers by means of a guided and focused discussion of specific readings on both reflective practice and teaching English in the primary classroom.

In Chapter 10, Claudia Saraceni analyses the interface between teacher training and teacher development, focusing on the main differences between these two aspects in the context of IELTE at a UK institution. The author introduces an integrated and reflective approach to academic practice, based on an action research project for teacher development. The chapter offers practical suggestions for teacher critical awareness development.

Chapter 11 takes us back to Spain. Villacañas de Castro discusses the implementation of a project consisting of the creation of video identity texts by fifty-one EFL student-teachers to work on identity transformation and emancipation. The aim was to give them the chance to experience critical forms of EFL education that contrasted sharply with those they had been exposed to in the past, and which had shaped their inherited educational common sense.

We end our journey in Brazil with Chapter 12. Coelho Liberali analyses the relationship between globalization, superdiversity, language learning and teacher education in Brazil. The chapter is based on the *Multicultural Education*

*Project*, a research project that works with pre-service multilingual teacher education (English-Portuguese and French-Portuguese) and is organized as a network of actions involving planning, conducting and evaluating teaching-learning activities in a multilingual perspective.

Each chapter ends with 'questions for change'. Why do the authors finish their chapters with questions? Readers will find that each contribution is a story that can resonate with other contexts. Therefore, the discussions and conclusions shared by the authors may serve as a trampoline to reflect and act in our own IELTE settings. This is why authors have been invited to pose some guiding questions to encourage reflection and action.

As the book comes to a close, I put forward some concluding thoughts and outline possible future directions in IELTE programmes and research. First, I refer to student-teacher engagement, identity formation and teacher educators' development as growing dimensions in IELTE enactment. Second, I discuss, in particular, collaborative action research as one way of strengthening the links between formative practices and research. Last, I invite teacher educators to engage in programme evaluation, informed curriculum innovation, online IELTE pedagogies and multidisciplinarity at the grassroots level.

We hope that you will find yourself represented through the pages that follow and that the voices of the teacher educators and future teachers recorded here will resonate with your own contexts and trajectories. Before I go, I would like to thank Robert Wright for his tremendous help and support with the preparation and proofreading of the manuscript, which has led to this book. I would also like to thank María Brauzzi and Kasia Figiel from Bloomsbury for their insights and guidance.

# 1

# Pre-service and Novice Teachers' Perceptions on Second Language Teacher Education

Mariel Amez and Elsa Dobboletta

## Objectives

1. Explore the stated beliefs of teacher-learners and novice English language teachers in the Teacher Education Programme (TEP) in Rosario (Santa Fe, Argentina) regarding the knowledge base of Second Language Teacher Education (SLTE).
2. Examine to what extent such beliefs are congruent with current research on the knowledge base of SLTE and can inform local proposals for initial English language teacher education (IELTE) curriculum reform.
3. Reflect on what directions should be followed in the ongoing curricular reform process for IELTE to address the demands of local context.

## Introduction

Curriculum reform in education is characterized by its complexity, which has often meant that changes planned by policymakers have had little impact on classroom practices (Freeman 2013; Kirkland and Sutch 2009; Wedell 2009). In this vein, current studies on the curriculum for IELTE have highlighted the importance of acknowledging local contexts and teachers' professional identities as part of the process of reform (Franson and Holliday 2009; Johnson 2009; Smolcic 2011) as well as of considering teachers' knowledge and beliefs to conceptualize the knowledge base of SLTE (Borg 2006a, 2009; Graves 2009; Tarone and Allwright 2005).

In Argentina, as the National Education Act passed in 2006 dictates the extension of compulsory education to encompass secondary school (Ruiz and Schoo 2014), educators meet new challenges to cater for diversity and achieve inclusion. The case of IELTE requires a transition from English Language Teaching (ELT) for a small elite to the provision of ELT for everyone. In addition, national language policy (see Banegas 2014; Ibáñez and Lothringer 2013; Porto 2015; Porto, Montemayor-Borsinger and López-Barrios 2016) advocates a plurilingual and intercultural perspective and a reflective and research-engaged teaching pedagogy, thus widening the scope of change to be introduced.

The process of IELTE curriculum reform in Santa Fe, our province, is still ongoing at the time of writing this chapter. Whereas on the whole this has been a participatory process involving policy makers, ad hoc specialist committees, IELTE heads of department and teacher educators in current programmes, in contrast the voices of students in TEP and those of recent graduates have been acknowledged perfunctorily or not at all. Yet it falls on them to carry out the implementation of the curricular change in primary and secondary education, which has already been put into effect.

The aim of this study is twofold: to explore the beliefs of advanced teacher-learners and novice English language teachers in Rosario (Santa Fe, Argentina) regarding the knowledge base of SLTE and to analyse to what extent such beliefs are congruent with current research on the topic. We believe that the conclusions can prove a welcome, contextually bound contribution to the curriculum under construction, as they allow us to glean the strengths and weaknesses of the current TEP and the demands of classroom teaching. Furthermore, they can contribute to the body of research on context-specific SLTE curriculum practices, which Nguyen (2013: 37) characterizes as scarce, though the apparent dearth in this respect could perhaps be attributed to limited accessibility to publications from non-central contexts.

## A multidimensional conceptualization of the knowledge base of SLTE

The comprehensive conceptualization of the teaching knowledge base by Shulman as 'a codified and codifiable aggregation of knowledge, skill, understanding, and technology, of ethics and disposition, of collective responsibility' (1987: 4) sets the grounds for most of the subsequent research on teacher education. He submits that the sources for such knowledge are to be found not only in discipline-specific scholarship, in the materials and settings of the institutionalized educational processes and in the practice itself, but also in 'research on schooling, social organizations, human learning, teaching and development, and the other social and cultural phenomena that affect what teachers do' (1987: 8). The seven seminal categories he proposes (content knowledge, general pedagogical knowledge, curriculum knowledge, pedagogical content knowledge, knowledge of learners, of contexts and of educational ends, purposes, and values) have been widely examined with reference to IELTE programmes (e.g. in Latin America in Álvarez Valencia 2009; Banegas 2009; Fandiño 2013).

The knowledge base of SLTE has been the subject of extensive research in its own right, with Graves (2009) as a case in point. She sets apart the knowledge base of SLTE, that is, what the education of language teachers involves, from the knowledge base of language teaching (LT), which refers to the education of language learners, though she suggests that both are inextricably linked. She draws attention to the fact that different conceptualizations of language as well as the teacher-learners' identities as L1 or L2 speakers will determine differences in the curriculum of SLTE and that the rationale for the inclusion of content should be its relevance to language teaching. Yet she argues, from a sociocultural perspective, that 'the issue is not what is relevant in the curriculum but who makes it relevant, how and why' (2009: 120).

Also from a sociocultural standpoint, Freeman and Johnson (1998) highlight the commonalities between the knowledge base for general teacher education and for SLTE. They focus on the activity of teaching and put forward the existence of three interrelated domains: the teacher as learner of teaching, the social context and the pedagogical process. At the crossroads with cognitivism, they posit that student-teachers' prior experiences of learning (both in early schooling and during SLTE) as well as their wants, needs and expectations have a key role in shaping the knowledge base.

In more recent studies, the contextual dimension has gained prominence. Johnson (2009: 114) advocates the need to 'take into account the social, political, economic and cultural histories that are "located" in the contexts where L2 teachers learn and teach' to prevent the imposition of external methods and recipes, while at the same time challenging local constraints through engagement with wider professional discourses and practices in processes of reflective inquiry. In this line, the discussion of the knowledge base of SLTE is further enriched with the contributions of critical and postmethod pedagogy. Franson and Holliday (2009: 40), for example, argue for a decentred approach to 'recognize and explore the cultural complexity and diversity' within the personal experiences of teachers and learners, as opposed to an essentialist view of culture abounding in stereotypes.

Richards (2010) further discusses the notion of context, which he understands to encompass both structural influences (e.g. school culture, management style and physical resources available) and personal influences (including learners, other teachers, even parents). He also delves into two dimensions of professionalism: one that is institutionally prescribed and refers to qualifications as well as a commitment to attaining high standards, and another that is independent and concerns the teachers' reflection on their own values, beliefs and practices. After IELTE, he posits, SLTE continues as a process of socialization in a particular context as the teacher becomes a member of a community of practice.

The role of socialization experiences, in fact, is another aspect that currently features prominently in the literature. Farrell (2009) draws attention to the part they play in the first years of teaching to consolidate teachers' beliefs about language teaching and learning. Conway, Murphy and Rath (2009) espouse the view that learning to teach should occur within a continuum of teacher education spanning initial, induction and in-service education and development, and they document a number of countries that have set up quality induction programmes. The purpose of such programmes is to assist novice teachers to address the challenges of their early years without being drawn into dominant practices of the professional context and to strengthen their commitment to lifelong learning. In order to bridge the gap between SLTE and the realities of the school classroom where novice teachers take their first steps, a number of options have been described in Farrell (2015a), all of which revolve around the need to integrate theory and practice through the development of principled reflection by teacher-learners and novice teachers.

Yet other directions found in recent analyses refer to the consideration of changing local circumstances instead of the pursuit of an all-encompassing static model for the knowledge base of LT to be replicated worldwide. Álvarez Valencia (2009), for example, postulates the existence of multiple, context-bound knowledge bases in dialogic interaction, which he illustrates through the metaphor of an orchestra with the teacher as conductor who, through reflection, decides what to play and how to play appropriately for a given audience and setting. In the same vein, Nguyen (2013: 37) observes that 'the development of the knowledge base of SLTE needs to be viewed as changing, contextualized and situated', and Fandiño (2013) recommends that IELTE programmes should undertake the development and improvement of national (or even regional) knowledge bases by infusing inquiry into daily practice in order to respond to the educational needs and interests of the community. It is in this light that we undertook the study discussed below.

## The ELT education scenario in Argentina

IELTE programmes in Argentina are generally undergraduate qualifications (Banfi 2013), which in Rosario are taught in three higher education institutions following a common provincial curriculum implemented in 2001 and currently undergoing an amendment process. Students who want to become teachers of English in secondary schools need to complete a four-year degree course, totalling 2,880 contact hours distributed in over thirty subjects, most of which are taught annually (from April to November). These subjects can be grouped in three fields: general pedagogy, or, in Shulman's terms, general pedagogical and curriculum knowledge, (delivered in L1 by education specialists, with 18 per cent of the curriculum load), linguistic competence and content-specific pedagogy, related to Shulman's content and pedagogical content knowledge, (delivered in L2 by teachers of English, with 68 per cent of the curriculum load) and teaching practice (14%) realized in four teaching practice workshops, the last of which features the practicum in tandem with a small-scale research project, which address issues encompassed in Shulman's knowledge of learners, of contexts and of educational ends, purposes and values. The main purpose of these workshops is to provide practice in reflective inquiry as well as to coordinate the organization and management of gradual practical experiences and the liaison between the TEP institution and schools.

Upon graduation, entry to the profession in the state sector is contingent on a selection process based exclusively on credentials and service period (see Muscará 2013; Doberti and Rigal 2014). In the case of EFL, given that vacancies are allocated per class, each totalling usually three contact hours a week, newly qualified teachers stand in competition with senior teachers who have already achieved tenure and are looking to increase the number of classes they teach.

As a result, novice teachers have to resign themselves to be summoned at short notice to fill in for absentee teachers for a few days at a time in schools unknown to them, as the only path to build a service period, while embarking on ministry-approved courses which provide credentials that will make them more eligible in the future. Terigi (2009: 137) uses the term *phased entry* (*inicio escalonado* in Spanish) to refer to this process, which she sees as a stumbling block to effective induction or mentoring. The private sector, in contrast, offers a number of options ranging from private primary and secondary schools to language schools or in-company teaching, where entry and permanence may be subject not only to performance and achievement but also to connections and personality, and where working conditions and stability vary widely. As can be seen, no provisions are made for an initial, induction and in-service continuum in SLTE (Conway et al. 2009), while the demands of the institutionally prescribed dimension of professionalism discussed by Richards (2010) can prove conflicting at times.

## The research experience: Recording their voices

We set this study at IES N° 28 Olga Cossettini in Rosario, Santa Fe, where we ourselves graduated and where we have been teacher educators for over twenty years. This institution offers the oldest IELTE programme in the city, dating back to 1936, but as mentioned above, the current curriculum under revision was implemented in 2001. Our role as researchers can then be described as 'socially located' (Holliday 2007), since we are bound to a place, time and culture. Our research process was guided by the tenets of the interpretative inquiry paradigm, whose core endeavour is 'to understand the subjective world of human experience' (Cohen, Manion and Morrison 2000: 21).

We contacted the participants of the study by email and enlisted their voluntary participation. We administered two similar web-based self-report survey forms: one was addressed to student-teachers who had already completed their practicum and were about to graduate, and the other one to novice teachers who had graduated within the previous two years. The survey combined quantitative data, in which the respondents rated their TEP on a four-point scale and indicated their employment status, with qualitative data in the form of open-ended questions that can be grouped as follows:

1. What should a good EFL teacher know?

2. Why did you rate your TEP as you did? What declarative or procedural contents should be added, removed or intensified in a curriculum reform of the TEP? What challenges do you face at work? Do you feel prepared to meet them? (the last two only for novice teachers)

We would like to point out that the classification of respondents into teacher-learners and novice teachers does not intend to sample opposing perspectives on the issues under discussion but rather displays a continuum along the situated academic and workplace domains. The analysis of the answers has been carried out considering both groups part of a 'small culture' sample, which, following Holliday, refers to 'those aspects of social cohesion, values and artifacts that distinguish one social group from another; only a small culture can provide the network of meaning for the social phenomena found as data' (2007: 34).

A total of twenty-one (N = 21) responses from student-teachers and twenty-one (N = 21) from novice teachers were analysed. Twenty respondents in each group were working as EFL teachers and most student-teachers (sixteen) and all graduates did so for more than ten hours a week. Even though all of them expressed their aspiration to work in state education, at the time only five graduates and two teacher-learners (who held other degrees, one as a translator and one as an EFL primary school teacher) had been able to secure a teaching position.

## In their own voices: The knowledge base of LT

The question 'What should a good EFL teacher know?' was designed to identify key issues in personal constructs about the knowledge base of LT that participants had developed in the interaction between their prior language learning experiences and the current TEP.

No significant differences could be appreciated in the answers from both groups, probably due to the fact that answers were informed by the respondents' personal experience as teachers, even though the statements varied regarding wording and length:

An English language teacher should be a language expert and have a thorough knowledge of the language system. But she should not overlook the fact that her role is to teach; therefore she should keep updated in methodology, philosophy, pedagogy and new trends in education. I believe that a good teacher is constantly looking to better herself and develop her skills to do her work.

[A good EFL teacher should have an] excellent command of the language, knowledge of the L2 system and culture, flexibility and open-mindedness to adapt to different educational contexts.

[A good EFL teacher should know] a little of her subject and a lot about the reality of her school and her students.

Answers were collated tagging salient expressions and then conceptualized in terms of the main constructs about the knowledge base in current research discussed above. The two broad domains to emerge from an analysis of the responses are the conceptual, or *knowing what to teach* (associated with content, knowledge or theory) and the operational, or *knowing how to teach* (associated with pedagogy, skills or practice). Within these two domains we were able to detect, regardless of convergence and frequency of mention, these salient categories: general knowledge and subject matter knowledge, general pedagogical knowledge and pedagogical content knowledge and curricular knowledge on the one hand, and on the other, language proficiency and teacher communication skills, pedagogical and decision-making skills, and the context of curriculum development, underlying which we identified a strand that brings together attitudes and values.

Table 1.1 illustrates these categories with samples of our selective coding of the responses. Even though they have been presented in two discrete listings, the order chosen highlights their correlation, and in each dimension of content knowledge found in the responses, there stands a counterpart in terms of skills.

**Table 1.1** The knowledge base of LT as represented in our selective coding of responses

| Knowing what to teach | Knowing how to teach |
| --- | --- |
| *General knowledge and subject matter knowledge* | *Language proficiency and teacher communication skills* |
| • the world; what is going on | • high standard of language ability in the English language (fluency and accuracy) |
| • the language system (grammar, phonetics, lexis) | |
| • the language (linguistics, sociolinguistics) | • communication skills to facilitate language teaching |
| • cultural, historical and geographical aspects of the target language | |
| • language for specific purposes | |
| • learning technologies and education | |

| *General pedagogical knowledge and pedagogical content knowledge* | *Pedagogical and decision-making skills* |
|---|---|
| • theories of learning and principles of second language acquisition (psycholinguistics)<br>• theories of teaching (didactics)<br>• learners' physical, social, intellectual and emotional development (psychology)<br>• learners' cognitive styles; affective factors; multiple intelligences; learning and communication strategies<br>• disabilities, diversity, inequalities | • selecting and designing teaching materials<br>• planning varied and appealing lessons<br>• teaching not only grammar and vocabulary but also values and culture<br>• assessing learning<br>• incorporating learning technologies to facilitate the students' learning process<br>• motivating and supporting learners<br>• establishing rapport with students and bonds between cultures<br>• managing group dynamics |
| *Curricular knowledge* | *The context of curriculum development* |
| • national and provincial education and language policies<br>• the state school system<br>• inclusion and equality programmes<br>• schools and schooling (knowledge of the 'territories of teaching' – rules and roles) | • evaluating situated educational sociocultural contexts (the institution, the local community, the state, the nation)<br>• identifying learners' needs<br>• making informed instant decisions in unexpected situations (adaptive expertise)<br>• motivating students to develop a positive attitude to learning the target language<br>• developing a repertoire of strategies to manage language learning in different school contexts and different classroom situations |

**Attitudes and values:** creativity, patience, flexibility, open-mindedness, responsibility, passion, commitment to lifelong learning, enquiring disposition

## In their own voices: The enacted curriculum and the knowledge base of SLTE

The second set of questions in the survey aimed to elicit an appraisal of the IELTE programme from which we could glean the participants' perceptions about the knowledge base of SLTE.

For the qualitative analysis, again teacher-learners' and novice teachers' answers were collated by tagging salient expressions under emerging common themes, and few significant differences were found between both groups other than a greater focus of students on the enacted curriculum. In contrast, graduates provided a more holistic appreciation, further informed by the description of the challenges they typically faced at the workplace.

Initial quantitative results from the participants' evaluation of their TEP were calculated to set the ground for the ensuing discussion. Both student-teachers and recent graduates reported a high appreciation of the programme they studied (mean 3.33, SD 0.48 and mean 3.28, SD 0.64, respectively, on a four-point scale where four is the maximum). The qualitative study supports this assessment as, on the whole, participants proved to be fairly satisfied with the programme and suggested amendments only in certain curricular aspects but did not demand a massive transformation of the official programme. Their accounts also exuded a sense of pride relative to their institutional belonging, which reminds us that all programmes are enacted in a cultural, historical and subjective setting (Álvarez Valencia 2009; Nguyen 2013) and each realization is therefore unique:

> Most of my teachers were passionate about what they did, and that passion is enough to motivate students, and much more important than colourful screens, digital platforms or pleasant music. The human and academic quality of IES is fabulous (of course there are exceptions); that is why I would like to teach there one day.

The evaluation of the TEP was developed by participants within the framework allowed by an official prescriptive programme, and appears to be strongly underpinned by the teacher-learners' identity as L2 speakers (Graves 2009). They alternatively advocated reducing the curriculum load of pedagogic subjects delivered by education specialists in Spanish or increasing that of language-specific subjects (grammar in particular) or culture-oriented subjects (social studies or literature). There was also a call for the articulation of content and assessment criteria in some subjects and suggestions for an interdisciplinary approach to certain topics to foster their comprehensive treatment, which can be related to the pedagogical process domain described by Freeman and Johnson (1998). A number of respondents also considered it essential to add content related to learning technologies, while individual suggestions ranged from intercultural studies, oratory, debate workshops, Spanish grammar, Latin, business English, neuroscience and language philosophy to teachers' voice care, first aids and CPR (cardiopulmonary resuscitation).

The most recurrent shortcoming recorded was that the programme failed to prepare them for the challenges in the 'real life of a teacher', which, in the perspective of our respondents, are clearly aligned with the structural and personal influences identified by Richards (2010) in his discussion of context.

In connection with responding to social demands, particularly in terms of diversity and inclusion, participants expressed major concerns regarding the organization and management of teaching experiences. The strongest comments denote an evident mismatch between the apparently ideal scenarios selected for the teaching practice and the array of actual school settings where in-service experiences usually take place:

The TEP often prepares us for classrooms with ideal students, and we are not prepared to deal with the issues that affect students today.

The schools we have been to [as teaching practice] were the perfect place to deliver an English lesson. That is not always the reality we face.

Today new teachers need to have the skills to face reality. Behaviour problems, learning problems (dyslexia, for example), given that we work under the motto 'Inclusion'. I believe the teaching workshops should be more comprehensive and cover not only planning but also problem situations such as absenteeism, grade repetition, discipline, exam design and correction.

There was also a demand for earlier immersion in the schools' contexts instead of postponing it until the last two years of the TEP. While participants felt professionally prepared to plan lessons and to design teaching materials, they voiced their shortage of strategies to understand and cater for students' needs, to cope with the absence of resources and family support and to address learning disabilities, misbehaviour, lack of interest and unexpected situations:

When you face reality you realize there are very difficult and complex situations that you have no tools or skills to handle.

Another real-life challenge in which the TEP was found lacking refers to coping with the administrative demands of the education system. Almost unanimously, participants regretted the absence of career guidance. They felt they were left to their own devices, not just to find work, but also to make sense of the intricate procedures and regulations that appear as a stumbling block to gain access to employment in state education and, later on, advancement in the form of tenure. Other administrative aspects that were mentioned included legal rights and obligations, leaves of absence, form-filling and paperwork in general (syllabi, projects, reports, etc.). As expressed by one of the respondents:

When we finish our studies we feel lost amid papers, rules and red tape. We need a course or workshop which explains what to do with our degree once we leave the institution.

Proposals to enhance the TEP were also consistent with Richards' (2010) views on context, especially in terms of personal influences. Recommendations featured a unanimous claim for a subject dealing with student diversity and special needs, particularly intellectual and physical disabilities and social inequalities:

> Nowadays there are many cases of students with special needs and sometimes it's hard to know how to work with them.
>
> [There is a need for] a subject to deal with disabilities, how to tackle them in class, how to integrate students with special needs.

Our participants' take on the knowledge base of SLTE, as interpreted above, is in keeping with the theoretical framework discussed, as well as with recent contextually bound studies to which we have had access. To mention but a few examples, Banegas (2009) concludes that language proficiency is a central constituent in contexts where English is a foreign language; Faez and Valeo (2012) find that beginning teachers consider grammar as a significant element of the programme they studied; and Nguyen (2013), Higuita Lopera and Diaz Monsalve (2015) and Erten (2015) describe the challenges of responding to students' diverse needs and backgrounds as well as understanding the administrative dimension.

## Conclusion

We started this study looking for distinctive constituents of the knowledge base of SLTE that were determined by our context, as expressed by those at the chalkface with a recent experience of the TEP in our institution. We struggled to make sense of the data, which to a large extent constituted an appraisal of our everyday work as teacher educators, and at first emerged empty-handed. The stated beliefs about the knowledge base of LT we have been able to reconstruct are well aligned with current research, and the demands for an IELTE curriculum that prevents the reality shock that novel teachers face are well documented in studies involving native and non-native teacher-learners alike. No significant differences are mentioned that would justify the inclusion of contextual adaptations in the on-paper curriculum. On the other hand, an area that does require significant change, not only in the TEP itself but also in the current legislation, is the transition from teacher-learner to in-service teacher and the only answer to that seems to be a continuum approach to teacher education and career that integrates IELTE, induction and continuous professional development.

However, it is in the participants' silences that we find the most revealing insights. When they describe the conceptual and the operational dimensions of the knowledge base, they fail to account for the way in which both nurture each other in the pedagogical process as learners make sense of their learning experience. When they complain about the absence of tools to address the everyday challenges of the classroom, they seem to be demanding magical recipes that will make their job simpler, rather than elements to transform their teaching experiences into instances of inquiry and reflection. We feel that in both cases the responsibility for these omissions lies largely with us teacher educators.

We therefore feel it is necessary to underscore the decisive role played by teacher educators in the enacted TEP. We are the ones who will make the curriculum relevant. We need to practise what we preach and align our practices with the spirit of critical and reflective inquiry that we lecture about. We need to take stock of teacher-learners' prior beliefs and expectations and explore together the sociopolitical, economic, cultural and ethical issues that are part and parcel of teaching and schooling. We need to engage in a constant dialogue that will enable both our students and ourselves to become knowledge generators rather than consumers and to negotiate and construct our teaching identity within a specific social and institutional context.

This study aims to take some small steps in that direction. If we reconceptualize curriculum change as an opportunity for student- and in-service teachers and teacher educators alike to take a reflective stance on IELTE, we will make some progress towards developing our sense of agency. We believe that it is only through grassroots innovation that we can take on-paper changes into the classroom in a manner that will result in an improvement in education rather than the perpetuation of a status quo.

## Questions for change

1. What are the distinctive challenges and opportunities that your local context presents to EFL teachers and curriculum planners? How are they accounted for on paper and in the enacted curriculum?
2. How can teacher educators take into account teacher-learners' prior learning experiences?
3. Trace your own professional trajectory. Include the different settings you have taught in and the different students you have met. How different is your context today from when you first started?
4. What do you remember about your first days on the job? What do you know now that you wish you had known then? What dreams did you have that you have given up on since? Would you like to renew any of those aspirations? How can you do so?

# Enhancing Student Engagement with Academic Learning in EFL Pre-service Teacher Education Courses

Chunmei Yan

## Objectives

1. Demonstrate the value of student engagement at higher education level through a pre-service teacher education course that attempted to enhance student engagement with academic theory learning in China.
2. Yield valuable insights to the stakeholders of teacher education both in China and beyond on how to create deep student engagement.

## Introduction

Higher education institutions have been endeavouring to attain institutional effectiveness in such areas as active and collaborative learning, student–faculty interaction to enrich educational experiences and supportive campus environments (Wolf-Wendel, Ward and Kinzie 2009). Within these endeavours, student engagement is widely deemed as critical to academic success (Sharma and Bhaumik 2013; Zhang, Hu and McNamara 2015), indexed by an increased sense of belonging, and individual and collaborative engagement (Singh and Srivastava 2014). As a dynamic system of social and psychological constructs as well as a synergistic process, it is represented in multiple dimensions, including behavioural, cognitive and affective engagement. Given its strong correlation with positive learning outcomes and personal development of students, student engagement is a useful proxy for identifying what happens in a learning environment to achieve quality learning (Wentling, Park and Peiper 2007; Zepke 2013).

In contrast with the ideal goal of student engagement, however, there has been some documentation of undergraduates' lack of deep engagement with their academic studies as an ongoing and growing educational concern (e.g. Mann and Robinson 2009; McCune 2009). Instructional and student factors have combined to cause this situation in the climate of massification of higher education, such as instructional deficiency and large classes due to staffing and funding issues (e.g. Cullen 2011; Tormey and Henchy 2008), and students' pragmatic motivation for certification (Taylor et al. 2011).

Countermeasures to enhance student engagement are multiple. A key one is, as Geitz, Brinke and Kirschner (2016) put forward, a combination of goal orientation, motivation, self-efficacy and self-regulatory capacity. Hence, understanding student perspectives is imperative (Benesch 2001). Various instructional strategies are found to foster deep learning, such as valuing more than intellectual maturity in education (Taylor et al. 2011), employing active learning strategies (Carr, Palmer and Hagel 2015), integrating signature assignments into core courses throughout the curriculum (Pinahs-Schultz and Beck 2015), providing autonomy support (Hospel and Galand 2015) and personal tutoring (McFarlane 2016). In today's digital era, technology is widely used to develop critical thinking skills and self-regulatory capacity learning skills (Demirbilek 2015; Heaslip, Donovan and Cullen 2014; Nguyen and Ikeda 2015; West, Moore and Barry 2015).

Pre-service teacher education, as Mann and Edge (2013) have pointed out, is an extremely important but somewhat neglected area of teacher education. In particular, English as a foreign language (EFL) student-teachers' on-campus academic learning experience has been under-researched. The gap between theory and practice has been a long-standing challenge (Borg 2010). In China, Wang (2009) noted that the inconsistency between pre-service teacher education programmes with the demands of the Basic English curriculum reform has resulted in novice teachers' inability to understand the fundamental concepts and implementation requirements of the reform or adapt to practical classroom teaching in schools. Therefore, there is a pressing need to examine how to improve teacher education courses.

In contrast with this urgency of research, there has been a dearth of research in pre-service teacher education on how to enhance student-teachers' engagement with learning. Ellis (2010) suggests that we are a long way from knowing which teacher educator role has the greatest effect on teachers and teaching. There is a need for research to enrich the literature on how student-teachers' campus academic learning can be enhanced to develop change agents who will positively influence their future students holistically.

As a hybrid teacher educator researcher myself, I usually try to fill this gap by looking at how student-teachers' engagement with learning of coursework can be enhanced in one of my EFL pre-service teacher education courses. My objectives intend to answer three research questions:

1. What was the level of student engagement with the course?
2. Which course features contributed to student engagement?
3. Which areas needed improvement to further enhance student-teachers' engagement?

The answers to those questions will yield valuable insights to the various parties concerned in pre-service teacher education, including researchers, policymakers, teacher educators and student-teachers. Such answers will help in understanding the interplay between agency and the academic context, which facilitates or constrains the development of student engagement. On the other hand, some valuable insights emanating from research of this kind can help open a path of sound teacher and teacher educator development via designing quality education courses.

# Contextual information

## The initial EFL teacher education programme

The pre-service teacher education programme under investigation was based in a Central China Normal University, one of the six national teacher education institutions affiliated to the Ministry of Education. Founded in 1903, the university is dedicated to preparing school teachers of more than sixty subjects at junior and senior secondary levels across China. The university consists of twenty-four schools and departments, and over sixty research centres. Since its establishment, it has trained over 200,000 graduates with bachelor's, master's and PhD degrees in different parts of China. In 2011 student enrolment was 30,000 (11,000 of which were postgraduates and 1,800 were international students). To enhance the pedagogical competence of prospective teachers, the university established twenty-nine zones in eleven provinces/cities for their teaching practicum and teacher research.

The pre-service teacher education programme under investigation is based in the English Department of the School of Foreign Languages, which aims to develop EFL teachers who will engage in English teaching at secondary and tertiary levels. Three levels of teacher education programmes are offered for pursuers of BA, MA/MEd and PhD qualifications. The department boasts over forty full-time teaching staff in four major professional and academic areas, that is, linguistics, translation, literature and teacher education. Of the over forty teaching staff, thirteen specialize in English teaching methodology and teacher education with master's qualifications, while six hold PhD degrees in EFL methodology or teacher education. Various teacher education programmes have been developed to serve the needs of both pre-service and in-service teacher development within central China and beyond, covering big cities like Shanghai, and rural areas.

The duration of the pre-service EFL teacher education programme is four years, divided into eight semesters like any other EFL teacher education programme in China's tertiary institutions. The first three years focus on on-campus courses to develop student-teachers' professional skills for their future teaching career, with language development and subject knowledge. The teaching practicum takes place at the start of the fourth academic year. Coursework includes two major types of compulsory and optional courses: *tongshi jiaoyu* (general education) courses (e.g. Computer Literacy, Advanced Chinese, Physical Education, Moral Standards Development and Fundamentals in Law) and specialty courses (e.g. Language Development Courses, Linguistics, Pragmatics, Stylistics, Cross-Cultural Communication, English Literature, Translation and English Teaching Methodology). The total number of required credits is one hundred and sixty-six: sixty-eight (41%) general education courses and ninety-eight (59%) specialty courses. The number of contact hours totals 3,048: 1,146 hours (38%) for general education courses and 1,902 hours (62%) for specialty courses. The pervading pedagogies are a combination of content-based lectures and group discussions to promote quality-oriented education (e.g. student-centred teaching, task-based teaching, formative assessment, multimedia technology, etc.). Class performance and end-of-module paper-and-pencil exams/essays constitute two parts of course assessment. This practice is common in China's higher education where summative assessments prevail, that is, assignments generally crowd towards the end of courses without detailed feedback.

## The teacher development course under study

This study served as a means of applying reflection on my own instructional practice in a two-credit optional course offered to undergraduates named *School English Teachers' Professional Development*. The course has run since 2009 to five cohorts of undergraduates, delivered in the second semester of the third academic year. The participants had no school teaching experience, and their access and familiarity with professional and academic literature was rather low as their prior learning was predominantly focused on language proficiency and subject knowledge development.

The overarching goal of the course was to bridge the gap between theory and practice to develop aspiring teachers' vision, and less transparent non-cognitive traits and skills essential to academic and professional success such as sense of responsibility, professional competence to enact educational ideals, and positive mindsets to cope with professional and life challenges. Three linked expectations of ascending importance were set:

1. To develop a critical understanding of key concepts, issues and approaches in both pre-service and in-service language teacher development.
2. To make informed decisions in pursuing their professional development based on a good knowledge of teacher development approaches.
3. To explore ways of improving schools as agents of change, in particular in Chinese school contexts.

These expectations were intended to develop thoughtful contributions to changes needed in schools today with a sense of agency solidly grounded on knowledge of the pertinent issues in student-teachers' professional learning and future career, as well as critical reflection on the interrelationships between theory and practice.

As Mann and Edge (2013: 5) argued, 'It is the realization of an idea in *action* that constitutes genuine innovation.'

To make the concepts relevant, practical and comprehensible to the participants who had no school teaching experience and limited English academic proficiency, I scaffolded three pedagogical conditions for cultivating multidimensional student engagement. The first one was dynamic communication about course goals and potential benefits (cognitive and affective). Continuous monitoring of their operationalization was conducted during the course. The second condition was enactment of instructional innovations to maximize the practical value of research and theory, including reading professional articles and response writing, peer review and group presentations. Reading professional literature and writing aimed to cultivate academic proficiency and a sense of agency after substantial exposure to insightful readings. Seven responses were assigned. Peer review was used as a supplement to teacher feedback in order to develop reflectivity and self-regulatory capacity. Five reviews were mandated. To demonstrate standards of effective review, I communicated my reviews on the first responses via QQ, a social media platform widely used locally. Group presentations on their readings aimed to develop collaborative spirit. Seven twenty-minute-long group presentations were conducted. A tutoring session was offered for each group presentation beforehand, and post-presentation discussions were organized for mutual exchange of views.

The third condition was assessment innovations, which valued all the learning activities (10 per cent for class attendance and performance, 30 per cent for reading professional literature and writing responses to the readings, 30 per cent for collaborative presentations on designated readings, and 30 per cent for peer review of five responses). The learning tasks culminated in an integrated learning portfolio at the end of the course for overall assessment.

This study focused on the offering to Cohort 2013. Initially twenty-five students signed up for the course; ten students dropped out after two weeks owing to their concern about the challenges and pressures involved. Two young colleagues from the College English Department, who had just returned from the United States as instructors of Chinese, joined in the course.

## Ways of understanding students' perceptions of the course experience

I conducted an informal pre-course survey to underpin the course participants' aspirations for more interactive and practical learning activities. Multiple course artefacts served as evidence of participants' learning experience, covering participants' presentations, writing responses, peer reviews, participants' course evaluations and my reflection on the whole course design and operation. To supplement the written data, I carried out one focus group and four individual interviews in Chinese. Interviews were recorded and transcribed verbatim.

The data sets were analysed inductively to identify, categorize and explore main themes. First, I carried out inductive coding of data from the participant evaluations and interviews. Initial analysis yielded codes and code relationships that were explored further through iterative comparative analysis between the different data sources. Refinement of codes was developed as I explored the data in more detail. The codes were classified into three main categories in relation to participants' level of satisfaction with the course experience, contributing factors and areas for improvement. The credibility of interpretations was enhanced through reflexivity and seeking critical comments and confirmation from the participants. Pseudonyms were employed for extracts to ensure anonymity.

## Observations of student engagement with the course

The course presented a new field of study and was taxing for the participants devoid of teaching experience. The only male student wrote about his initial resistance, struggle and panic over the major writing task he had rarely practised:

> The thought of quit occurred to me before. I always fear English writing for my inadequacy in critical thinking and self-reflection. But the knowledge of being taught by such a wonderful teacher convinced me to hold on, and I'm always proud of this decision. (Song)

In spite of difficulties, the course was considered as 'transformative', 'insightful and thought-provoking', yielding multiple well-earned benefits. The most important one was a better understanding of issues for school teachers and the habit of reflection. Wang became more actively and persistently engaged over the course duration. She said, 'If I hadn't attended this course, I wouldn't have got a more comprehensive understanding of teachers' work and wouldn't have made so many reflections.' Completing the challenging assignments yielded a sense of achievement, and an awareness of their weaknesses, potentials and future development directions. The necessity of positive mindsets and learning skills was commonly emphasized, as expressed below:

> The course enables me to pass through the surface level of this profession and penetrate into its essence, perceive problems from a positive perspective and boosted my confidence as a prospective teacher. Besides, it makes me aware of the room for further improvement. The vision I have obtained from the teacher, the mindset and the positive energy will never end. (Zheng)

The process of attitudinal change during this course experience was noteworthy. Introduced for the first time to self- and peer assessment, the students were disconcerted to be delegated significant responsibility for assessment decisions. A student described the effect of peer influence in the preface to her portfolio to commemorate the experience:

> I experienced a psychological change during the response writings. Initially I regarded it simply a formality. I just read the paper and wrote down some of my feelings and thoughts without in-depth thinking. But when one girl's response came to me, everything changed. Her writing was so informative, fluent and logical. She even cited several references in her response. Suddenly I felt ashamed. Attitude! I read that response more carefully and found so many points I can learn from her. We chatted and solved the puzzles in writing the

response. So I understood I can really learn from the peer review. The difference between excellent and mediocre people is their attitude towards everything they go through. This course would benefit me for the whole life. (Deng)

A number of factors were found to have contributed to the positive impact of the course. Above all, as Ling commented, 'The great course experience was the result of the course tutor's strong commitment to scaffold course infrastructure that can engage students in various coherent transformative learning activities as autonomous deep learners.' The teacher's commitment and personality as a role model were the main contributing factors. As Song said, 'The power of model is beyond calculation.' Unlike most high-profile professors, the instructor's personality and character appeared to be an appealing magnet that powerfully drew students into the course journey and inspired them to 'seek a vibrant life', including passions in pursuing excellence, commitment to educating students, sincerity and gentility in communication with students, criticalness about professional and academic issues, open-mindedness to different views and readiness to share personal experiences, as evidenced in the comments below:

She is a role-model. Diligence, integrity, optimism, and patience are what I see in her. For four months, I have been charged with positive energy. Her encouraging words are always helpful when I am frustrated about uncertainties in my life and study. What she has instilled into my mind will always resonate in my mind. (Luo)

She made us know that there is one kind of people who earnestly devote themselves to the educational course. She shared with us her work, files and notes, the trying circumstances of our school, her daily efforts to strike a balance between work and life. All the sharing has motivated us to live a vibrant life. I easily gave up, but now I am awakened by the power of attitude, and trying to mould myself and look forward to the day that my efforts sprout. (Chen)

The second contributing factor was the multiple course features, covering the curriculum, topics, instructional methods and assessments. The course was perceived to be a sound implementation of relevant theories with a curriculum relevant to students' future career and life. As a student noticed, 'Theories are deeply embedded in the practical tasks and activities.' The topics were pertinent to their own development. The teaching methods fostered 'a relaxing and inspiring learning atmosphere'. As Ming commented on brainstorming, 'We can speak aloud our own thoughts and ideas. We have much fun in learning new things with laughter.' The group discussions were commonly endorsed as prompting students' reflection, and kindled their sense of agency as prospective school change agents, a crucial quality of a teacher, as revealed in Wang's account below:

> The group discussion and communication with us in class set us thinking. I have realized that every one of us has the potential to initiate change. We need to be open-minded to embrace new ideas that may even change our previous deep-rooted beliefs and active to figure out alternative ways to make things better. I have a sense of responsibility to update myself equipped with upright character and sufficient academic knowledge to embark on the teaching career.

The participation of two colleagues from our school and a couple of visiting scholars and their ideas and experiences inspired the student-teachers. The two colleagues' presentation on their reflective teaching offered the student-teachers a contextualized understanding of the professional learning approach and incentives to apply the approach in their own teaching.

The third contributing factor was the formative assessment the course employed. The workload posed by the assignments caused initial resistance, but after it gained momentum, the student-teachers' inner drive was gradually fuelled by the awareness of the assignments' value in cultivating learning awareness and lifelong learning skills. Zhong said: 'The assignments gave me a sense of achievement, courage and energy to face difficulties in the future, there is nothing that can frighten me! Haha!' The reading and writing assignments were initially considered 'strenuous' but subsequently applauded as capable of fostering a learning incentive in some 'lazy' students, instead of just using reading assignments. For example, Lei perceived the value of theory through reading, saying, 'I began to see the link to my practice, and I moved from "having to do it" to "wanting to do it". Reading informs your planning and your practice.'

The collaborative research project was commonly deemed as a more effective learning approach than lectures. It demystified the research process by allowing application of theory to practice and enhanced the participants' research ability and collaborative spirit. The course instructor's guidance and peer collaboration were important for successful research assignments:

> The research is demanding for us, and various problems crop up constantly. But we faced them together, and we improved our problem-solving ability, collaborative spirit and exploratory capability. The teacher provided much useful advice and concrete help through after-class discussion and a seminar for questionnaire design. (Yao)

Alongside the positive elements, several drawbacks surfaced. The time constraint caused by the short course duration was the first commonly perceived limitation. The time constraint to some extent undermined the depth and effect of each activity. For example, because of the pre-set schedule, each topic was addressed briefly, the input from the instructor was insufficient and deep understanding and insights of weekly papers had little time to emerge. The research experience was 'only a start' and their research inexperience was evident.

Second, the theoretical nature and abstractness of some topics and professional articles constituted a hindrance to understanding because of students' limited knowledge about school realities and lack of school teaching experience. For example, their understanding of constructivism was still limited to the literal level as declarative knowledge. This challenge could be tackled by providing practical experiences, such as the involvement of more in-service teachers sharing ideas and experiences and student-teachers' school visits. On the other hand, provision of real-life practical learning resources, such as written, audio and video materials might help achieve a solid mastery of the concepts and methods introduced. Cai's opinion was typical:

> The in-service part serves as a preparation for us, but it is clear that we often get stuck since we are not familiar with school management system and school environments, so we could invite more in-service teachers to share with us. I hope we can have the chance to observe real classroom teaching to get a clear idea of teaching and learning, and better prepare us for future teaching.

The quality of reading and response writing emerged as a concern for a couple of students. More careful choice of professional papers was mentioned. Some 'theoretical and superficial' papers presented a gap between the theories in those papers and their future teaching career. Additional choices of papers were suggested for each topic based on their interest. The weekly writing pace could be made more flexible or less frequent. As Jun explained, 'Quality writing takes time, involving careful reading, creative thinking, good academic writing skills and elaborate modifications.' Another solution was the addition of video-based discussions to reduce the number of paper responses.

The quality and sustainability of peer feedback also presented a challenge, according to three students. Some students still saw it as an externally imposed task to be assessed; therefore they simply completed the required number of reviews. Grading posed an 'all-"A"s' phenomenon because of the pressure of maintaining a good peer relationship. Besides, personal differences in review criteria caused the issue of authority of reviews. Peer reviews were still limited to the two partners concerned, and communication of the reviews publicly was considered necessary to generate a wider effect of peer review:

> Once I tried to assign a 'B' to my classmate and I became so worried that I wrote lots of explanations for her understanding. The all 'A' phenomenon shows that Chinese people are always bothered by interpersonal relationships and try not to harm others' faces. Another problem is that some of them pay so much attention to grammaticality that their reviews become fastidious and extreme. It is a pity that we never cared to communicate about these problems. (Ye)

## My reflection on the course innovation

Student engagement is not only a means of achieving learning outcomes, but also an ultimate goal of course learning. This study explored how teacher education courses could promote deep engagement with educational theories in which students had previously lacked confidence owing to their limited professional experience and inadequate proficiency to deal with professional and academic literature. It demonstrates that learning-oriented curriculum design and course experiences can transform instrumentalism into genuine intellectual, emotional and social engagement (Gardiner 2015), which may help enhance the value of theories for students and their potential application in practice. Aligned with the view of Northcote and Lim (2009), fostering deep engagement is a purposeful contrivance by reform-oriented teacher educators to scaffold a professional learning community strategically and create engaging educational learning infrastructure to impact students osmotically. Innovations necessitate teacher educators' strong beliefs, positive sense of self-efficacy and selfless commitment to busting a cul-de-sac of educational stagnation in the epidemic 'publish or perish' climate. Resonant with Wong's (2004: 165) argument, the study corroborates that 'learning styles are not cultural, but contextual'. The Chinese students embraced active and reflective thinking, open-mindedness and a spirit of inquiry as documented in some research (Tam et al. 2009; Zhang 2006), and their learning patterns appeared to be more easily adapted to new circumstances. The common endorsement of the portfolio-based formative assessments confirms the value of 'starting small' (Carless and Zhou 2015) in reforming assessment, one of the most conservative aspects of higher education pedagogy due to the high-stakes nature of assessment and long-standing traditions.

On the other hand, akin to previous observations (e.g. Carless 2011; Sambell, McDowell and Montgomery 2013), the study highlights some challenges, suggesting that strategic efforts are facilitated or constrained by contextual realities (Palfreyman 2006). The participants' ingrained reliance on teacher input and lack of real-life school experience hindered their comprehension and application of relevant concepts and issues. The incentive problem (Kwan 2011) typified by some students' pragmatic, assessment-driven learning strategies reveals their long-term exposure to traditional learning and assessment models in the exam-oriented education system. In this study ten students dropped out after one week for fear of the likely workload of reading and writing entailed in this optional course, and also for the lack of the habit of deep learning and formative assessment. As Zhu and Engels (2014) explained, organizational cultures affect students' and teachers' perceived need for innovation, their views about innovative instructions, and responsiveness to their implementations. They were wary of unfamiliar assessment approaches, which were different from their prior experiences of assessment methods, or where outcomes might be less predictable and prompt concerns about low grades or even failure (Bevitt 2015). Peer feedback, similar to Tsui and Ng's (2000) study, was not without problems, indicated by students' lack of knowledge and skill to provide corrective feedback. The increased workload and intensified pressures on staff corroborate Gibbs' (2006) observation.

All these issues provoked the question concerning sustainability of such pedagogical and assessment innovations. In this experience, it remains uncertain whether the participants' deep engagement through such innovations can lead to permanent change. However, the study strongly supports Ruegg's (2015) argument for the powerful effect of course instructor's active engagement in a dialogic process to promote autonomous learning. The whole process entails the instructor's wholehearted commitment along with strong educational belief and ethical fortitude. Acutely aware of the inadequacy of individual effort, I felt the need for coherence and collaboration among staff, and between the programme and cooperating schools to make far-reaching changes in student learning. For more systematic programme-wide adoption of innovations rather than fragmented and isolated application, epistemological change at the programme level is imperative.

## What is the next step?

The study describes a teacher education course that sought to enhance participants' autonomous learning dispositions and skills as prospective teachers through engagement with various learning activities. The course generated some social and academic accomplishments and also posed yet-to-overcome challenges. The course experience may be helpful to participants who might like to try similar innovations with their students, and who have first-hand experience and feelings about how they played out in instructional activities. As the course instructor, I gained valuable insights on how to facilitate student-teachers' coursework learning and narrow the theory-practice gap. But meanwhile, there will be potential difficulties in sustaining and scaling up such innovations, which suggests that the first priority needs to be placed on establishing high-quality teaching and learning environments.

# Conclusion

This chapter depicts a theory-focused teacher education course that employed professional literature reading-based activities and portfolios to enhance student-teachers' engagement with academic learning. The implementation of innovative pedagogies and assessments hinged upon the course infrastructure constructed by the teacher educator, who made efforts to offer students deep learning approaches and meaningful learning experiences. All the efforts would cultivate hybrid teacher educators (Zeichner 2010) with increasingly enriched professional expertise in research and practice.

Last, given the limited breadth and depth of impact of one single course, transformation of the programme-wide learning culture is needed to bring about the desired student engagement and attainment, which will be an ongoing enterprise involving all parties concerned.

# Questions for change

1. How could we encourage our student-teachers to produce concrete examples and deep thinking about the issues and strategies for improving their practices?
2. Since transformative learning is incremental in nature, can the espoused and enforced learning experiences be sustained after the students complete their programme of study in a system that has been subject to slow incremental change, to compromise and to inertia?
3. How can we achieve coordinated, systemic synergy of pre- and in-service teacher education?

# Empowering Beginning EL Teachers in Literacy Pedagogical Practices

Donna Lim, Linda Mary Hanington and Willy A. Renandya

## Objectives

1. Share insider perspectives on teacher education from a country in Asia with a well-respected education system.
2. Demonstrate how approaches to teacher education emerge from and serve the needs of the social context in which they are delivered.
3. Demonstrate how teacher education helps prepare teachers to be agents of change and how such change depends on shifts at a wider sociocultural level.

## Introduction

In this chapter, we examine the provision of initial English Language (EL) teacher education for those preparing to teach in primary schools (lower primary) in light of national developments that impact teaching in Singapore. We focus on a course designed to support the development of children's literacy and to help prepare beginning teachers to implement the new EL syllabus. We highlight key pedagogical principles, such as the Shared Book Approach (SBA) and a modified version of the Language Experience Approach (MLEA), introduced in the course.

In the second part of the chapter, we outline three main challenges faced by beginning teachers and those preparing them at the initial stage in their careers. The first is the potential disconnect they may face in the transition from learning about broad-based principles of literacy to the adaption and application in specific school contexts. A second issue is the tension between teaching and testing. The third relates to the background of our pre-service teachers and the issues that arise due to a lack of subject content knowledge.

We, the authors of this chapter, are teacher educators in the sole institution in Singapore that trains teachers for the state school system. As practitioners, not policymakers, we reflect on these challenges and describe ways to help our student-teachers address them. We further outline recent policy decisions with the potential to ease the tensions observed. In doing this, we consider the sociocultural forces that affect our student-teachers' perceptions and practice and discuss our role in widening their perspectives and encouraging their critical thinking.

## The Singapore context

Singapore is a small nation with a strong emphasis on education. Since it has very few natural resources, Singapore compensates by focusing on and making significant investment in its human resources. Education and training at all levels are the mainstay of this focus on preparing citizens to be active and effective members of the workforce and able to drive Singapore's economy.

The multi-ethnic and multilingual resident population of Singapore of about 5.54 million comprises 74.3 per cent Chinese, 13.3 per cent Malays, 9.1 per cent Indians, and 3.2 per cent people from other ethnic groups (Singapore Department of Statistics 2015). Although English, Mandarin Chinese, Malay and Tamil are all official languages here, the EL plays a central role and its status is one of the unique features of the context described in this chapter. Singapore used to be a British colony and after independence in 1965, English was deliberately chosen as a neutral language that the new leaders felt would bring together various ethnic groups that formed the resident population and at the same time function as a global conduit for international relations (Iswaran 2009). Important for this discussion, in 1987 it became the medium of instruction from primary school to university except during Mother Tongue (MT) lessons (students are required to learn one MT, which is defined as the language reflecting the ethnicity of the child's father). English thus enjoys an important status and permeates society in Singapore today.

Its status is also reflected in a shift in its use as a home language. Although use of the MT as the main home language still predominates, statistics released in 2015 show that 36.9 per cent of those aged five and above now speak English more frequently at home than they do their designated MT. This compares with 32.3 per cent in 2010 (Lee 2016). However, the continuing use of different languages at home has implications for the role of EL teachers in schools.

## Policy and the primary school in Singapore

In Singapore, children start primary school at about seven years of age. Their six years of primary schooling culminates in a national examination: the Primary School Leaving Examination (PSLE). Classes typically are composed of students from different ethnic backgrounds whose exposure to the EL outside school varies widely.

The system of primary school education is highly centralized. The larger goals of the English curriculum are detailed in the EL syllabus of 2010 (Ministry of Education [MOE] 2010) and realized through the Strategies for English Language Learning and Reading (STELLAR) programme developed by the MOE to cater specifically to the needs of Singapore students. STELLAR adopts internationally accepted research-based literacy strategies and adapts them to suit the Singapore context. The MOE supports teachers in the delivery of lessons through provision of teaching resources and guidelines as to their use (Pang et al. 2015). Newly qualified teachers need to apply the broader principles of literacy development learnt during their training programmes within the remit of STELLAR, and specific training is given by MOE early in their deployment to school to help with this transition.

Other national educational reforms have also impacted teacher education. In 1997, Prime Minister Goh Chok Tong called for thinking and continuous learning skills to form the bedrock of education (Goh 1997). While mastery of core knowledge and skills were to be retained, these were to be embedded in an environment that prepared students to be self-directed learners who would continue to learn throughout their lives. Thinking Schools, Learning Nations (1997), as this initiative was called, became the overarching framework for initiatives that followed, for example, the Teach Less, Learn More initiative of 2004 (Tharman 2004), calling for a move away from teacher-centred pedagogies towards more student-centred classrooms.

A recent debate of particular importance for teacher educator centres is testing. In 2013, Prime Minister Lee Hsien Loong acknowledged that intense competition among students resulted in the focus of education being 'too much on examination and not enough on learning' (Lee 2013). Following this, plans are underway to replace the PSLE scores with wider grade bands in the hope of reducing competition between students (Yang 2016).

## Teacher education in Singapore

Two characteristics of the teacher training system in Singapore make it quite unique. First, those wishing to become teachers in the country's state school system apply through the MOE, which determines eligibility for training based on the suitability of the candidate and also on the national school context and its projected needs. Second, there is only one teacher training institution providing pre-service training for these individuals: the National Institute of Education (NIE), an institute of Nanyang Technological University. The institute cooperates closely with the MOE and a major implication of this close relationship is the alignment of national educational policies, pedagogical content and school-based practices in the training of teachers.

Singapore espouses four desired outcomes of education: that those leaving the school system should be confident individuals, self-directed learners, active contributors and concerned citizens (M.O.E. 2016). These outcomes reflect the strong socializing role of the school in shaping behaviours and attitudes. Our student-teachers are products of the system in which they were educated and their understandings have been formed by social and cultural circumstances. Now, they are being socialized to the norms, expectations and culture of the school as future teachers. The latter is evident in the localized nature of approaches to literacy that are described in this chapter and through the extended periods they spend in school, first observing, then teaching under the guidance of more experienced practitioners.

In many ways, teacher education processes reflect apprenticeship models described by Lave and Wenger (1991) in their seminal work on situated learning. Yet at the same time, just as those they will teach, our student-teachers are expected to be self-directed learners and active contributors. These qualities strongly suggest that their training should require their cognitive engagement. Although they were once seen as two different domains, Billett (1996) argues that sociocultural and cognitive literatures are not mutually exclusive. In our courses, we engage the participants at a critical level with a range of theories about literacy and approaches to literacy development. While they need to understand and respond to the local context and culture, they also need to be able to distance themselves from it and question what is effective and appropriate, and why. Thus we argue that sociocultural perspectives alone do not fully capture the complexities of the teacher development process. However, an approach to training that goes beyond acculturation to existing norms gives rise to the tensions described later in this chapter.

Our discussion focuses on a four-year degree, which is one of the pre-service programmes offered by the NIE. This programme combines development as a teacher with academic subject specializations common to degree courses and those training to be primary school teachers taking one academic subject. However, in school they are expected to be able to teach at least three curriculum subjects competently: EL, Mathematics and one other subject. The ability to teach the three subjects is developed through a series of courses under the umbrella term Curriculum Studies (CS), the name given to our methodology courses. For EL, there are four CS courses: Teaching Reading and Writing (for lower primary), Teaching Reading and Writing (for upper primary), Teaching Oral Communication and Teaching Integrated Language Skills for upper primary. In addition to CS courses, student-teachers take other courses, for example, Educational Psychology. In this chapter, we talk specifically about the CS course on literacy instruction for lower primary.

## Profile of student-teachers in degree programmes

The profile of student-teachers in degree programmes is quite diverse. While the majority are embarking on their pursuit of a degree directly after completing their high school education and attaining Cambridge 'A' level certification, others have completed diplomas at polytechnics and a few are teachers with diplomas and several years of teaching experience. Low et al. (2011) found that the motivations of those joining the service stemmed from altruistic reasons, with love for kids, interest in teaching and fulfilling a mission being the top three factors. Such findings supported those from earlier studies (Thornton, Bricheno and Reid 2002; Thornton and Reid 2001a, 2001b).

Those attending CS courses for EL may come from different academic disciplines. While some may be studying EL as their academic specialization, others might be taking very different subjects, such as a science subject or mathematics, yet in school they are required to teach English. We find that this can lead to classes that vary in the level of subject content knowledge for participants.

## Initial teacher preparation in EL methodology for young learners

During the first year of their programme, our student-teachers concentrate on their academic subjects. They take four (CS) courses in their second to fourth year and cover these in tandem with further academic courses. Here we discuss the first of these courses: Teaching Reading and Writing (for lower primary).

Since few of our student-teachers have had experience of teaching in primary school classrooms, their understanding of the literacy development of young learners is minimal. Furthermore, this is the first time they are introduced to classroom methodologies and are asked to relate content knowledge to teaching practice. Therefore helping them bridge the gap between theory and practice is especially critical.

Learning outcomes of the course are understanding the principles of language learning, the development of literacy and the ability to select appropriate strategies and teaching resources to enact the teaching reading and writing for learners aged seven to nine. In the course, we focus on two anchor strategies: the SBA and the MLE, as they are key elements in the STELLAR curriculum. In this way, training at NIE is the beginning of an apprenticeship and acculturation process that continues through their programme and into school.

### Shared Book Approach

The first strategy our student-teachers need to learn is the SBA. This well-established strategy supports early readers and focuses on enjoyment and meaning-making gained from reading books (Holdaway 1979). SBA seeks to replicate bedtime reading, the benefits of which are well-established (Mol et al. 2008). It exposes children to quality literature and facilitates their discovery of text through the use of pictorial cues and mediating talk (Wong 2010).

Our student-teachers learn how to use this approach to develop children's reading skills. This involves creating the intimacy that is an important aspect of bedtime reading by gathering and managing groups of children and sitting close to them while they read the story from the picture book displayed on an easel. SBA models proficient reading by asking key questions to encourage children to think about the text and make predictions, draw inferences and establish personal connections. It also helps them use visual, graphophonic, semantic and syntactic cues in making meaning. Finally, it requires the use of specific techniques that facilitate children's acquisition of sight reading skills and focuses attention on points of the story, text and picture cues that are significant.

Using the reading text (or picture book) as an anchor, our student-teachers learn how to develop subsequent lessons targeting specific language skills (e.g. vocabulary, grammar, listening, etc.) using content that is now familiar. For example, a grammar-focused lesson around a retelling task provides a natural context for the use of past tense or a lesson that explores vocabulary introduced in the book. They learn how to reinforce the chosen skill and provide students with the opportunity to use and demonstrate understanding of it in speech and in writing as appropriate.

## (Modified) Learning Experience Approach

According to Morrow (2012), the Language Experience Approach (LEA) rests on the following premises:

- What I think is important.
- What I think, I can say.
- What I can say can be written down by me or by others.
- What is written down can be read by me and by others. (Morrow 2012: 153)

LEA harnesses the reading-writing connection to support literacy development of young learners. It stems from oral language derived from a common experience provided to a class of students. Because the students' contributions determine the text they produce, their rate of success when reading is significantly increased. LEA was initially developed in a context where the target students already possessed the ability to think and speak in English. This approach has been modified to suit the Singapore context where English is not necessarily the dominant language used by children when they come to school (Ng and Sullivan 2001) and is known as the MLEA.

Our student-teachers learn how to use MLEA to support young learners of EL coming from different linguistic backgrounds and with varied prior exposure to English. LEA and MLEA seek to provide a common experience for students, which will then become the stimulus for their writing. In both approaches, the children dictate their description of, or responses to, the experience and the teacher performs the role of scribe by writing down what they say. The difference is that with MLEA, the teacher discusses with the children what is to be written to a greater extent and in the process explicitly teaches language structures and vocabulary. This approach requires a great deal of sensitivity on the part of the teacher so that the children still own their story and yet are provided with tiers of support that make the final individual writing task more accessible. In our course, we help the participants develop sensitivity to such issues.

## Approaches to course design and delivery

Inherent in the design of our course is the concept of theory application. Deng (2004) argues for the need for a greater understanding of this concept within the context of the training model of initial teacher preparation in Singapore. He posits that the connection between theory and practice is 'inferentially complex' and using a technical (and remote) lens to connect the two cannot do it justice. Theory application entails more than equipping student-teachers with skills and procedures they execute in the classroom. Complexities and uncertainties need to be factored into the teaching model with the aim of nurturing student-teachers' capacities to reason and make informed decisions when teaching. Disregarding this could lead to distorted notions and images of the real classroom.

In our course, we take our student-teachers through fundamental theories that underpin literacy instruction such as developmental stages of literacy, home-school transition and reading and writing processes, prior to introducing the two anchor strategies described in the previous sections. Emphasis is placed on understanding the pedagogical principles of the strategy so as to strengthen their knowledge of the *why* and not just the *what* of teaching.

Typically, we first model the target strategy. Wong (2010) describes the stages of SBA reading lessons and MLEA lessons that are typically modelled. These include pre-, during- and post-stages. During modelling, some student-teachers act as school students while others are lesson observers. During the subsequent debriefings, participants contribute from their role as either the 'student' or the lesson observer. Emphasis is placed on not just the procedure observed but also the pedagogical principles that underlie the process.

Next, we delegate ownership of the teaching strategy to the student-teachers through micro-teaching sessions. To ease the tension and cognitive overload at this initial stage, they form small groups and plan a lesson using the target strategy, which is then delivered to the rest of their tutorial group. A debrief is done with tutors facilitating discussion of the lesson, much like the earlier debrief described.

Finally, for the course assignment, we ask student-teachers to develop lesson plans for target students that integrate the theories they have learnt and strategies needed to realize them in class.

From end-of-course feedback, we often receive particularly favourable comments about demo teaching and micro-teaching. This is demonstrated in one of the responses:

> I find the tutor demo and micro-teaching extremely useful. Besides reinforcing what were taught during the lectures, tutor demonstrations also provide a clearer idea how certain things are to be carried out. On the other hand, microteaching sessions allow us to translate what we have learnt into practice and learn from our peers. We should have more of this. (Student-teacher 2014)

Ideally, the strategies we introduce belong to the classroom, and should be delivered in this context and deconstructed for optimized learning. However, actual practice in school takes place later in the degree programme and therefore demo teaching and micro-teaching sessions mimic target conditions and allow for the complexities and uncertainties alluded by Deng (2004) to be factored into the initial teacher preparation. Having student-teachers role-play students in an intended class has the additional advantage of allowing them to gain a partial perception of these strategies as received by students.

## Challenges and responses

In the previous section we outlined the key approaches introduced and strategies employed in one course addressing EL literacy development for young learners. Course designers thought very carefully about how to structure the course and how to simulate classroom teaching, something that was much appreciated by the participants. However, despite the development of a classroom application, our student-teachers' transition from the controlled environment of the university tutorial room to the classroom is not without its challenges. In this section, we address three main challenges: adjusting to school expectations and requirements, the tension between teaching and testing and the participants' own EL knowledge.

## Adjusting to the school context

> The course encouraged reading aloud from authentic children's books during EL lessons. I had planned to do this during our teaching practicum but I found that I didn't have the time. Furthermore, the school wanted me to stick to the recommended lessons so as to keep pace with the rest of the other classes. (Student-teacher 2015)

One of the most significant challenges newly qualified teachers may face, as shown in the quote above, is the potential disconnect between broad-based principles of literacy development espoused by the teacher training institution and school-based specific parameters drawn up to suit the school context. As they start to apply a pedagogy they have learnt about with particular groups of students and in an environment constrained by a wealth of other school contingencies, they sometimes feel there is a disconnect between what they have learnt and what is expected.

As teacher educators we also struggle with related issues. We wish to introduce our student-teachers to global concepts and trends in the development of children's literacy, yet we are very aware that they will need to operate in the local context where decisions have already been made about how best to develop early literacy based on the student profile. The integration of demo and micro-teaching goes some way to address this issue, but the tension between global and local is not eased by the relatively short duration of the course (the equivalent of thirty-six hours of classroom teaching), which can mean our student-teachers have not fully internalized the pedagogies covered and links to STELLAR programme approaches. This situation is exacerbated by their having to take other methodology modules for two further subjects (e.g. math modules) alongside academic courses (e.g. Phonetics) in their chosen discipline.

While we as teacher educators can take some measures to help our student-teachers, wider policy decisions are likely to have a greater impact. One such decision was announced in 2015, when plans to allow for primary school teachers in Singapore to specialize in two, rather than the current three, subjects were announced. This change will be gradually phased in over the next few years with the purpose of freeing time for teachers to plan better lessons (Musfirah 2016). This also impacts courses offered by the NIE, and the degree programme is currently being restructured. With this significant move, additional time available resulting from the reduction in pedagogically oriented courses will hopefully allow for deeper reflection and internalization of what is covered for the remaining two subjects.

## Teaching or testing

> Student-teachers often ask why we don't focus on teaching PSLE type of questions in the course. We often have to help them distinguish between testing and teaching. The teaching must first be done well before the testing can come into the picture. (Tutor 2014)

A second challenge for beginning teachers is the potential tension between teaching and testing, as shown in the quote above. In Singapore, primary education culminates in a high-stakes national examination, the PSLE, at the end of six years. Singapore prides itself on meritocracy and school results, rather than personal connections or home location, determining the secondary school a child can attend. While PSLE results demonstrate the social mobility education aims to achieve (Wong 2011), it is the narrow gateway to 'a highly stratified system of secondary schooling' in which 'the implications of each track for future careers are very significant' (Bray and Lykins 2012: 23) and, as a result, extreme pressure is placed on the child, parents, teachers and the school to ensure optimal academic performance. This race for results is an interesting example of a sociocultural phenomenon that developed a life of its own.

In the classroom, beginning teachers also find themselves under pressure to cater to this sociocultural imperative that is results-driven even though it may run counter to what they have learnt. They struggle to reconcile an ideology of teaching for life and the immediate practicalities of teaching to achieve good test results. In the process, the latter may take precedence and thus they start preparing students for test-taking rather than nurturing learning through the in-depth teaching of skills. Sociocultural expectations in the immediate and wider environment mean they resort to what seems to be a faster route to achieving short-term goals. 'The long term goal, the process of learning, is silently sacrificed' (Teacher educator 2016).

Questioning norms and recognizing the importance of other forms of assessment require an understanding of its purposes and the alternatives. Assessment literacy is an important component of our CS courses, and in the one we have described, participants learn how to match early literacy assessment approaches (assessment as well as learning) to the purpose of lessons. In this way we hope to empower them to make informed decisions about assessment practices. However, Lee and Hung (2016) point out that curriculum innovation in schools requires leadership and the provision of sociocultural support for change to take place. The same is true of attitudes and expectations in relation to testing. Fortunately, the issue is starting to be addressed at a wider level.

At the ministry level, the difficulty teachers have balancing the STELLAR approach with the traditional exam-centric one has been acknowledged and a commitment has been made to provide better support for assessment literacy through in-service training (Pang et al. 2015). Prime Minister Lee's criticism of the focus on examinations (Lee 2013) proposed changes to PSLE scoring. This new focus on assessment literacy is a first step that may in time impact expectations and norms, although clearly changing an entrenched sociocultural phenomenon that is driven by the perceptions of critical stakeholders such as parents is not an easy task. The acting education minister (Schools) acknowledged this in a recent parliamentary debate on the issue: 'Parents and community have to make the shift too' (Ng cited in Davie 2016).

## Developing subject content knowledge

> However, I am not so confident about teaching writing because writing is such a complex process which requires competency in many other areas. It feels like I would need to learn more about writing before I would be confident in teaching it. (Student-teacher 2015)

A third challenge pertains to the subject content knowledge of student-teachers, as illustrated by the quote above. Based on national educational needs, the decision about which subjects an individual trains to teach often lies not with prospective teachers but with the MOE. Because of the need for EL teachers, English becomes a default subject for many. In the degree programme, many non-English specialists are therefore in our CS courses.

In the interest of time and the pedagogical aspects needing introduction, we have to presuppose a certain level of EL subject content knowledge. For example, the course focuses on *how to* teach grammar during MLEA and not knowledge about grammar per se. However, in reality, some course participants do not have the prerequisite knowledge. Their own school experience, based on earlier versions of the curriculum, may not have prepared them for requirements in the current EL syllabus. For example, those who experienced a more immersive approach to language may lack the meta-language emphasized in the current syllabus. This then means that they may face difficulty giving explicit grammar explanations to their students.

The issue of subject content knowledge was recognized during the development of the 2010 EL syllabus. To address this issue, the NIE was asked to provide help for those not specializing in EL as an academic subject. Short subject content knowledge courses are now compulsory prior to CS courses.

While this change has gone some way to address shortfalls, these courses, taken at a time when they are adjusting to the demands of university life and those of other subjects, do not always result in student-teachers being conversant enough with the prerequisite knowledge to enact it during CS.

It remains critical to call attention to the lack of subject content knowledge and to emphasize the need for further development of this knowledge for our student-teachers throughout their teaching careers, in tandem with EL methodology. This need has also been recognized by the MOE, with the NIE and another institution primarily responsible for in-service training, and a framework for continuing development is being drawn up. This is intended to ensure teachers are receiving cohesive and comprehensive training in both subject content knowledge and methodology throughout their careers.

## Conclusion

In this chapter, we have discussed a particular aspect of initial teacher education for teachers training to work with lower primary-aged children in the context of Singapore. While both rigour and depth of thought have gone into the design of the course we have described, challenges nevertheless persist. We have highlighted three such challenges from initial teacher preparation to eventual school teaching, the potential tension between teaching and test-taking, and the lack of EL subject content knowledge. We have outlined measures we take as teacher educators to help prepare our student-teachers for such challenges and have also shown how broader policy decisions and further support in schools are vital if change is to take place.

From our discussion, it has also become evident that the proverbial adage 'it takes a whole village to raise a child' also applies to teacher education in that it takes a whole community to develop a teacher. While as teacher educators we can begin to change mindsets and help teachers become more self-directed and therefore agents of change, our impact can only reach so far. National and ministry level changes are critical.

## Questions for change

1. What are the unique features in your country/province that impact decisions about the use of English both with education systems and in the broader environment?

2. Do you face similar challenges to those outlined in this chapter in your own work? How do you deal with such tensions either as a practising teacher or when helping novice teachers with whom you may be involved?

3. Identify two policy decisions that impact EL teaching in some way. What are the impacts in terms of your work as a teacher educator, curriculum developer or classroom teacher? How might you research the impact of such changes or the measures you have taken to accommodate them?

# 4

# Strengthening the Link between University Curricula and English Language Student-teacher Preparedness

Alice Kiai and Angelina Nduku Kioko

## Objectives

1. Examine the alignment of university English Language Teacher Education (ELTE) programmes in Kenya to the secondary school English curriculum.
2. Discuss ELTE in Kenyan universities within the framework of sociocultural theory.
3. Highlight issues that Kenyan university English language teacher educators need to address in their research and curricula innovation.

## Background

Kenya, a country of diverse languages and cultures, has a population of about 43 million people. Of these, approximately 26 million (60.4%) are aged 0–24 years (KNBS 2015). This means that Kenya has a youthful demography, with a large population comprising children and young people of school-going age. The current system of education in Kenya includes eight years of primary schooling, four of secondary, and a minimum of four years at university.

The language in education policy in Kenya dictates the use of the language of the school's catchment area as the language of instruction (LoI) in the first three years of school, and the use of English as the LoI at all other levels of education. Thus, success in education is dependent on a learner's mastery of the English language, and this makes ELTE an important area of educational research in Kenya. The success of the English language teacher has a strong impact on the success of the teachers of other subjects. As Kioko and Muthwii (2001: 208) noted, 'Some of the wastage in education can definitely be blamed on the language situation in the country, since the medium of instruction has a great impact on success in other subject areas.'

This chapter examines ELTE in two Kenyan universities – one public, one private – as examples of universities preparing future secondary school English language teachers. This chapter was inspired by our joint engagement of over ten years each in university ELTE. Our experiences and observations suggested a weak link between English language teacher preparedness and university curricula, as captured by the following snapshots:

1. 'When I cleared my undergraduate [studies], I never knew there were different types of grammars. I just know … grammar of English, that is all. So we were saying that such courses should be taught at a lower level before teachers are let out to go in the field.' (Voice of a graduate student, with a Bachelor of Education (English) degree).
2. 'Why did you not teach us these methods when we were in college?' (Cry of a practising teacher, after an in-service workshop).
3. A 2015 review of the Department of English curriculum in the private university, using expected learning outcomes, revealed the need for cross-faculty collaboration to fully address the skills needed for effective language teaching in secondary schools.

These snapshots allude to the existence of a gap between the course content in universities and the skills expected of English teachers. This is in line with Ong'ondo's (2009) observation that during teaching practice, student-teachers were unfamiliar with the content of the secondary school English language syllabus.

The current (2002) secondary school English syllabus covers skills in listening, speaking, grammar, reading and writing. The syllabus emphasizes the need for learners to use English correctly, appropriately and expressively in different contexts. It states that proficiency in English is a 'desirable life-long goal' (K.I.E. 2002: 7). To achieve this, the syllabus, with a focus on achieving communicative competence, integrates English and literature as one subject.

Through the voices of educators and student-teachers in the two universities, we relate the student-teachers' experience to the university coursework and the teaching practicum, and interweave these with the basic tenets of sociocultural theory in ELT. Finally, we propose ways of strengthening the bond between university curricula and student-teacher preparedness.

## Sociocultural theory

Though Vygotsky's ideas have been subsequently developed by scholars from various fields, he is seen as the father of sociocultural theory (Swain, Kinnear and Steinman 2011). Vygotskyian sociocultural theory is a psychological theory that connects internal and external processes. Learning is seen as a process of meaning-making as opposed to the internalization of discrete skills. The learner is an active meaning-maker who moves from a point of dependence on more knowledgeable others (MKOs), such as teachers, peers and technology, towards a point of independence, in which knowledge is internalized, and infused with personal values. Learning arises in the process of interacting with others, and the quality of that interaction is important. It is ideally supported through mediation and scaffolding in which the MKO models the desired behaviour in order to provide direction and clarity, and gradually guides the learner towards greater independence and critical/abstract thinking. These tenets of sociocultural theory will guide the discussion of the voices of educators and student-teachers in this chapter.

## University curricula

Students admitted into the four-year ELTE programme in the public university are required to take fifty-three courses, distributed as follows: four university-common courses, nineteen courses from the Faculty of Education, thirty from the Faculty of Arts – fifteen from the English department and fifteen from the literature department. The private university is very similarly structured; however, students are placed on four, three and two-year programmes based on existing qualifications that merit course exemptions.

In the public university, students access English courses from the Department of English and Linguistics and literature courses from the Department of Literature, within the Faculty of Arts. In the private university, they access both English and literature courses from the Department of English, Faculty of Arts. In both universities, students access education courses from the Faculty of Education. Teaching staff in the Faculty of Arts do not necessarily require a background in education but must be content specialists. Occasionally, in the private university, the English and literature content specialists, with an education background, are invited by the Faculty of Education to teach the English and literature subject methods courses to their students, but there is no such collaboration between the Faculty of Education and the Faculty of Arts in the public university.

Classes in the Department of English and Linguistics in the public university have over 300 students, combining both Bachelor of Education and Bachelor of Arts students, while the average class in the private university has fifteen Bachelor of Education students only.

Prior to their final year or semester of study, student-teachers in both institutions undertake teaching practice for one term (three months) in a secondary school. They are assigned two to three university supervisors and observed four to six times. Supervisors are expected to have a background in education; however, students are not necessarily supervised by staff from the English or literature departments.

For uniformity, the private university conducts an induction programme for supervisors at the start of the process and hosts a midterm meeting for university supervisors and student-teachers to share experiences and handle emerging issues. Supervisors in both institutions are equipped with standard instruments for use in lesson observation and provision of standardized feedback to the student-teachers. Because of large student numbers, some public universities are currently implementing a mentorship programme in which more experienced teachers work with university supervisors to induct and support student-teachers during the practicum.

## Teacher educator and student-teacher voices

To place the reflections on the snapshots described earlier into perspective, we conducted interviews with six educators of English and literature – three from a public university (TE1, TE2, TE3) and three from a private university (TE4, TE5, TE6) – and with six recent student-teachers – three from a private university (ST1, ST2, ST3) and three from a public university (ST4, ST5, ST6).

We developed semi-structured, open-ended interview guides for teacher educators and student-teachers. The guiding questions for teacher educators sought to elicit participants' educational background, their perceptions about themselves as teacher educators, their supervisory/mentorship experiences during the practicum, their views about the challenges facing their respective teacher education programmes and their ideas about how these programmes could be improved. The student-teacher interview guide essentially sought to elicit participant perceptions about the adequacy and relevance of the teacher education programmes, including the practicum, and their views on how the programme could be improved.

We purposively selected participants on the basis of their roles as teacher educators and student-teachers in the two institutions, especially those who had relatively recent practicum experiences (2014–15). We carried out face-to-face audio-recorded interviews among willing and consenting participants who were individually approached for this purpose. All sampled teacher educators had over ten years of university teaching experience; were holders of Bachelor of Education degrees in English and literature; and had relevant masters' degrees. Four had doctorates in either linguistics or literature. The sampled student-teachers comprised two males and four females: five Kenyans and one Ugandan, two on a three-year programme and four on a four-year programme. All of them had English and literature as their teaching subjects.

We transcribed the interview data and met at intervals to brainstorm, to isolate the themes from the responses and to agree on the selection of quotations from the 'voices' in order to support our interpretations and discussion. We uncovered interesting differences in teacher educators' perceptions of themselves, and student-teachers' views of teacher educators as models, and we gave voice to participant perceptions about their university curricula. In the sections that follow, we present the perceptions of teacher educators and student-teachers on the interaction between university curricula and teacher preparedness for both teaching practice and the actual teaching experience.

## Educators' perception of themselves as teacher educators

While all teaching staff from the private university perceived themselves as teacher educators, all the teaching staff from the public university perceived themselves as content experts only. The perception of the private university educators is informed by the nature of their work (TE1) – that all their students are student-teachers – their own education background (TE2), and the long experience of teaching student-teachers (TE3). As TE1 put it,

> I am nothing else but a teacher trainer, myself ... whereas I am participating in the lecturing career. ... I form teachers. I remember one of the adverts on Citizen Media which said ... only professionals make professionals – so I am really a teacher. (TE1)

On the other hand, the perception of the English and literature educators from the public university seems to be related to the nature of their classes, where both teacher educators and general Bachelor of Arts students learn the same courses in the same class, and to the fragmented structure of the programme where language content and teaching methods are offered in different faculties. The following quotes illustrate the views of the teacher educators based at the public university:

> My focus is on the students' acquisition of content. ... I have a course description and my intention is to have them understand that content. What they will do with that content, I don't spend time thinking about it. (TE4)
>
> I don't talk to them of what they will do in the classroom, though the majority of them will be teachers. ... I teach them the theory on language usage and structure. I am not strictly a teacher trainer. (TE5)
>
> I don't consider myself a teacher trainer. I don't teach them to teach. ... I equip them with content. (TE6)

These voices reveal that language educators at university level in Kenya lack a unified view of themselves as English language teacher educators; this is particularly so among those in the public university who perceive themselves as language content providers and see it as the responsibility of the student-teacher to decide what to do with the content in the field. As Westbrook et al. (2013: 29) observe, only a few studies have focused on how teacher educators are trained, how they develop their practice or how they develop a community of practice through collaborative networks. The view of self as content specialist rather than teacher educator among university teaching staff generally relates to three factors: first, that those who teach English and literature content need not have an academic/professional background in education; second, that the ELTE programme separates content and pedagogy, with minimal cross-faculty dialogue; and third, the English and literature curriculum is delivered to an eclectic group of learners, who are not necessarily viewed as future teachers. In a situation like this, the MKO is not likely to provide appropriate scaffolding to the student-teacher.

## Student-teachers' perceptions of teacher educators as models

Private university student-teachers perceived more than 50 per cent of their educators as excellent models. They associated excellence with qualities ranging from approachability and willingness to help; mastery of content; ability to moderate language and content complexity to suit learner levels; timely provision of feedback; and passion for the subject and/or profession. ST3 captures some of these expectations:

> Be strict of course ... to maintain class discipline, but not ... to an extent that students even fear you – and again, we expect our teachers to use language we understand. ... They should ... even engage in some occasions, or be with them [student-teachers] for some trips. (ST3)

Public university student-teachers felt that less than 50 per cent to about 50 per cent could be considered excellent models. This is what ST5 and ST6 said:

> About 50 per cent, most of them were excellent but others taught for the sake. ... Majority didn't complete the course work, frequent absenteeism, and no time to interact with students. (ST5)
>
> Less than 20 per cent. Some of the lecturers were only majoring in theory yet the training requires demonstrations and how it should be done when teaching. (ST6)

Public university educators were viewed less favourably due to their failure to complete the syllabus, absenteeism and poor teacher-student interaction. Excellence, to their student-teachers, involves:

> Organized presentations, consistent tests and feedback, consistent class attendance. (ST4)
>
> Provide guidelines on what trainees should do when faced with challenges in the field. (ST6)

Since not all teaching staff consider themselves teacher educators, they do not necessarily have, or seek, expertise in language teacher education. Such 'educators' will not model to student-teachers the different ways of teaching their subject content. As Westbrook et al. (2013: 60) note, student-teachers benefit from experiencing and observing good practices. Student-teachers who have learnt under *transmission-oriented* ways, for instance, cannot educate others in interactive practices. That teachers in Kenya graduate without much of that experience is evident from the many in-service interventions for teachers in the field. However, since the same educators run these in-service workshops, researchers have noted that many such interventions are inadequate (Njagi 2014). Citing six East African studies, Westbrook et al. (2013: 61) observe that 'teacher educators, themselves strangers to interactive practices, used expository methods with basic group work and advocated a prescriptive teaching sequence with little emphasis on critical and independent thinking for trainees'.

# The curriculum

The participants voiced their perspective on various aspects of the university curriculum process: the relevance of the content, resources, simulation exercises and the practicum.

## Relevance of course content

Participating educators from both universities noted that the focus of course content at university did not always prepare students for the reality of secondary school English teaching. In their view, the role of the university was not only to prepare students to be teachers of English but also to prepare them for graduate studies and for subject specialization:

> The critical approaches to literature, Marxism and all those, you need them as a literature student, but you are not going to teach them. (TE2)

TE2 further observed that the curriculum is content-based rather than skills-based, and cited this as a contributing factor to student-teachers' use of lecture methods while teaching in secondary schools. TE3 also noted that there was a disconnect between the way phonetics is taught at the university and the expectations of oral skills teaching in secondary school.

Educators in the public universities were explicit that the content and pedagogy in the secondary school English syllabus had not influenced the content and delivery of the programme in their department, as exemplified by TE5:

> The integrated English syllabus has been around for a long time and we have not responded. When we revise programmes we respond to what is happening in linguistic theory. ... Even when the syllabus for secondary school changes we don't respond. ... My department is in humanities, not under education; we are a service department ... we give what we want to teach, not what the secondary school syllabus requires. (TE5)

This response voices the failure of the university curricula to align itself to the needs of the industry/employer, and therein to the skills inventory that the student-teachers need to succeed in their career. When the student-teacher is learning to teach English and literature, how can the English and literature lecturers at the training institution be ignorant or negligent of the secondary school English/literature syllabi? Currently in Kenya, this lack of alignment between university curricula and market/industry needs has attracted a lot of attention in the media. Stakeholders from various fields lament the chasm between the knowledge, skills and attitudes that learners exit tertiary education with, and what the related professions need.

Recent local studies have actually revealed that teachers face challenges teaching the integrated English syllabus. Ongong'a, Okwara and Nyangara (2010) observe that though the official secondary school English language requires integration, there are minimal amounts of integration in the classroom. Macharia (2011) attributes this discrepancy to inadequate pre-service teacher education, poor understanding of integration philosophy, overloaded curriculum and difficult content. Kioko (2015) emphasizes the powerful role of teachers in implementing integration, once they have understood and embraced it. Indeed, the integration of literature and English receives robust defence from several scholars (Manyasi 2014). Yeasmin, Azad and Ferdoush (2011), for instance, cite positive effects such as stimulation of learners' imagination, ability to infer meaning, familiarity with universal issues and motivation to read.

Despite these challenges, student-teachers in both institutions largely indicated that the university courses and experiences had generally prepared them for the work of a teacher of English in Kenya. In the private university, ST3 cited the courses in the Faculty of Education as helpful in turning them into professionals:

> Anyone can become a teacher, but few can teach. 'ED' courses prepare someone to teach.

ST1, however, was critical about the handling of English subject methods as a Faculty of Education course:

> I wanted to come to you and say, why is it that you people are not teaching us subject methods – the English part of it? It was not education, as such.

The responses from student-teachers in the public university were similar. Some courses were directly relevant to secondary school teaching while others were not. In this, they concurred with their teacher educators that many of the courses were largely theoretical. They were all in agreement that their educators did not demonstrate the relationship between the content of the courses taught and the syllabus they would teach at secondary school. Therefore, it is possible that student-teachers leave the university without making this connection. One student-teacher expressed the following:

> 50 per cent courses in the English department are general and theoretical; no practical language teaching and learning in them. … No effort is made to link …

students read from hand-outs and some of it required practical classes and these were not available. (ST5)

Given the responses on content relevance, we sought to obtain participants' perspectives on the organization of the curriculum content. Student-teachers from both universities identified courses they felt should have been taken prior to the practicum. For instance, all participants in the private university wished they had been taught the English Grammar and Usage course before the practicum. Neither institution has post-teaching practice sessions to address identified gaps.

## Resources for teachers

The teacher educators felt that the observed gaps could be addressed by making resources available to student-teachers:

> Given that university curricula does not necessarily evolve in tandem with that of secondary schools ... it is the publishers who take the initiative ... to help them understand better how to use that [text]book. (TE3)

Student-teachers' use of resources is, however, not always problem-free. According to Kiai (2013), experienced teachers use guidebooks infrequently, and some even discourage novices from using them, yet such resources can boost their confidence.

The participants also pointed out the rich resources available via modern technology. The value of technology in the language classroom is undeniable; however, as Westbrook et al. (2013: 30) report, for various reasons, positive teacher attitudes towards blended learning do not always translate into successful use of ICTs.

## Micro-teaching

In both universities, the subject methods courses include practical sessions referred to as *micro-teaching*. These sessions give student-teachers opportunities to present mini-lessons, and obtain feedback from their instructors and peers. Each student-teacher is required to prepare a mock-lesson lasting from ten to twenty minutes based on a practice scheme of work. The other students role-play secondary school students during the lesson, which is video recorded and replayed to the class so that the student-teacher can engage in self-assessment. Depending on their performance, student-teachers may repeat lessons more than once. This provides for incorporation of feedback, self-correction and growth in confidence. This is what TE1 had to say about it:

> After they have taught, we replay. ... We let the owner evaluate themselves, and then, after that ... the whole class is invited to add input; to say what the person did right, what the person did wrong.

TE3, however, laments that the time for practice and feedback is insufficient in the one-semester course:

> Many of our students, when they go for TP, are still very nervous. They are not very sure.

Student-teachers in the private university indicated that in their subject methods classes of about fifteen to twenty-five students, they were able to practise two to four times each, and they improved as they went along. ST2 indicated that the constant focus on preparation of schemes of work and lesson plans during the course made the exercise enjoyable during teaching practice; however, she advocated more practical teaching:

> I think there should be more practice because we do a lot of theory. ... They can maybe create more time for the practicals – maybe two terms of micro-teaching.

Student-teachers from the public universities, however, indicated that though micro-teaching was part of the course outlines for the subject methods courses, they did not engage in the practical sessions because of the number of students in the classes: some of the subject method classes had as many as three-hundred students. Thus, the learners did not get opportunities for collaborative learning experiences in class. Often, their first experience of standing before learners occurred during teaching practice. The student-teachers brought this out clearly:

> It would have helped to have had more peer teaching in class. (ST4)
>
> I wish there was adequate training on how to teach comprehensions from a literature perspective since they employ oral literature and written literature techniques. Practical sessions through micro teaching ... would help the teacher to manage class well. (ST6)

Though micro-teaching is clearly a valuable experience for student-teachers, it appears to be insufficient, even when implemented. Strengthening it will be an important step in reducing student-teacher uncertainty and promoting self-confidence.

## The practicum

Teaching practice gives teacher educators an opportunity to gauge the practical competence of student-teachers. Participants from the private university perceived their student-teachers' competence as above average. TE2, however, observed that student-teachers specifically lacked competence in handling integration of English and literature; they tended to mimic university-level teacher-student interactions, and they set higher expectations of their learners than what the learners could accomplish. For example, they sometimes adopted group work without adequately preparing their students for the activity, and as TE2 observed:

> Something like – 'what I know at University, they should also know' … the student-teacher tells these Form Twos, 'go and research on this'. … It is a blanket assignment – 'go and research on oral narratives from your community' – so, isn't that what we do here? … In school we are dealing with homework, which is guided and very specific.

Teacher educators in the private university also noted weaknesses in student-teachers' handling of content and their teaching methodologies in language skills and grammar. For example, TE2 observed that student-teachers faced challenges in addressing learners' questions on grammar rules and on exceptions to rules. They sometimes accepted incorrect structures and failed to go beyond the textbook examples to add value and clarity to their grammar lessons. TE3 indicated that student-teachers were ill-equipped to teach writing, or to be writers themselves, whereas TE1 described them as lacking a reading culture:

> I must say that the teachers of today are not reading much, so they don't have depth in reading. … They will deliver little, though accurate, but little; it is not varied … they are challenged by variety.

Again, the picture from the public university is slightly different. TE4, TE5 and TE6 strongly felt that their students were not adequately prepared for the job. They expressed disappointment in their learners' preparedness in both areas of content and teaching methodology, with TE4 describing student-teachers as

> slaves of the textbooks. The majority are ill-equipped both in terms of knowledge, content and integrated approach … what is frustrating is that some of the knowledge gaps are very basic. (TE4)

TE5 reported disappointment and disillusionment because English and literature are taught in different departments, yet students are expected to implement integration in the field.

Despite the challenges and perceived shortcomings identified, student-teachers from both universities reported that the practicum experience inspired them to become, rather than discouraging them from becoming, teachers:

> It encouraged me since I got a chance to practise what I had learnt; identify my weak and strong areas; and … interact with students of different abilities and background. (ST5)

ST1 was happy with the planning, which gave students practice in a school for a whole school term. She noted that this gave her time to obtain feedback, internalize it and improve, as compared to the short sessions she had experienced in her primary school teacher education. ST2 reported that the experience was inspirational because it was interactive:

> At first I never thought that I would teach, but after TP, it was interesting and interactive. … What I enjoyed most were lesson preparation and delivery … because during micro-teaching … we'd write many lesson plans … it was like a hobby, writing them.

ST3 said that he experienced motivation to continue when he realized that students understood him. He further observed that in his final year, he found a course on Educational Administration and Planning more understandable because of the challenges he had encountered during his practicum.

Though they also found in the practicum a great learning experience, student-teachers from the public university did not perceive the supervision of teaching practice as very effective. This could partly stem from the lack of supervisor-induction at the start and the absence of midsession monitoring meetings. Again, though the university required at least four supervisions – two in each teaching subject – not all the university supervisors were from the language departments, and at times teaching staff without an education background participated in supervision.

In other areas, they expressed similar views to those of participants from the private university:

> Teaching practice should be regular, not once. Learning to be more practical and not just theory i.e. what is taught, learners should put into practice during learning. (ST5)
>
> Adequate time for training before going into the field … addition of one or two units relating to teaching practice. (TE6)

Student-teachers from the private university who experienced peer support during the practicum commented positively about it:

> The students who were close to me ... the sharing ... what you think is the best food from your mother's house, eventually you realise that there is another one, across there. (ST1)

# University curricula and student-teacher preparedness

To improve teacher preparedness, university curricula design needs to respond to the issues discussed in the following subsections.

## Peer support and mentorship

TE3 observed that in many cases teaching is a fall-back position rather than a first choice. Educational institutions should, therefore, focus on infusing the profession into the life of the teacher-student from the onset of the programme, with rigorous orientation at the departmental level, as proposed by ST1:

> Maybe it is good to have resource persons to come and talk to the undergraduate [students] – those who are about to finish. ... As a Department we can have a bit of a sit-down which is not very formal ... just to talk as a family, and be advised by lecturers, as a family, outside the formalities.

One type of human scaffolding that teacher-students reported to have used successfully is peer support. ST1 recalls that she journeyed with two colleagues, in the same school, during the practicum, and that they would share and laugh about the day's experiences. She strongly advocated co-posting of students from the same department to schools, where possible:

> For us, we were three ... and we were staying in the same house. So we were able to help each other.

Westbrook et al. (2013: 61–2) cite eight studies that report positively on peer support: 'Peer support through informal groups, formal clusters or pairs of teachers at the same school gave teachers opportunities for joint observation, sharing teaching and learning resources, lesson plans and assessment practices.'

Further, a recent research project underscored the need for a national and university policy on teacher mentorship in pre-service education. It revealed that teacher-students 'were able to settle a lot faster regarding writing schemes of work, lesson plans, and general orientation to school rules. ... It helped them to build confidence in and the motivation towards the profession' (Building 2014: 2).

## Resources

Teacher educators in the public universities lamented the lack of facilities such as language laboratories to aid in teaching pronunciation and other oral skills:

> We no longer have the facilities like language laboratory to prepare teachers who are users of English as a second language to teach oral skills. They [student-teachers] feel intimidated. (TE4)

Over-reliance on a textbook is another resource area requiring redress. Beginning teachers require greater support and scaffolds, both human and technological, to transit smoothly into their career. Studies indicate that manuals and scripted lessons can provide support for novice teachers by bridging the gap between theory and practice, and reducing the need to recall large amounts of information (Westbrook et al. 2013).

## Alignment of university ELTE curricula to secondary school syllabus

The findings revealed that the students' future career as English teachers is subordinated to the university's focus on future graduate study opportunities. Thus, professional practice is not necessarily given prominence when revising the curriculum or modelling good teaching practices. As such, students who eventually become teachers are likely to experience a disconnect between what they have learnt and what is expected of them in the classroom. According to TE2, the 'good' students work out for themselves the requirements of the school-based syllabus. Westbrook et al. (2013: 42), however, point out that 'teacher education programmes need to be tailored to teachers' existing knowledge, practices and circumstances, so that learning relates to their classrooms and to the pedagogy they are to teach'.

Adequate modelling and preparation of teachers for implementation of the integrated approach has remained problematic for universities. This is how educators expressed the perception of this gap:

> There is no link between literature [department], English [department] and ComTech [department] in the training. English lecturers do not use literary texts to teach language, literature lecturers do not highlight language structure

patterns during their literature lessons, and ComTech lecturers do not connect with the content from English or Literature. They [student-teachers] ... are against integration. (TE6)

To address this gap, the educators from the public university called for closer collaboration between the departments participating in ELTE; for involvement of subject content specialists in the teaching of subject methods; for a specific programme of study for student-teachers, differentiated from general Bachelor of Arts; and for a re-definition of class sizes where large numbers make practical sessions impractical.

## Strengthening micro-teaching

TE3 advocated that micro-teaching be handled as an independent course. He observed that micro-teaching is treated as part of graded coursework within subject methods; therefore, students sometimes collude with each other not to ask difficult questions. This would be overcome if the grading of micro-teaching played a subordinate role to that of provision of adequate practice for student-teachers. The desire for more practice also came from student-teachers, with ST2 calling for two terms of micro-teaching.

## Continuous professional development

Most student-teachers felt that the practicum ended too soon; for instance, ST3 advocated for at least two practicum sessions to enable them to develop full confidence. ELTE can perhaps be generally improved by introduction of mechanisms that provide for continuous professional development, as proposed by Westbrook et al. (2013: 32):

> Traditional front-loaded ITE [initial teacher education] whereby student-teachers learn content and methods in a residential setting prior to the practicum in schools looks out-dated in comparison to the field-based models of CPD [continuous professional development], which more successfully integrate theory with teachers' actual classroom practices.

## Post-practicum and post-studies follow-up

In both institutions, there are no specific follow-up post-practicum sessions. TE1 and TE3 both concurred that if there were post-practicum sessions, they would take a bottom-up approach and elicit from the teacher educators and student-teachers the topics that they would like to cover:

> I'd rather do it workshop-style, rather than trying to pre-empt what they are going to talk about. (TE3)

Student-teachers from the public university also looked into future ways of growing their professional skills; they had the following to say:

> I intend to acquire these through experience and consultation from experienced teachers. (ST4)
> I intend to learn online, especially pronunciation of words which is a major challenge to many students in high school. (ST6)

## Conclusion

The findings emphasize the important role of MKOs in providing mentorship and scaffolding for student-teachers, as advocated by sociocultural theory. However, in both universities, student-teachers lack reference to teacher educators with a unified identity because of the compartmentalization of content and methodology. When teaching staff see themselves more as subject matter specialists than as teacher educators, it reduces effective interaction among the student-teachers and between them and the MKO. This, and other coursework-related challenges, have led to a situation in which many student-teachers lack confidence in their skills and face significant challenges teaching the secondary school English syllabus during the practicum.

More broadly, the expressed desire by student-teachers for a curriculum that better prepares them for the actual practice of ELT is reflective of the pressure that the English language teacher faces in an 'English as a second language' context. As the primary medium of instruction, the English language plays a central role in helping to access knowledge, skills and information required to meet the nation's educational goals. Overarching sociocultural factors, however, present challenges to the student-teacher. Such factors include lack of confidence in teaching certain areas of the language, such as pronunciation (Muthwii and Kioko 2002: 80); an accompanying focus on exonormative standards – the British Standard variety (which the Ministry of Education claims is the variety taught in Kenyan schools); a highly examination-centred education system; and a disconnect between the ministry requirements and the university curriculum.

Thus, student-teachers appreciate the significance of a skills-based approach in their preparation, an approach that prepares them to bridge the gap between theory and practice.

At the heart of enabling learners to access knowledge, skills and information in English are English language teachers, who need to be well prepared for the task. It is hoped that the suggestions offered will be useful in bridging the gap between university curricula and student-teacher preparedness in Kenya and similar international ELTE contexts.

## Questions for change

1. How can the faculties and departments that teach Bachelor of Education students engage in effective cross-faculty dialogue to promote scaffolding and modelling for English student-teachers?
2. Which aspects of the curricula in your context require review in order to be aligned to the methodology and content needs of English student-teachers?
3. What post-practicum programmes can improve student-teacher experiences?
4. How can micro-teaching and other practical teaching sessions be effectively handled where classes are large?

# 5

# Supporting Post-observation Feedback in the EFL Teaching Practicum

Georgina Ma

## Objectives

1. Highlight challenges faced by supervisors working on pre-service teacher education courses.
2. Identify five aspects of post-observation feedback for development.
3. Encourage supervisors to 'learn their craft' as well as institutions to commit to the professional development of EFL teacher educators.
4. Report on the impact of a professional development intervention on one supervisor's professional practice.
5. Develop the practice of post-observation feedback in the EFL teaching practicum.

## Introduction

My interest in conducting research on the post-observation feedback genre began almost a decade ago and can be traced back to the following quotation in an email correspondence from a student-teacher on a pre-service Teaching English to Speakers of Other Languages (TESOL) course that I coordinated at a tertiary institution in South Africa:

> When students are criticized or score poor grades and they then find other students have suffered less criticism for an equally good or bad performance they tend to be extremely unhappy. Most of them want credit for good performance and constructive criticism for poor performance. What they do not want is a feeling that they are being unfairly judged. (Harmer 2005: 60)

This student-teacher was unhappy with the consistency and method of evaluation of teaching practice, as well as the post-observation feedback provided by supervisors of the course, and wanted to bring this to my attention. Through my own learning experiences and my work as a teacher educator of pre-service teacher education courses, I was aware of the precarious role and reputation of post-observation feedback. Like many other language teacher educators, I had *fallen* into the role by accident when I was offered a temporary relief position. Armed as I was with nothing more than my professional education and language teaching experience, my induction into language teacher education was a typical 'look and learn approach' (Diaz Maggioli 2012) in the craft tradition of teacher education (Wallace 1991), where I observed and learnt to imitate the content and procedures that I needed to follow. The part-time role grew into a permanent one and I carved out my career in language teacher education. I learnt through observing experts in the field, drawing on my own experience, doing, making mistakes and reflecting on my practice. In the nine years that I worked as a pre-service teacher educator, my colleagues and I received no institution-initiated in-service professional development. The receipt of this student-teacher's email further raised my already acute awareness of the complexity of the post-observation feedback genre and spurred me on a research journey. I aimed to better understand the discourse of post-observation feedback and was committed to contributing positively to the professional development of supervisors working on initial English as a Foreign Language (EFL) teacher education courses.

The data presented in this chapter was collected during research conducted for a master's degree (Ma 2009) and doctorate of philosophy (Ma in progress). The focus of this research is to better understand the genre of post-observation feedback of the TESOL course from the perspective of supervisors at the institution. Focusing and gaining insight into the attitudes of supervisors to feedback, the way in which they deliver feedback, and the impact that professional development intervention has had on their practice, has enabled me to capture the current state of post-observation feedback and provide suggestions to support the practice of supervisors through their professional development.

## Professional development of supervisors

The teaching practicum plays an important role in the professional development of student-teachers in initial EFL teacher education courses (Ochieng' Ong'ondo and Borg 2011). A central component of the practicum is the support and supervision that is offered to student-teachers by supervisors during post-observation feedback. There is often much at stake in the feedback conference and it is a challenging event to manage (Copland, Ma and Mann 2009). Giving appropriate feedback requires great skill on the part of the supervisor; yet 'most supervisors of students teachers receive very little preparation or education, and many do not have the expertise to supervise beginning teachers effectively' (Freiberg and Waxman 1990: 8).

Teachers who are qualified and experienced in language teaching and are considered to display the right knowledge and practice in their own classrooms are often drawn into working as supervisors. It is assumed that they will possess the skills and ability to supervise student-teachers successfully or will be able to learn on the job (Bailey 2006). Many supervisors have learnt how to supervise student-teachers through their membership of a community of practice (Copland 2010: 471). However, each supervisor comes to an observation with different ideas about teaching, different levels of understanding of the theory of language teaching and different styles of teaching. As a result, each supervisor will approach feedback differently.

By making the assumption that experienced teachers will know how to supervise pre-service teachers effectively overlooks important issues that may affect the development of pre-service teachers as well as standardization and quality of pre-service teacher education programmes.

These assumptions have serious consequences for the quality of pre-service teacher education. It is argued that supervisors have considerable influence on how and what students learn (Feiman-Nemser 2001). Poor supervision may have serious consequences for the quality of initial EFL teacher education, which is likely to affect subsequent teaching and learning directly. In order to ensure that supervisors are well equipped to provide quality post-observation feedback to student-teachers, it seems logical to demand that supervisors too 'must learn their craft' (Clark 1990: 48).

Professional development interventions seem a logical way to provide supervisors with the opportunity to develop their practice. Keogh, Dole and Hudson (2006: 1) argue that

> not all experienced teachers are effective [supervisors], and ... they need to undertake professional development and education in effective [supervision] to enable them to provide fully-rounded practicum experiences for the pre-service teacher.

The development of supervisors 'is an area in which there is growing and challenging demand for formal and informal education at pre- and in-service levels' (Kurtoglu Eken 2010: 5). Some studies reviewed for this research project have identified development needs for supervisors and the post-observation feedback event (Arnold 2006; Timperley 2001; Wajnryb 1994; Wang 2001).

## Professional context

The research site for both studies was a university-based language school in South Africa. The context of the study is the TESOL course, an internationally recognized initial EFL teacher education course, which consists of 120 hours of tuition in teaching English using a communicative approach. The course is made up of a theoretical component and a practical component. The theoretical component addresses language awareness, teaching techniques and language teaching methodology. The practical component involves a teaching practicum, where student-teachers put theoretical knowledge into practice and develop their teaching skills by preparing for and teaching a series of lessons to EFL learners from the local community. The teaching practicum post-observation feedback event is the focus of both research projects reported on in this chapter.

A total of nineteen supervisors participated in the two research projects. They range in age from twenty-eight to forty-five. Most supervisors have a university degree as well as a recognized English language teaching qualification, such as a CELTA or TEFL certificate. Supervisors are experienced English language teachers with at least six years of experience in teaching EFL. Some supervisors have experience working as teacher educators or supervisors on other initial language teacher education courses and all have been working as supervisors on the TESOL course for a minimum of six months.

## Theory underpinning the research

This research was informed by a social constructivist, process-oriented approach to initial language teacher education (Farr 2011), where post-observation feedback is seen to play an important role in the development of student-teachers' professional competence. In a social constructivist approach to post-observation feedback, supervisors need to move away from a directive or transmission approach, which is 'expert-directed, subordinating, replicating, [and] dependent' towards a non-directive or exploratory approach. The latter approach 'builds on existing knowledge, allows for different learning styles, provides opportunities for problem solving, encourages autonomy and is reflective' (Brandt 2006: 362) and 'allows for dialogue between student and teacher of a kind that promotes thinking and reflection and evokes and explores understanding' (Freeman 2007: 100). In the social constructivist approach to teacher education, student-teachers are no longer seen as 'empty vessels waiting to be filled with theoretical and pedagogical skills' by supervisors (Yates and Muchisky 2003: 137). Instead, learning is a collective endeavour of a community engaged in developing a specific form of practice, in this case the professional development of supervisors. In addition to social constructivism, a critical lens has been applied to this research, with the view of reviewing and improving supervisors' practice of post-observation feedback within a community of practice. It is within communities of practice (Barab and Duffy 2012; Lave and Wenger 1991) that professional knowledge, personal knowledge and community knowledge come together to help experts and novices to 'construct and reconstruct understandings through their involvement in the practices of teaching and learning' (Diaz Maggioli 2012).

This research is underpinned by Carr and Kemmis's (1986: 184) view of action research that

> thought and actions arise from practices in particular situations, and that these situations themselves can be transformed by transforming the practices that constitute them and the understandings that make them meaningful.

Action research is defined by Kemmis and McTaggart (1988: 5) as 'a form of collective self-reflective enquiry' used by participants in social situations to 'improve the rationality and justice of their own social or educational practices, as well as these practices and the situations in which these practices are carried out'. This research approach was selected for this study as 'action research is a way of defining and implementing relevant professional development' (Lomax 1990 cited in McNiff, Lomax and Whitehead 1996: 11), which is the fundamental aim of this project.

The research follows the Lewinian approach to action research, which is cyclical in nature and comprises a series of steps (Kemmis and McTaggart 1988). These steps include the identification of a problem and subsequent resolution of the problem through a process of planning, acting, collecting data and reflecting on this data.

# The action research cycle

This section is divided into the four distinct parts of the action research project, namely reconnaissance, planning, action and observation.

## Reconnaissance

Research into the state of post-observation feedback of the TESOL course (Ma 2009) aimed to provide a snapshot of the macro aspects of the practice of post-observation feedback to better understand the discourse and to provide some empirical evidence of areas of the post-observation feedback event that could be developed. This small-scale, context-specific needs analysis formed the reconnaissance for the planning stage of the action research cycle and the data collected was used to inform the development of a professional intervention for supervisors.

Research revealed that while supervisors working on initial EFL teacher education courses are committed to the professional development of the student-teachers they supervised, the quality of their supervision is affected by their lack of experience and education. Supervisors operate using the transmission, product-oriented approach to pre-service teacher education. In order for supervisors to move from this approach to the social constructivist, process-oriented approach, five of the six macro features of post-observation feedback analysed need to be developed. The macro features include the supervisors' approach to feedback, talk, reflection, structure and content.

### Approach

The results of the analysis of the supervisors' approach to feedback highlighted that they adopted a directive approach. To talk about their roles, 71 per cent of supervisors used phrases such as 'provide student-teachers with', 'to re-enforce the guidelines', and 'tell them'. They see their role as telling student-teachers what worked and what did not work in the lesson. In a directive approach to supervision, the supervisor assumes a 'hierarchical position as regards to the teacher' and 'advises, proposes, recommends and suggests the teacher carries out certain things in the classroom' (Randall and Thornton 2001:107). Post-observation feedback should move away from a directive or transfer approach towards a non-directive or exploratory approach, which 'builds on existing knowledge, allows for different learning styles, provides opportunities for problem solving, encourages autonomy and is reflective' (Brandt 2006: 362).

## *Talk*

The talk in the recorded feedback sessions is supervisor dominated, with the supervisors speaking for longer turns and more than the student-teachers. On average, the supervisors' talk accounts for 76.5 per cent, with student-teachers' talk accounting for 23.5 per cent of the post-observation feedback sessions.

Turn-taking in the sessions is generally structured in the same way. All supervisors begin their feedback with generic questions, such as 'What did you think went well?' or 'What did you think was good about your class?' The student-teachers have longer turns at the start of the feedback sessions; however, as the sessions progress, the supervisors' turns increase in length and student-teachers' responses are limited to one-word or short-phrase responses.

In extract one, the student-teacher, ST1, takes longer turns in the beginning of the feedback session, with the observer, SA, responding with short verbal agreements.

**Extract 1**

| | | |
|---|---|---|
| 07:34 | ST 1: | Well it's difficult for me to: u:m: It's still difficult for me to visualize the theory and- and visualize it into practice. In other words your – for me to: to: to: the: you know, the whole lesson plan for: for: for this letter writing. To actually for me to visualize it- visualize it into practice, the: a:nd and then separate to that the actual practice in the end was like it's very difficult to bring the whole lot together- |
| 08:06 | SA: | Okay. |
| 08:06 | ST 1: | And actually get them to- to: do you know the: I tried to- to: to let them to you know the planning, the drafting, and the editing and that thing. But unfortunately, you know, whilst they got started, they did it so sl::ow:::::ly: Like I couldn't get them to do it qui:::::cker: You see what I mean? |
| 08:24 | SA: | All right. |
| 08:24 | ST 1: | It's difficult for me to: With this bunch. To do that kind of thing. And I tried. I understood, I made sure I understood what you mean by the: the planning- |
| 08:34 | SA: | Mmhmm. |
| 08:34 | ST 1: | the drafting, the editing. I understand in theory what it means- |

Extract 2 shows how three minutes into ST1's feedback session, the observer, SA's turns increase and the trainee's responses are reduced to short verbal agreements in response to the observer's feedback.

**Extract 2**

| | | |
|---|---|---|
| 09:25 | SA: | You handed out after you explained everything about it- |
| 09:29 | ST 1: | Yeah. |
| 09:29 | SA: | Okay. Remember, the model, the model has to be handed out before: anything else. |
| 09:34 | ST 1: | Okay. |
| 09:35 | SA: | So all of your explanations about the content of the letter, and the: different paragraphs and what you include in each one: and how: to say it. All of that I wrote here that, the students were almost required to make notes in a vacuum. Like you were speaking about this formal letter and you were speaking about all of the components and aspects thereof. But for: On their part it was like a listening comprehension. They had to listen to you giving a lecture sort of- sort of a lecture type discussion about something. And at the end they got given the text to look at. |
| 10:11 | ST 1: | Yeah. |
| 10:12 | SA: | So that would be: In a writing lesson we deal with written word not spoken word. So: for a majority or a large chunk of the lesson they: were: a:sked to: listen to you rather than deal with the written word. Okay? So remember this for everyone's lessons that the- the key of a writing lesson- or the key of teaching writing is that the students must have a model from the beginning and from that model you take bits of language, which is what you did. |
| 10:40 | ST 1: | Yeah. |
| 10:40 | SA: | But the students didn't have the model in front of them- |
| 10:43 | ST 1: | Okay. |
| 10:43 | SA: | So when you were speaking of first paragraph, second paragraph and all of this language that is involved in it. |

In a constructivist, process-oriented approach to pre-service teacher education, talk plays an important role in the development of student-teachers. The development of pre-service teachers can be linked to Vygostky's (1978) belief that mental and sociocultural activity in humans is bound together in a dependent and symbolically mediated relationship. Gebhard (1990) concluded in his findings on research done on the development of pre-service teachers that the primary instigator of change is talk. If supervisors want to be successful in their goal of developing student-teachers, they need to provide opportunities for student-teachers to talk about their teaching by providing a more collaborative environment during post-observation feedback.

### Reflection

> I don't think there is enough opportunity for students to do post-observation reflection. Students need more time to consider their lessons. I think feedback will be more productive this way. (SB)

This supervisor identifies the lack of opportunity afforded to student-teachers to reflect on their practice and suggests that by adopting a more reflective approach, post-observation feedback would be more successful. An analysis of the data (Table 5.1) confirms that the supervisors' use of prompts for reflection was much lower than that of other general speech acts such as suggestions, advice or warnings.

Reflection plays a major role in the development of pre-service teachers as it helps to develop thinking. Reflective teachers who are aware of themselves, what they are doing and how that affects learning are therefore more able to change and develop areas of their teaching. A reflective habit will not only help them to develop their practice but will also be an invaluable tool in their future careers as language teachers.

### Structure

Some supervisors alluded to following a framework for their post-observation feedback. These supervisors describe following a two-stage framework: a reflective prompt followed by feedback delivery. Closer analysis of the feedback reveals that parts of the feedback sessions lack structure and focus and are in some cases very repetitive. I do not dispute that repetition may be an effective strategy specifically employed during feedback; however, in the

**Table 5.1** Supervisors' total general speech acts versus total reflective questions

| Supervisor | Advice | Suggestion | Order | Warning | Request | Total general speech acts | Total reflective questions |
|:---:|:---:|:---:|:---:|:---:|:---:|:---:|:---:|
| A | 4 | 22 | 11 | 2 | 2 | 39 | 7 |
| B | 1 | 34 | 4 | 0 | 0 | 39 | 17 |
| C | 17 | 19 | 7 | 8 | 0 | 51 | 12 |

feedback sessions analysed, repetition did not appear to benefit the student-teacher or help move the feedback forward. This observation was confirmed by SA in his reflection on the structure of his feedback:

> I identify a main 'lack' in the lesson and seem to harp on about it. I mention how it was an issue. ... We then discuss something else from the lesson and I seem to come back to the 'lack' again and mention more about it. (SB)

Structure is the backbone of feedback. It determines the shape and purpose of feedback and without structure, feedback risks being clumsy and unproductive. Structure enables the supervisor to ensure the following: feedback meets the objectives and criteria of the teaching practice, the most important aspects are covered, feedback is approached in such a way as to ensure input is accessible to student-teachers and gives them opportunities to reflect and participate, and, above all, for the feedback event to be more successful.

## *Content*

The content of the post-observation feedback covers student-teachers' academic and professional identity, received and experiential knowledge and a range of topics relating to roles of the teacher, teacher talk, learner behaviour and other general topics. Post-observation feedback is, on the whole, relevant to teaching practice criteria, although individual supervisors focus on points that are not relevant to the criteria or the course but may benefit the student-teachers in their future careers. Transcripts of the feedback brought to light some issues regarding different supervisor preferences and contradictory feedback. Brandt (2008: 42) advises that 'feedback is more effective when ... it is focused and contains relevant, meaningful, concrete information, accurate and specific data and irrefutable evidence'. Post-observation feedback should 'provide information specifically relating to the task or process of learning that fills a gap between what is understood and what is aimed to be understood' (Hattie and Timperley 2007: 81). The content of the post-observation feedback needs to be standardized and aligned with the teaching practice criteria.

## Planning

Reconnaissance of post-observation feedback allowed me to identify the *problem* by highlighting five areas of post-observation feedback that could be better developed. Professional development was identified as one of several interventions that could be implemented. Planning for the intervention included a review of the literature on professional development, pre-service EFL teacher education and post-observation feedback.

The experience of designing and implementing a professional development intervention for my colleagues was quite daunting. Committed to my own and their professional development, I aimed to develop a clear, well-designed professional development intervention that included meaningful, practical and engaging activities to meet the expectations and needs of the participants and promote learning and development. Adults may come to professional development with many preconceptions, habits and rationalizations for their habits, as well as tensions, enthusiasms and expectations (Newton and Tarrant 1992: 140) that may affect their motivation and limit opportunities for learning and development. In order to minimize possible negative effects of these factors on the interventions or on the development of the participants, I involved the supervisors in the planning stage. Professional development interventions are more successful if the participants are able to feel some ownership of the intervention, by being involved either in the selection of the topic, tasks and activities or in the planning (Newton and Tarrant 1992: 144).

Kurtoglu Eken (2010: 5) argues that 'education needs to liberate itself from a crippling let-me-show-you, let-me-tell-you approach and adopt as its main principle exploratory and experiential learning processes, which promote personal and professional growth'. Experiential learning is defined as 'the process whereby knowledge is created through the transformation of experience' (Kolb 1984: 38; also Kolb 2015). It is a continuous process that is grounded in the participants' experience, where existing beliefs and practices are explored and tested against new experiences, resulting in the evolution of more refined ideas (Head and Taylor 1997). In order to achieve such processes, I planned for the interventions to include the following fundamental elements: a balance of theory and practice, synchronic and sequential coherence of input, utilization of participants' knowledge and experience as resources, examination and exploration of professional thoughts, beliefs and practices, dialogue, reflection and research-based practices (Malderez and Bodóczky 1999). In many ways my approach to the professional development of supervisors can be described as 'matching what is taught with how it is taught' (ibid.: 25).

## The professional development intervention

This professional development intervention is a systematic effort with the aim of bringing about change in the practice of supervisors, their attitudes and beliefs as well as the learning outcomes of student-teachers (Guskey 2002).

The professional development intervention was offered to teacher educators and supervisors employed for TESOL courses at the institution. It included twelve two-hour workshops, which ran over ten months. Each two-hour workshop was divided into two sessions: one focused on the *what* – the course content of the TESOL course, which aimed at developing the supervisors' content knowledge – and the other focused on the *how* – the delivery of post-observation feedback, which aimed at developing the supervisors' pedagogic content knowledge (Shulman 1986). Key topics in the *how* sessions included the following:

1. Approaches to giving feedback
2. Structuring feedback
3. Talk in feedback
4. Scaffolding student-teachers effectively
5. Reflection in feedback
6. Mitigating language in feedback

## Three key developments in one supervisor's practice

The following section provides an overview of three key developments in the practice of one supervisor who completed the intervention. The three key developments include (1) approach, (2) structure and (3) reflection.

### Approach

> I wasn't aware of much in terms of approaches to post-observation feedback before the workshop, other than my own experience of receiving feedback – and a brief description of suggested feedback on [an] assessor's course. (S1)

In this reflective writing task, S1 clearly indicated that he did not have much knowledge about different approaches to feedback prior to the workshop. Prior to the workshop, S1 appeared to take a very directive approach to feedback. His feedback sessions were supervisor-centred, which consisted of his telling the student-teachers what they did right and where they needed to improve. Feedback sessions were dominated by supervisor-talk, and although reflection was included, it was quite superficial. By adopting this approach, S1 slipped into the role of judge rather than mentor.

It is interesting to note that following the workshop on approaches to feedback, S1's feedback changed. As described in his reflection below, he was drawn to the alternatives approach, and evidence from the mid- and post-workshop feedback sessions indicate that he adopted an alternatives approach when giving his feedback:

> I was curious to learn some new approaches, and found the information shared very interesting. … I like the alternatives approach as it offers an opportunity not only to have trainees consider the alternatives, but also to include the trainees in the process of considering alternatives, which aligns it with a more collaborative approach. I would definitely use an integration of approaches though as there are stages in feedback that lend themselves to a directive approach. (S1)

### Structure

This supervisor identified the structure of feedback as an area for development.

> I learnt that the structure of my feedback was rather predictable and probably repetitive. I tend to follow a limited pattern – something like the hamburger model as this has previously been suggested to me. (S1)

In the quote above, the supervisor expresses the need for more variety in his feedback. He describes his feedback as being predictable and monotonous due to the overuse of the typical sandwich feedback model. Data shows that the structure of the supervisor's feedback changes over the course of the professional development intervention.

S1's pre-workshop feedback follows a three-stage framework, which is organized by the post-observation discourse categories: reflection, feedback and summary. S1's approach to the feedback session is highly structured and rigid. In the reflection phase, he poses reflective questions to the student-teachers and they reflect on their feedback in turn. In the feedback phase, S1 delivers his feedback to each student-teacher in turn and in the short summary phase, he asks the student-teachers for comments or questions.

The post-workshop feedback sessions reveal a distinct shift in S1's structure of his feedback sessions. He moves away from a rigid, directive feedback framework to a more integrated, collaborative framework, where the feedback is organized around the student-teachers and each feedback phase includes four sub-phases: (1) reflection, (2) questioning, (3) peer feedback and (4) individual feedback. The student-teachers are given more time to reflect using this approach and their reflection is more meaningful. As a result of the students reflecting more on their teaching and the inclusion of peer feedback, S1's individual feedback is reduced by almost a third per student-teacher.

In a reflective writing task completed following the workshop on the structure of feedback, supervisors were asked to reflect on the structure of their feedback and what they had learnt during the professional development workshop:

> What appeals to me most from this workshop is the practical suggestions for trying different structures. The feedback summary sheets were the most useful tool for me as they ensure that sufficient information to support feedback is recorded in an organised way. I used one of these templates this past weekend and found it very useful. (S1)

He expressed that he felt he could improve the structure of his feedback by utilizing different feedback structures for different lessons, which would provide some variety of feedback structure for the student trainees and make feedback more interesting:

> I know that there's more ways to structure your whole feedback. I don't think I've done that. ... That's something I should make a priority for myself when I do my next course. ... In the same way our trainees have to use different approaches for different types of lessons. I'd like to be able to deliberately have different approaches for different kinds of feedback. (S1)

## *Reflection*

> I tell the students that the best way to become good at teaching is to look at what you've just done while still fresh and to keep a record of that. ...It just generates a lot of awareness. And then gives us a lot to talk about afterwards as well. (S1)

In the quote above, S1 identifies reflection as one of the key tools that teachers can use to develop their practice. Overall, there was an increase in the quantity of reflection used by S1 following his participation in the professional development workshops:

> I think that I've brought more awareness to it so that I'm giving them that platform to ... contribute more before I lead them down the road. (S1)

S1 attributes the shift in his approach to reflection to the increase of his awareness of the importance and benefit of reflection as a result of the professional development intervention.

In addition, there is a shift in the type of reflection from more open to focused reflection. Prior to the professional development intervention, S1 tended to use open reflection by asking questions such as 'What worked well or didn't work well in your lesson?' where he encouraged 'general reflection and afford[ed] some space to the teachers to engage in talk related to their own individual observations and priorities' (Farr 2011: 73). During and after professional development intervention, there is evidence that S1 is more selective and focused in his reflective questioning by including a 'priority issue for discussion' when prompting student-teachers to reflect (ibid.: 75). Some examples of more focused reflection by S1 are included below:

> How do you feel they coped with that (sentence completion activity)?
> Could you think of a way that they could maybe generate more communication or discussion out of it?
> What do you think was the main reason for your time issues? (S1)

## Conclusion

This chapter provides an overview of my nine-year research journey into the discourse of post-observation feedback and the professional development of supervisors working with pre-service EFL teachers. Through this journey, I identified key areas of the professional practice of supervisors that required development, developed and implemented a professional development intervention and tracked the supervisors' practice to identify change. Data collected (Ma in progress) shows that there was positive impact on the practice of the supervisors who participated in the in-service professional development intervention. S1's reflection on the professional development intervention reveals that the supervisors benefitted from the education in numerous ways:

> I enjoyed belonging to a community that shares interest and desire to learn in the field. The workshops gave the supervisors an opportunity to discuss important aspects of feedback and assessment and we achieved a sense of agreement and standardisation. I developed a deeper sense of empathy with the student teachers I observe. (S1)

Shulman (1983: 45) claims that one virtue of a case study is its ability to evoke images of the possible. This chapter provides a model of professional development for supervisors and what is possible. The process has helped to deepen my knowledge of the practice of post-observation feedback and contribute meaningfully to the professional development of my peers within a community of practice. Through this process I have addressed some of the issues that I set out to tackle, but I have unearthed other issues that I had not expected. As McNiff (2010) suggests in the quote below, my research journey is set to continue:

> There is no end, and that is the nature of developmental practices, and part of the joy of doing action research. It resists closure. Each ending is a new beginning. Each event carries its own potentials for new creative forms.

## Questions for change

1. What professional development do you engage in?
2. What aspects of your feedback practice could be developed?
3. Do you engage in both face-to-face and digital feedback provision?
4. What support do supervisors require in order to better supervise student-teachers?

# 6

# Technology-mediated Initial Teacher Education

Gabriel Diaz Maggioli

## Objectives

1. Present initial teacher education processes under the light of a design mindset.
2. Provide a design-based template that has the potential to contribute to the development of rigorous and productive online learning experiences for aspiring teachers.
3. Explore both issues above from a Cultural Historical Activity Theory (CHAT) perspective.

## Introduction

The exponential boom of technology into higher education has seen the proliferation of a multitude of experiments aimed at quality provisions with reduced costs for universities and more accessibility for learners. However, it is my contention that the potential of this for teacher preparation programmes is still merely a mirage and that we are just witnessing the initial labour pains of their purported impact. While Learning Management Systems (LMSs) continue to surface claiming to respond to the sector's ever-changing needs, educators and students alike complain about the inability of these systems to capture the inherent complexity and messiness of the acts of teaching and learning. Because LMSs are, by nature, binary and electronic, they, if used as they come, carry with them the danger of becoming another behaviourist project where unreflective, *drag and drop* activities (Diaz Maggioli and Painter-Farrell 2013) predominate. However, when used as a tool for mediation, they can unleash learning unbridled.

This is because the development of awareness about teaching, as well as of the knowledge and skills needed to facilitate language learning, operates mostly within a horizontal logic, one that skews polarities in favour of a multitude of shades of grey and which is, at the same time, recursive and chaotic, as opposed to linear and sequential.

In this chapter, I introduce the notion that the inherent characteristics of the LMS medium pose a risk to learning when the system is used as a repository of content and teacher-learners interact in a perfunctory fashion. In this scenario, we may even advance the notion that teacher education mediated by technology has, so far, failed to provide teachers of teachers (ToTs) (Malderez and Wedell 2007) with the tools needed to effectively facilitate the learning of professional concepts, skills and dispositions for teaching. Most functions of LMSs rely heavily on binary processes: deduction and induction. These are oriented towards analytical and evaluative types of activities and, while this may be suitable for some content in teacher education, an important area of development is the teacher-learners' capacity to entertain alternatives and to imagine possibilities. In this respect, Cross (2011) advocates for the adoption of the concept of *abductive* reasoning to fill this gap. He explains:

> Deduction proves that something must be; induction shows that something actually is operative; abduction suggests that something may be. It is this hypothesizing of what may be, the act of producing proposals or conjectures, that is central to designing. (Cross, 2011: 27)

If learning to teach is a highly skilled, contextually bound endeavour that evolves through principled participation in teaching and learning activities, then ToTs need to seek those alternatives that best help them facilitate the development of professional knowledge, skills and dispositions that make adaptive experts of teachers. In this sense, the task of the ToT is not unlike that of the designer.

## Perspectives on learning to teach

Theoreticians and researchers have long put forward various theories on the nature and process of learning to teach. This process has been depicted as one of transmission and replication of skills; as the transmission and replication of theories; as a reflective endeavour *in* and *on* practice; and, more recently, as one of progressive participation in professional communities of practice

(Diaz Maggioli 2012). While there are more contemporary approaches to the conceptualization of teacher learning, I advocate for the last one since it most faithfully represents the processes I describe in this chapter.

With more countries starting English as a Foreign Language (EFL) instruction at the elementary level, the need for qualified professionals has become pressing worldwide. In contrast with this reality, both the recruitment into the profession and the attrition rates experienced by schools have rendered many efforts futile, at best. Although we cannot readily correlate the lack of qualified teachers to the (in)adequacy of the methods used in teacher education, we can, nevertheless, advance the idea that teachers seem to learn best when given the opportunity to become involved in the act of teaching early on in their careers (Bailey, Curtis and Nunan 2001; Diaz Maggioli 2012; Malderez and Wedell 2007). However, what does not seem to be a logical solution is seeking to circumvent this reality under the guise of increased learning opportunities afforded by technology-mediated provisions.

Instead, focusing on the pedagogy to which the technology can best be put to use looks like a promising alternative. Laurillard (2012) posits this very notion when she observes that of all the technologies impacting teaching (such as the development of writing, books, the chalkboard and, more recently, LMSs) only one (the chalkboard) was specifically developed with teaching in mind. All others were developed for purposes such as commerce, the spread of religion or the simplification of corporate training. This leads the author to say:

> Tools and technologies, in their broadest sense, are important drivers of education, though their development is rarely driven by education. Precisely because of their potential to change education unbidden, it is imperative that teachers and lecturers place themselves in a position where they are able to master the use of digital technologies, to harness their power, and put them to the proper service of education. (Laurillard 2012: 2)

ToTs should thus start by familiarizing themselves with the pedagogical principles behind various applications so that they faithfully replicate the social processes that are in operation in on-site realities. In this respect, a perspective that sees teacher learning as an increase in the opportunities to participate in the processes of teaching and learning seems to make sense in that it acknowledges the fact that in order to *learn*, one must be able to *do*. This doing, however, is not purely unreflective mimicry, but stems from the opportunities for interaction with more seasoned participants in the activity (Lave and Wenger 1991) and is enriched by the opportunities for mediation afforded by the negotiation of meaning that normally occurs in the development of any activity. It is through participation that one acquires both the language and the frame of mind needed to succeed in an activity. Compare this scenario to situations where participants are only given prescriptive procedures to follow or theories to replicate, such as those that happen in short-term teacher education courses. In these, learning appears constrained as participants are denied the chance to expand their individual repertoires in favour of the faithful replication of a fixed, external model. In contrast, a perspective that favours progressive internalization by the participant of inherent characteristics of the activity allows for the expansion of the participant's ability to effect changes in the activity. It is in these opportunities to externalize novel ways of approaching the activity that the internalized mediational systems previously available through social interaction become a higher form of cognition that not only allows the individual to develop but also changes the structure of the whole activity and its participants.

In other words, participation in any form of human activity that is mediated by less, equally, or more capable others as well as by concrete and mental tools affords individuals the possibility of new learning, which, in turn, opens pathways for various zones of proximal development (Vygotsky 1978, 1986). These eventually lead to changes in both the activity system and the individual's cognition.

## LMSs and teacher learning

Educational provisions delivered through LMSs should thus allow for the replication of this reality in the process of teacher education. Most of the LMSs currently available are best described as *teaching* management systems in that most of the applications available seem to keep track of students' work, thus simplifying the work of teachers. Some of these applications include grade books, online grading and correction tools, applications that allow statistical analyses of student participation, individual or group email facilities, depositories of course materials, systems for the submission of assignments, evaluation authoring tools and applications for keeping track of students' completion of tasks and assignments. In contrast, tools for learning tend to include only wikis, forums, facilities for setting up small group work and, in very few cases, videoconferencing tools.

At this stage we might wonder what kind of technology-mediated environment has the actual potential to counteract the 'machine-deep' (Diaz Maggioli and Painter-Farrell 2013) nature of the ones currently available. While the answer to this quandary is still tentative and further research is needed in order to truly understand the effects of what is proposed in the following sections, preliminary results from a recent action research project seem to confirm that a change in the logic of course design for online delivery may favourably enhance online opportunities in learning to teach.

## Popular course formats for online learning

Technological developments happen at incredible speed, and with each iteration of innovation, come a host of tools and applications that render previous ones obsolete. However, it is not the tools themselves, but the uses they are put to, that provide actual affordances as tools evolve through use and take on functions unforeseen by their creators. However, for those affordances to be effective, the intervention of an expert, in the Vygotskyan sense, is needed. Motteram (2013: 179–80) explains this concept when he says that

> computers are the sticks and flints for the modern world, in that they can be used by people in ways not originally part of the designed affordances of the tool, but are different from a stick in that they are already complex in nature and already have at least one cultural function in society; they often end up having many.

Online course delivery has taken on many facets. Many courses, including Massive Online Open Courses (MOOCs) rely heavily on pre-recorded lectures, input in the form of e-publications, and self-administered and machine-graded checks of comprehension, with or without the addition of tasks that are peer- or instructor-moderated. Other courses encourage the use of forums for students to post answers to the tasks set by the instructor but fail to foster further interaction by having the instructor as the sole receiver and assessor of the tasks. More pedagogically sound courses, in contrast, purposefully design opportunities for students to interact with and offer each other feedback, with the instructor acting as moderator of those discussions. All these forms of online delivery are guided by carefully crafted learning goals followed by a sequence of activities aimed at attaining those goals. In other words, instructional design is sequential and convergent, whereas the development of knowledge for teaching is cyclical and divergent (Shulman 1986).

Hence, regardless of the format, the design logic behind many of these courses seems to follow Tyler's (1949) rationale, which prescribes the following stages:

1. Determine the purposes of the course (i.e. course objectives that would act as measures of learning).

2. Identify the educational experiences that would best help achieve the purposes of the course.
3. Design and organize these experiences.
4. Evaluate the attainment of the purposes of the course.

Such an approach to course design is limiting in that it does not actually allow ToTs to effect the needed changes in the aspiring teacher's cognition. Much of the research on teacher learning (Borg 2006b; Sanchez 2010) concludes that by the time we arrive in the teacher education classroom, we already have a fixed mindset about what it means to be a good teacher, and it is this mindset that we use to develop our teaching style. This mindset, which Lortie (1975) calls 'the apprenticeship of observation', is developed through the thousands of hours we spend as learners. In this sense, we seem to come to understand good teaching as that which helped *us* learn best (and not necessarily that which helps *our students* learn best). Bailey et al. (2001) indicate that the preconceptions derived from this apprenticeship of observation are very difficult to change and that for them to be challenged and reconceptualized, extensive *engagement with the activity of teaching*, coupled with opportunities for reflective self-assessment, is necessary. It is evident that LMSs and many of the courses designed for them fail to take stock of these needs.

## Applying a designer's mindset: An action research project

In the fall of 2015, I undertook a self-motivated action research project in order to assess the suitability of applying an alternative framework to the development, delivery and assessment of a technology-mediated teacher education course so as to promote more engaged forms of participation. I was then teaching a blended *EFL Methods* course at an undergraduate institution in Uruguay with online support, on-site input sessions and a teaching practice component. What motivated the intervention in this process was the dissatisfaction I experienced with the delivery of this course using the current institutional guidelines for course design. This dissatisfaction was also voiced by the participating student-teachers who complained that they felt that the course was mostly a reading and answer questions/do task course, and not a venue for the development of skills in teaching EFL.

The group was made up of nine recent high school graduates who possessed, on average, a B2 + level of English (Council of Europe 2001). Throughout the process, I engaged the collaboration of two critical friends. These were colleagues who taught other sections of the same course and with whom I met throughout the rewriting of the course and its teaching over two semesters. Their comments and suggestions helped me reflect on my own design process and clarified and validated many of the claims I make here. Student-teachers' voices helped develop the design process on an ongoing basis through written answers to focused questions at the end of sessions as well as by a survey administered at the end of the course. The questions were oriented towards finding out what students had learnt that they did not know before, through this online experience. The survey focused on aspects of course design, participation and learning, as well. Of the nine students in the group, five completed the survey.

## Intervention

In order to better support my students, I organized the new course using a designer's mindset. Simon (1986: 129, see also Dorst 2015: viii) writes that to design is to '[devise] courses of action aimed at changing existing situations into preferred ones'. The aim of this intervention was to probe whether students' participation in the online environment reflected their ongoing engagement with practice as well, so that the course was not just oriented towards the attainment of content objectives but also enhanced their participation in the activities of their communities of practice.

For the purpose of this chapter, I will illustrate the intervention using one of the units in the course. The unit on *Planning for Students' Learning* was taught immediately before the first supervisory visit. The original course had favoured a backward design (McThige and Wiggins 2007) logic, which specifies that first you establish the evidence for learning, then you design assessments to gather that evidence and only after these have been established, do you design the learning activities. The course was structured around a generative question: 'How can lesson planning help me teach?' and it had, as its culminating performance task, the planning of a forty-five-minute EFL lesson, which was then taught and supervised. The module, which lasted one week in a fifteen-week semester, targeted three essential understandings, which, in turn, yielded three lessons: (1) how to write learning objectives, (2) how to design assessments to secure the attainment of objectives and, finally, (3) how to sequence teaching and learning activities. Each lesson started with explicit learning goals. It then presented an individual task where students learnt about theory. This task was neither graded nor shared. Its main purpose was to engage students with readings and/or video lectures. The individual task was followed by one or more discussion tasks via a forum, where students expanded their discussion of the main ideas in the readings/lectures. The forum was moderated by the instructor who provided guidance both publicly (on the forum) and privately (via individual messages to students). Finally, there was an application task where students put theory into practice. There was a final reflective self-evaluation students had to complete after having received feedback from the instructor. In their self-evaluation, they also had to devise an action plan to overcome the difficulties identified during the assessed lesson. Figure 6.1 shows the organization and sequence of the module.

Participation in the old version of the course was adequate in that students completed the tasks on time to fulfil assessment requirements. Their postings on the discussion forums were, at times, perfunctory, barely skimming the surface of the concepts they had read about. Also, even though there was a minimum number of words required, they generally fell short of that figure. Most noticeable in their participation, though, were their attempts to account for the theory by referencing their own practice. However, this reference was tangential as they failed to make relevant connections between theory and practice. In general, they forced an illustration of the concept from their experience. What follows is an example of a response to the learning objectives of a peer:

TASK: Select one of your objectives and account for your selection of methods of assessment for that objective.
STUDENT A's posting:
Objective: To engage students in natural communication through pair work.
Assessment: Present an exercise involving matching prepositions to the correct picture, and given a certain time to think about it. Correct two or three pairs and ask them to be the 'teachers' and begin correcting others. This can help them to develop a certain amount of autonomy and it will also help me to save time and help those who could not understand.
STUDENT B's response:
Hi.
I believe the assessment methods you propose should yield good results. They seem to be consistent with your objectives, and cover a wide spectrum of possibilities. I like the use of collaborative learning techniques as a means to encourage autonomy and help others. I guess there will be a lot to pay attention to as they play, so, monitoring their activity would certainly offer indicators of their level of understanding of the subject.

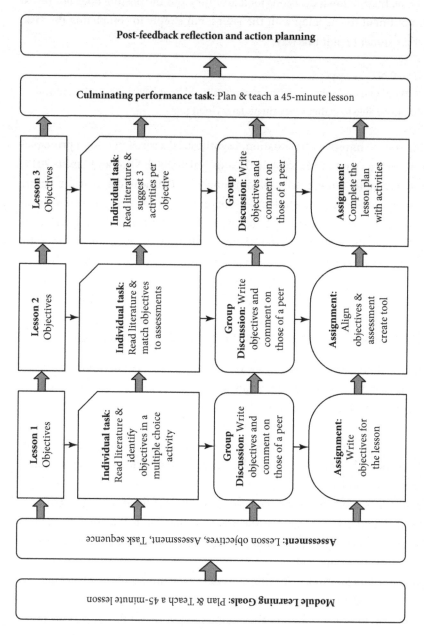

**Figure 6.1** An online module following the understanding by design logic.

As it can be seen from this interaction, students failed to provide theoretical support for their decision making and concentrated only on the practical side of the issue. Instructional decisions look arbitrary and the posting does not reveal a commitment to engaging with the issues, but simply to completing the task. Another student put it this way:

> STUDENT C's response:
> What you say looks good. The students should be able to do the tasks and you should be able to gather assessment data. Good job!

In order to improve this situation, I synthesized a series of design principles (Cross 2011; Dorst 2015; Kaptelenin and Nardi 2009; Otto and Smith 2013) into a workable, though principled, framework that would orient the nature of the interaction among students while respecting the necessary non-linear and iterative nature of learning to teach. Additionally, I resorted to Laurillard's (2012) learning modes to ground my mediation via technology on solid pedagogical principles. The modes of learning Laurillard proposes include acquisitional learning; inquiry-based learning; discussion-based learning; practice-based learning; collaboration-based learning; and production-based learning.

The framework I developed highlights the following design features:

1. *Understand*: students become aware of the theoretical underpinnings of the issue at stake mainly through acquisition, practice and discussion-based learning (and, at times, inquiry-based learning).
2. *Observe*: students observe how theory is imbricated in practice and vice versa. They derive their own conceptualizations, thus building a knowledge base about the issue. Inquiry-, collaboration- and discussion-based learning are useful modes at this stage.
3. *Empathize*: students seek to position themselves at the receiving end of their intentions so as to assess the potential effect of their actions on their students' learning. Inquiry- and production-based learning modes figure prominently in this feature.
4. *Imagine and brainstorm*: having considered the impact of their teaching actions, student-teachers envision possible solutions to the issue or problem. In order to do this, they might need to revisit the knowledge they constructed through understanding, observation and empathy. All modes of learning can be synthesized at this stage, as students will have to go back

and forth gathering information, evaluating and synthesizing, in order to create something new during the *Design* phase.

5. *Design:* imagining and brainstorming provide the fodder for the initial design of a solution to the learning issue or problem they are seeking to unravel. In so doing, they revisit their learning through other design features, so that they can inform their collaboration and production.

6. *Try out:* the actual implementation of their *prototype* leads student-teachers to engage with the activities of teaching and learning in a more realistic manner so that they can assess the viability of their design. Inquiry and discussion modes predominate in this feature as students begin moving from a peripheral to a more central position in their community of practice.

7. *Reflect and commit:* the final feature of the design framework involves looking back at all the other features, taking stock of what has been understood and learnt, and committing to applying this new learning in the future.

The different design features, though sequentially organized, encourage a more systemic approach to learning, as they foster ongoing movement back and forth among the various steps towards achieving a proposed, workable solution to the issue or problem.

Table 6.1 summarizes how the design features of the course (Column 1) and the various different learning modes (Row 1) interact and shape the turf where new learning takes place. However, bear in mind that this conceptualization is my own and it is based on my contextual positioning. Other contexts may require different interactions.

**Table 6.1** The intersection of features of design and learning modes

| | Acquisition | Inquiry | Practice | Discussion | Production | Collaboration |
|---|---|---|---|---|---|---|
| Understand | ▓ | ▓ | | ▓ | | ▓ |
| Observe | | ▓ | | ▓ | | ▓ |
| Empathize | | ▓ | | | ▓ | |
| Imagine and brainstorm | ▓ | ▓ | | | ▓ | ▓ |
| Design | | | | | ▓ | ▓ |
| Try out | | ▓ | | ▓ | | |
| Reflect and commit | | ▓ | | ▓ | | |

## Results

Data gathered from the discussion forums, focused questions and survey show a more positive response to the course, its design and implementation. For example, five of the respondents to the survey found the *empathize, design* and *try out* tasks to be the most useful. The second most useful tasks, as indicated by four of the participants, were the *observation, imagine and brainstorm* and *reflect and commit tasks*. This was confirmed by the ongoing answers to focused questions during the development of the course. For example, on the impact of the *try out* task the participants responded:

> The theoretical material explored, and the collective and collaborative feedback following the initial design (and subsequent) tasks were truly priceless. IMO, crashing against the wall really helps to put one's feet on the ground after dealing with theory. Implementing the design was a real 'reality check' that allowed me to see my own learning impacting that of my students. (Student 2)
>
> IMO, the presence of interactive material really improved the experience; with handpicked videos, articles and such, it was easier for me to notice the mistakes and good habits in someone else's class so I was more aware of the advantages and disadvantages of the procedures involved and this made me more confident about what I did in my own lessons. (Student 1)
>
> Having the opportunity to have your peers AND your teacher provide feedback on the whole process was, IMO, the strongest part of the course. I felt reassured by having this support network and the various readings and handouts about lesson planning, but at the same time, my decisions were questioned many times. This helped me think more about the learners than about my own lesson plan. (Student 3)

The nature and quality of the discussion board posting also changed dramatically, both in terms of length and in terms of the theory-practice connection. Though too lengthy to be reproduced here, the following features were characteristic of the postings in this version of the course:

1. Students seemed to operate from a theory-to-practice-to-theory again perspective. They used theoretical principles to guide their design and then attempted to theorize their practice by considering how the practice confirmed or disputed what they had read. In the process they made explicit connections between their design, the contextual needs of their students and the theory.
2. The length of posting increased by at least 70 per cent in terms of number of words with many exceeding by 200 per cent the mean number of words

of postings in the previous version of the course. For example, initial posts averaged ninety words and they grew to 150 and, in some cases, 200 words.

3. Postings made more reference to the impact of the community on their learning. In responding to peers' postings, student-teachers spoke of their own implementations, the opinions of cooperating teachers and referenced the experiences of other students in the class. Whereas in the previous version of the course the highest frequency pronouns in the postings had been *You* and *I*, in the new version there are frequent references to *they*, *he* and *she* to nominate peers, students and cooperating teachers. Likewise, more references to *we* are seen in the new postings to refer to the student-teacher and his/her students.

4. The overall quality of the final lesson design and its teaching appeared more solid. More realistic potential problems were anticipated and proposed solutions were also more genuine, taking elements from context into consideration. The sequencing of tasks and the implementation of assessment were also more grounded on the reality of the classrooms where student-teachers taught.

5. Finally, student-teachers incorporated their students' needs and motivations more in their instructional design. Whereas in the previous version of the course classes had been scientifically sound (in that they reflected the theory studied), those in the new version took the theoretical principles and their actual students' needs as the point of departure for instructional decision making.

## An activity theoretical perspective on the results

The result of this focused action research project shows how a change in one aspect of the activity can yield changes to the whole activity while expanding learning opportunities. In this sense, we could advance an activity theoretical interpretation of how the change was made possible. Leontiev (1978) saw activities as hierarchical systems containing actions or chains of actions that serve the purpose of fulfilling certain aspects of the object or motivation. These actions, in turn, are composed of a series of operations. In the case of the present inquiry, the activity that is the focus of research is mediation of student-teacher learning using a design framework as the tool, whereas the motive is enhanced learning by student-teachers implying their reconceptualization of the task of language teaching. While activities have motives oriented towards an outcome,

**Table 6.2** Examples of activities, actions and operations in this study (adapted from Hashim and Jones 2007).

| Activity level | Instructor mediation of students' learning using a design framework. | *Motive:* enhanced (re) conceptualization of new concepts by student-teachers. |
|---|---|---|
| ↓ ↑ | ↓ ↑ | ↓ ↑ |
| **Action level** | Design framework to support learning. | *Goal:* provide mediation to student-teachers' (re) conceptualization efforts. |
| ↓ ↑ | ↓ ↑ | ↓ ↑ |
| **Operation level** | Affordances of each component of the design framework for student-teacher concept development. | *Conditions:* affordances of the design mindset to enact various scaffolds. |

actions have specific goals that can be satisfied when operations in the script are implemented under certain conditions – in our case, those afforded by the elements of the design mindset. The relationships between all these elements in this inquiry can be represented thus (Table 6.2), borrowing from the work of Hashim and Jones (2007):

Engeström (2000) indicates that while object-oriented activity is durable, goal-oriented actions and operations are short-lived, even when contextually standardized or habitual scripts may bind the continuity of actions. To the author the relationship among the constituent elements of activity is a crucial one as 'activity systems realize and reproduce themselves by generating actions and operations' (op. cit.: 964). Data from this inquiry seem to support the notion that, given the chance to participate in teaching activity guided by design elements, learning is expanded as students move through their individual and collective ZPDs via a variety of scaffolds: modelling, peer mediation, applications, developing metacognition and so forth.

## Conclusion

While the chapter has presented a small-scale intervention that still requires further research, we may conclude with Otto and Smith (2013: 3) that a design mindset applied to online teacher education holds more promise than other practices because 'design is clearly *future oriented*; its success is measured by the relevance the designed products and conceptual solutions have for people's everyday lives'. In light of the evidence presented here we can claim that a design mindset presents such a viable solution.

## Questions for change

1. How may a design mindset help organize face-to-face interaction between ToTs and student-teachers?
2. Would a design mindset help facilitate the ongoing professional development of teachers? If so, how?
3. What, in your opinion, are the most forceful arguments in advocating for a design mindset to the design of on-site and online ToT-student-teacher interaction?

# 7

# Exploring Student-teachers' Professional Identity Development through Discourse in an Online Language Teacher Education Programme

Graciela Inés Manzur and Cecilia Zemborain

## Objectives

1. Explore the identities and subject positions of three student-teachers who developed as online students, in the process of becoming qualified ELT teachers.
2. Study the interrelations of their discursively constructed personal, academic and professional selves, as online students and teachers in face-to-face teaching practice.
3. Gain insights into how their practicum experiences have influenced the ways in which they interpreted and lived their teaching practices and their identity as teachers.

## The exploratory experience in context

Our interest in L2 teacher identity emerged from our intertwined academic activities as L2 teacher researchers. Having explored the relevance of narrative discourse in identity construction, we decided to study three student-teachers' identity development by interpreting the narratives they created during their one-year practicum.

Between 2012 and 2013, we started to work as teacher educators for *Lenguas Vivas*, the only tertiary institution offering online Initial English Language

Teacher Education (IELTE) in Patagonia, a large southern region of Argentina. In an area with long distances, a sparse population and a vast number of unqualified teachers, this online initial teacher education programme affords the only opportunity for practising teachers to obtain an academic qualification in English Language Teaching (ELT) (Banegas and Manzur Busleimán 2014).

This online teacher training programme was our first experience in the field of online L2 teacher education. We thus became engaged in novel educational and social practices that were inherent to the singularities of this online learning community. Student-teachers are from different corners of the country and are either practising teachers or people with no teaching experience in ELT. Identity development thus emerges from technologically mediated learning experiences intertwined with diverse geographical, social and cultural contexts. As Menard-Warwick (2014: 41) states, teachers' identities relate to the contexts where they 'have learned, used and taught languages'.

This chapter focuses particularly on three student-teachers that completed their practicum during 2015. The rationale for selecting these three student-teachers was twofold. First, we aimed to obtain a comprehensive picture of how these student-teachers made sense of their L2 teacher identity throughout the whole course of studies. Second, we sought to shed light on the effects the online learning experience had on student-teachers' teaching practices in the classroom.

Two of the student-teachers included in the study reside in two different locations in the south of Argentina while the other is from the east of the country. Two of them were practising teachers at the moment of enrolling in the online teacher education programme, while the third had no teaching experience. We believe that this difference in their teaching background enriched the study as it allowed us to explore their identity construction in relation to their conceptualization of their teaching practice. In this respect, we concur with Kanno and Stuart (2011: 236) that there exists an 'intertwined relationship between novice teachers' identity development and their changing classroom practice'.

We adopted a phenomenological approach since the study focused on the individual and social construction of meaning of L2 teaching and of online learning, as experienced by these three student-teachers. We thus aimed to understand their perceptions, as subjectively reflected in the narrative account of their experiences as students and as (future) L2 teachers (Davey 2013: 33). The study also adopted a hermeneutic perspective as it highlighted the relevance of the historical, social and cultural contexts that shape student-teachers' interpretations and representations of language teaching as related to online learning (Davey 2013: 34).

# Gaining sense of teachers' identity through identity and discursive frameworks

## An integrated approach to identity

Research on the field of teacher identity has emphasized that narrative discourse is integral to the process of teacher identity formation (Alsup 2006; Block 2015; Clarke 2008; Davey 2013; Menard-Warwick 2014; Norton 2013; Varghese et al. 2005; Vitanova 2010). During the practicum and at the end of their course of studies we engaged student-teachers in narrative writing to help them (de) reconstruct their beliefs, world views, feelings and pedagogical practices in order to gain a clear sense of their different selves. In narrative discourse, our emotions, cognition and volition are engaged.

Throughout the year we became aware of the different feelings, perceptions, attitudes and world views that imbued the three student-teachers' learning experiences and interactions in this online learning community. Davey (2013: 6), citing Clandinin and Connelly (2000), states that teacher identity can be understood as 'the stories we live by – as stories in which ongoing experiences are shaped, interpreted, reinterpreted and theorised as we live through them'. Hence, in line with Bedacarratx (2009), Dörnyei and Ushioda (2013) and Ushioda (2009, 2011), we supported a holistic view of student-teachers and regarded their identities as individually, socially, academically and professionally constructed.

In turn, in line with post-structuralist theorists, such as Foucault (1980 as discussed in Norton and Toohey 2011: 6), many identity researchers postulate that identity is dialogically constructed, that is, socially negotiated within the context one is part of (Alsup 2006; Block 2015; Clarke 2008; Davey 2013; Menard-Warwick 2014; Norton 2013). Thus we also focused our exploration on these student-teachers' identity development within the online learning community to which they belong.

The analysis of the complex and dynamic nature of the three student-teachers' identities in this chapter is informed by the descriptive framework proposed by Davey (2013), originally conceived for teacher educators. We adopted this approach since the kaleidoscopic conceptualization of identity it provides is coherent with the holistic view aforementioned. Following the five intertwined dimensions of Davey's methodological framework and the aspects each of them attend to, we examined student-teachers' narratives in relation to the following:

1. *The becoming dimension*, through which we explored teachers' motivations, aspirations and desires to become qualified L2 teachers. We also analysed the effect of their first teaching experience as language student-teachers and the process of transformation they underwent through their teaching practice.

2. *The doing dimension*, by which we focused on how the student-teachers envisaged the work language teaching implies. They were asked to describe the tasks, functions and responsibilities language teachers' work comprises and how they perceived and experienced these different features during their practicum. We also took account of how these aspects impacted the construction of their professional identity.

3. *The knowing dimension*, through which the participants in the study reflected on the specific kinds of knowledge (regarding subject matter and pedagogy) they think they have learnt or need as language teachers. Their reflections also referred to the pedagogical aptitudes and attitudes they perceive as characteristic of the teaching profession.

4. *The being dimension*, which encouraged the three student-teachers to become aware of their sense of professional selves, as related to how they perceive and experience the different roles they assume and the images they convey as language teachers. They also reflected upon the feelings that those roles or projected images aroused. We thus focused on student-teachers' affective involvement in their teaching experiences to explore how their 'sense of the personal' is related to their 'sense of the professional' (ibid.: 116).

5. *The belonging dimension*, which allowed these student-teachers to explore their collective identity. This means considering the extent to which they identify with the communities they form part of. They were able to examine group affinities, which involve gaining recognition or not by members of their communities as well as being aware of the commonalities, and differences with other professional communities.

## A discursive approach to identity construction

In line with a sociocultural perspective, we maintain that this integrated view of professional identity involves analysing the dialectical relation between the internal influences of teachers' inner self, the external influences emerging from the wider sociocultural and political contexts as well as from the teachers' own professional community. In this case, we find it particularly valuable to explore how the three student-teachers experienced their learning-to-teach practices and constructed their identities in the merging of online and face-to-face contexts. Since we regard teacher identity development to be 'an amalgam of personal agency or commitment on the one hand, and externally imposed, normative pressures on the other, all held in dynamic tension and changing over time' (Davey 2013: 17), we considered it necessary to analyse the different discourses the two student-teachers engaged in during their practicum.

For the purpose of analysing the discursive construction of the student-teachers' identities, we resorted to Appraisal Theory or the Language of Evaluation Theory, developed by Martin and White (2005), from the fundamentals of Systemic Functional Linguistics. Due to its focus on the interpersonal dimension, this theory, we believed, would help cast light on the interactions and subject positions the student-teachers in the study created while participating in their learning and teaching contexts.

We contend that the relevance of Martin and White's (2005) framework to our study lies in the assumption that our sense of self is inextricably linked to the social self. It is particularly valuable in the fields of teaching and research for providing more thorough and systematic analytical categories to examine the evaluative functions of language resources, as Ngo and Unsworth (2015) state. Through its three interacting domains, namely attitude, engagement and graduation, Appraisal framework attends to the different intersubjective stances the speakers/writers adopt. We noticed that feelings played a key role in student-teachers' pedagogical experiences and in their identity development. For this reason we decided to focus on the attitudinal sphere, which pertains to *affect*, *judgement* and *appreciation*, each offering a positive or negative assessment of people and their behaviour, of events and objects.

We therefore paid attention to the three semantic areas involved: affect (related to emotion), judgement (related to ethics) and appreciation (referring to aesthetics). *Affect* relates to the emotional responses as well as to the rhetorical purpose of seeking common consent and of building rapport in interpersonal relations. *Judgement* focuses on normative assessment and comprises 'social esteem' and 'social sanction'. The former comprises positive and negative evaluations in relation to 'normality' (how unusual a person is), 'capacity' (how capable a person is) and 'tenacity' (how determined someone is). The latter involves positive or negative assessment in relation to 'veracity' (how credible a person is) and 'propriety' (how ethical a person is). Regarding the third semantic region, namely *appreciation*, focus is placed on positive and negative evaluations of objects and entities. It includes three categories of analysis: 'reaction' towards objects; 'composition', which refers to the consistency and complexity of objects; and 'valuation', that is, the value attached to objects.

Bearing these aspects in mind, we sought to analyse student-teachers' emotional responses towards online learning and teaching practices, their normative assessment of behaviour and aptitudes as well as their positive or negative evaluation of objects in relation to their quality, complexity and value.

## Examining student-teachers' identity construction through their own voices

The student-teachers' narratives devoted to each domain of the identity framework helped us explore the different feelings, perceptions, attitudes and world views that imbued their learning and interactions in this online learning community. In so doing, these student-teachers were also engaged in an awareness-raising activity about the identities they adopt and build.

We have decided to use pseudonyms to refer to the participants in the study. We will name them Ana and Daniel, the student-teachers with teaching experience, and Lucía, the one with no previous experience in ELT. Ana had been working as an EFL teacher for fifteen years before starting her course of studies. She was married and had two children. Hence studying to become a qualified teacher implied devoting herself to her family, work and studies. On the other hand, Lucía was single and had already returned to her hometown after a two-year stay abroad. She was uncertain about her future and was thus in a process of self-discovery. Daniel was from a small town in the east of Argentina. He was married with a child when he decided to pursue his undergraduate degree in ELT. He had worked around the world in restaurants and hotels. These working experiences fostered a strong cultural awareness in him. Moreover, his teaching practices in a rural area led him to perceive language as a social activity. The three of them had tertiary studies in other fields, so enrolling in the ELT online programme was not their first undergraduate experience.

We focused the discursive analysis on the linguistic resources and contents around the five dimensions presented by Davey (2013). With the aim of achieving an in-depth understanding of the processes the student-teachers underwent in their teacher identity construction, we examined the narratives regarding each dimension as interrelated. We not only analysed each student-teacher's narratives, but also underlined any difference or commonality between the three student-teachers' reflections that we judged significant to the analysis.

## Being as a constant becoming

In point of their motivations and aspirations for becoming English language teachers, the three of them claimed that they first regarded teaching as a job opportunity. But then they described the decision as *conscious*, thereby denoting awareness and reflexivity. Their initial motivations changed as different attitudes towards teaching and learning unfolded.

In Ana's and Daniel's narratives, it is interesting to notice that both learning and teaching were positively assessed and described in terms of mental processes related to a pleasing experience:

> I really enjoyed teaching young learners. (Ana)
> I love this job. I love to be in contact with children and families. ... This contact makes me feel more alive. (Daniel)

Ana also refers to teaching as a personal achievement, collectively fulfilled, and the practicum as generating fears. She experienced her teaching practice as complex (composition-complexity) and valuable (positive valuation):

> My tutor helped me overcome my fear. I owe a lot to her, as well as to my local observer. (Ana)

Being a teacher in a rural community made Daniel regard teaching as 'a challenge' (composition-complexity), not only for the different tasks and functions he should perform but also for the need to foster meaningful learning, relevant to students' context. He also saw teaching practice as a personal and professional transformative process. He focused on the need to make students feel 'comfortable, relaxed' (affect, related to the in/security variable and the feeling of trust) and 'motivated' (affect, related to the dis/satisfaction variable and the feeling of pleasure). His emphasis on such feelings seemed to emerge from the value given to the sense of community, as shown in the following statement in which the affective dimension has a positive valuation:

> It is also important the kind of relation that teachers have with their students. The emotional aspects of our relationships are *imperative*. (italics added)

As regards online learning, Ana's reflections also showed a positive evaluation through a mental process:

> I enjoyed learning that way, interacting with mates and tutors by means of the fora. (Ana)

Like Daniel, she described learning to teach a foreign language as 'a challenge' (composition-complexity) but 'worth the effort' (valuation). She attached special significance to the English language through a mental process, 'I *loved* the language' (italics added), and to the practicum by focusing on the capacities she developed, as shown in these reflections:

> As years went by, I *was able to* notice how the way I had been taught (not only English but my other subjects at school) did not promote learning at all. (Ana; italics added)

The bare assertion 'did not promote learning at all' is monoglossic in nature, that is, it does not recognize dialogistic alternatives, which reflects Ana's definite and negative viewpoint about traditional teaching approaches, thereby showing commitment to such a stance. She also adds:

> I am not saying that I am the best teacher now, but a *better one* than I used to be. At least, I *can* face a classroom filled with teenagers. (Ana; italics added)

She judges herself in terms of her capacity (judgement-social esteem): 'I ... can appreciate the changes, the improvement, in my teaching.'

For Daniel, online learning and his practicum were 'stressful' and 'demanding' at times (composition-complexity) but also 'effective' and 'very valuable' (positive valuation). In his narratives, he emphasized the relevance of language competence, pedagogical knowledge and of social skills in the teaching profession as well as the key role his undergraduate studies played in developing them. It allowed him the opportunity to gain sense of theory through the practices in which he was involved.

Both Ana and Daniel perceived online learning as a process of growth and transformation, which in turn implied identity development. Strong emotional involvement is perceived in these propositions:

> My learning experiences have played a main role in my own development as a person and as a teacher; all my experiences have played the role of educating me and of constructing my actual knowledge of the world. (Daniel)
>
> I'm quite sure I wouldn't have gained self-knowledge in a traditional teacher training programme, graduating from an online teacher training programme helped me get rid of the intolerance towards my and other's mistakes. (Ana)

In Lucía's narrative, deciding to pursue a career as an English teacher meant a major responsibility, a commitment to herself and to others. It also implied a sense of realization:

> I could let the teacher in me out and improve her. I could make a difference for students who struggle with language and be the living proof that communicates it is possible and the reward for those hard years of learning is endless, rich and life changing. (Lucía)

From this reflection, we observed that she described the language learning process in terms of students' effort, as shown by 'struggle' and 'hard years', while the result of this process was 'a reward', that is, rewarding (reaction, positive impact), 'rich' (positive reaction-quality) and 'life changing' (positive valuation).

Thus, her intentions to become a teacher grew out of her desire to help students acquire the language and, even further, be an agent of transformation, as shown by 'I could make a difference' or 'be the living proof'. Through her narrative, we interpreted this desire to be the result of a process of realization, which started with the perception of teaching as a job and changed to that of teaching as a mission.

As regards the practicum, she described it as the 'only real experiences in teaching' she had during her course of studies, but with a relative degree of authenticity as 'human relations are rather forced, time is extremely limited and you are undergoing an examination process. It is somehow staged'. This rather negative appreciation was counterbalanced by the chance to construct her teacher identity, to a certain extent: 'Nonetheless, you are able to show a good part of your teacher-self.' In this respect, we believe teacher educators should pay special attention to the analysis of initial teaching practice as betwixt and between the processes of becoming a teacher, thereby analysing the transformative transition. As Kanno and Stuart (2011: 236) state, the amount of hours devoted to classroom practice makes student-teachers' path from student identity to teacher identity a challenging process. We consider that this challenge should also be analysed in relation to the kind of learning experiences student-teachers are invited to engage in during their course of studies in general, and the practicum in particular.

## Knowing, doing and belonging as (trans)formative processes

When examining the student-teachers' narratives, we became aware of the close relationship between student-teachers' visions of language teaching and learning and their past and present experiences as learners. For Ana, her learning experience as a young learner – based on repetition, accuracy in writing and speaking (particularly spelling and pronunciation) and error correction – drove her into being 'afraid of failure'. Through this expression, Ana ascribed power to trigger such feeling to her learning experiences. In the attitudinal framework, fear is construed as *irrealis affect*, that is, a state of being that is not a fact. She claimed that with time she learnt to 'manage it and turn it into self-knowledge, very helpful to find solutions when anyone else would only see drawbacks'. She thus judged herself as capable of changing her attitudes and attached the positive value of becoming insightful. She declared that these experiences helped her realize what 'a teacher shouldn't be like'. She resorted to modulation to express social sanction (propriety-ethics).

As a result of these learning experiences, she displayed growing independence and through this online language teacher education programme, she positively judged herself in terms of capability and tenacity:

> I am more aware of my own capabilities and the way I can overcome difficulties, looking for support ... according to my needs. (Ana)

For this student-teacher, online learning meant more than learning the English language and gaining pedagogical knowledge. It involved becoming resourceful and more autonomous. She also manifested having learnt to express herself and to interact in the dynamics of online learning.

In consonance with Ana, Daniel also learnt from a negative experience at school. He described this teacher's behaviours through 'his verbal abuse' and 'violent attitude' (negative judgement, social sanction) that made him 'hate the subject' (affect expressed through a mental process). The experience led him to pay special attention to feelings and emotions and to value the potential of empathy in the learning process:

> Rapport is not only achieved through theoretical knowledge. To my mind, it is created through teachers' ability to feel empathic towards their students' (judgement-positive social esteem).

A salient aspect to note is how Ana valued interaction and social construction of knowledge, not only due to the readings available in the programme but also because of experiencing it. Another attitude that called our attention is her need to justify stances and viewpoints when showing alignment with theoretical assumptions:

> I know somebody can react to this by saying 'But you have read about Constructivism and Sociocultural Theory and that is what you are expressing here'. Yes ... but I've also experienced it myself. (Ana)

Like Daniel, Ana was able to give significance to theory through her own practices, but unlike him, she seemed to judge it as a negative social sanction, related to the category of veracity (truth) or legitimacy.

Lucía's narrative reflected different attitudes from those of Ana and Daniel. Through modulation, she attached different degrees of importance to what knowledge base she considered to be distinctive:

> I think we should have a correct use and deep knowledge of the language as well as cultural aspects. ... Keeping updated, a little bit of everything, *is* also *a* must (social sanction, obligation).

She evaluated 'good pronunciation' as 'desirable' and 'pedagogical and didactic knowledge' as 'crucial'. She even gave more value to certain subjects: phonetics ('was of utmost help') and language ('was extremely nurturing').

Contrary to Ana and Daniel, Lucía did not describe online language learning as transformative; rather, she identified benefits of some of its distinctive features but in relation to the drawbacks. For instance, she found the possibility for organizing study at her own pace to be 'a benefit' but 'definitely very challenging'. She felt that online learning led to 'depersonalized' but 'more mature' teaching and learning experiences. She described online learning not only in terms of advantages and drawbacks but also in relation to face-to-face learning. She detailed some of the difficulties she encountered during her first year of studies: learning the forum netiquettes; not knowing how to clarify a doubt; getting used to the lack of physical presence and face-to-face relationships; and finding an effective way to profit from her tutors' help.

She resorted to positive judgements to refer to the strategies she found useful to handle online learning, and to negative appreciations to mention unsettling experiences. Her subjective involvement is less overt or direct when she reflected upon the difficulties, as seen in these reflections:

> The sole idea of sitting for hours trying to make something out of notes and books *was demoralizing* enough, but as *I have learnt* during my teacher formation course, *I am just a different kind of learner.* I believe *I managed quite well* for such a new thing, but some of these *complications* resulted in my *first failure* on a subject. (Lucía; italics added)

Lucía devoted special time to describing her abilities as a learner and her learning styles, which seemed to give her a sense of self-assurance and self-knowledge. Unlike Ana and Daniel, the past learning experience that impacted Lucía's vision of teaching was a pleasant one, with a teacher she felt she identified with: 'I like to picture myself with a lot of Sara, my own teacher, and another good bunch of myself.' She sought to project a persona of 'someone unusual – in a good way', (positive judgement, related to the normality valuation of social esteem). She also emphasized the importance of fostering a friendly learning environment in the classroom.

The three student-teachers stressed the relevance of motivation in L2 teaching and learning, but the focus of their teaching aims varied: Ana centred her attention on helping her students use the target language meaningfully and enjoy learning, while Lucía placed more emphasis on providing a safe learning atmosphere and positive attitudes. In Daniel's case, he emphasized both aspects: the need to provide significant and authentic learning experiences as well as a friendly environment. Of the three sets of meaning in the typology of *affect* that groups emotions, un/happiness, in/security and dis/satisfaction, we could say that Ana's aim tended to focus on the dis/satisfaction variable, concerned with ennui, (dis)pleasure, interest and respect, while Lucía's aim was oriented towards the in/security set, concerned with eco-social well-being – anxiety, fear, confidence and trust (Martin and White 2005: 49). Daniel pursued both aims.

Although the three student-teachers were aware of the abilities they developed in this online teacher learning community, they construed different evaluations of the dynamics of online learning spaces. For Ana and Daniel, the characteristics of the online learning community led them to develop certain teaching and learning skills while for Lucía it was the difficulties she encountered in her first year of studies that fostered skill development. We may then establish a relationship between her past face-to-face learning experiences and the ones lived online with their teaching aims and intentions.

When analyzing her narratives regarding the *doing* dimension, we identified attitudes and stances that followed the same line of thought depicted in the other dimensions. Thus, Lucía, who had no teaching experience, was uncertain about the tasks her job as a teacher would involve but mentioned duties related to didactic issues: lesson planning, materials design, classroom management and support to students. When describing these duties, she resorted to monoglossic assertions (the term monoglossic is explained earlier in this article) to imply these responsibilities as taken for granted:

> Unavoidable duties and responsibilities are being ready for a lesson, which means, delivering content efficiently, in the way students need; of course, teachers do not only provide content, but also support.

She expressed different degrees of relevance to other tasks. She seemed to perceive collaborative work among colleagues as useful, not as a way of working that is expected from teachers: 'Sometimes we need group support from other teachers.' However, she was emphatic when making reference to constructive relations between families and the educational institution: 'Definitely a good dialogue between parents and the institution we are teaching in is crucial' (positive valuation). Thus, she was aware of the relevance of the social context but not of the role of educational policies and policymakers in teachers' work.

Due to their teaching experience, Ana and Daniel showed more subjective involvement in their narrative. Ana regarded teaching work and decision making as part of an 'institution culture' in constant change (created and recreated through time by each and every individual taking part in it). She mentioned school authorities, policymakers, teachers, students and families. The conception underlying this reflection is that of the school as a community, constructed by the subjective and power relations built by all its members. In these relations, Ana perceived teachers' work as dependent on authorities' decisions. Due to the characteristics of the rural context in which he lived and taught, Daniel also regarded school and teaching as significant for the community and their culture.

What is noteworthy was Ana's confidence to take a stance and voice her suggestions and viewpoints, supported by her knowledge and experience:

I don't have a classroom of my own. Something I'd love to because it would allow me to arrange students and resources differently, always according to the type of lesson to teach and group of children. Although, I've been insisting on it, the answer has been the same: 'No. I understand the reasons, nonetheless I still believe it would be beneficial for students, who will be immersed in an English atmosphere.'

Here goes a suggestion for schools' principals: If the school you run/manage offers English to the community, then take your time to learn something about that language and the way to teach it ... or hire somebody who can do it for you.

She showed more determination in the second fragment, and discursively constructed the tensions teachers may be involved in as part of their profession. Her propositions also denoted a certain degree of openness to alternative views, as an invitation to reflect together and introduce change. This may stem from the sense of autonomy she claimed to have gained during her online language education studies.

The three student-teachers related their sense of personal, academic and professional selves to the communities to which they belonged. Ana and Daniel made reference to the need to build a positive interdependence among colleagues to create a sense of belonging. Their teaching experience allowed them to start gaining sense of their professional identity. Being close to becoming a qualified teacher strengthened their sense of self-image. Ana considered initial teacher education to be 'a landscape' in her 'personal map', which prepared her for the next steps she would like to take: designing a book for young learners and teaching online. Through positive valuation, Daniel described it as the 'opening of a new phase', which allowed him to 'overcome insecurities' and to see himself 'as someone new who has a *valuable* personal training path' (the highlighting is ours). However, both regretted not receiving enough recognition from their colleagues for having studied in an online teacher education programme. In Lucía's case, as she did not have any teaching experience, her language teacher identity was fully based on the online learning community. Her peers' recognition contributed to her persona, as she maintained that her mates regarded her as a source of reference.

The exploratory journey through the discursive construction of the three student-teachers' identity development shows the intrinsic relations among the five dimensions integrating professional identity (being, becoming, knowing, doing and belonging). It helped us gain insights into the impact online language teacher education has had on their personal and professional identities.

## Conclusion

In view of the growing body of research regarding language teacher identities and online education, exploring L2 student-teachers' identity as developed in digital environments is of paramount importance. Therefore, the findings of this study may be of interest not only for teacher researchers but also for teacher educators, particularly those involved in online teaching. As we have observed throughout the chapter, online language teacher education, with its own specificities, shapes student-teachers' perceptions of time and space, and their interpersonal relations as well as their ways of communicating, constructing knowledge and experiencing learning and teaching practices. Therefore, professional identities are construed at the crossroad of their online and face-to-face learning experiences.

Furthermore, in line with our sociocultural perspective, we stress the need to explore student-teacher identity in the contexts in which they are constructed. Online learning spaces stem from socially situated practices that influence identity construction. Thus, reflecting on such practices can help student-teachers, as well as language teacher educators, become aware of the processes each student-teacher undergoes in the construction of his or her professional identity within the learning community to which he or she belongs.

We believe this chapter contributes to a deeper understanding of teacher identity formation in online initial language learning teacher education. As Johnson and Golombek (2016) state, L2 teacher education shapes teachers' viewpoints, beliefs and teaching practices within the sociocultural contexts in which they learn to teach.

## Questions for change

1. How do teacher educators shape L2 teacher identity in general and in online language teacher education in particular?
2. How do curriculum designs in an online teacher education programme shape student-teachers' professional identity and foster awareness of their sense of self?
3. In what ways does the learner identity of student-teachers shape their language teacher identity development?
4. How does the professional identity of student-teachers hinder and/or promote the possibility of present and future innovations in ELT?

# 8

# Self-regulation and Language Teacher Training in Colombia

Liliana Cuesta Medina, Carl Edlund Anderson
and Jermaine S. McDougald

## Objectives

1. Review relevant literature on self-regulation with a focus on development of self-regulation in language teachers.
2. Explore a hypothesized gap/mismatch between emphasis on self-regulated learning (SRL) in teacher training programmes and actual practice in the field through analysis of data collected from Colombian teacher educators.
3. Propose strategies and approaches to address the challenges identified and to promote the development of self-regulation in language teachers and their learners.

## Introduction

Self-regulation and a capacity for SRL are widely recognized in educational research literature as critical not only for contemporary learners but also for teachers. Yet, the emphasis placed on instilling skills and strategies for SRL in learners often ignores a more fundamental problem of teachers who are not only unprepared to educate their learners in SRL but, in fact, lack SRL abilities themselves. Successfully meeting these challenges requires understanding the distinct situations of younger learners, who can develop SRL habits and skills from the beginning of their formal educational processes, and adult learners, who need to unlearn years of dependent learning habits as well as learn new SRL habits, especially if these adults are to foster SRL in others.

Learners who can manage their actions, ability known as *metacognitive awareness*, can also adjust the strategies deployed in their learning to ensure goal attainment and learning satisfaction (Baker and Brown 1984). Such individuals can more readily identify their own strengths and weaknesses and maximize use of their mental structures to examine task-specific knowledge, proficiency levels (current and desirable) and available resources (internal and external) needed in a given learning situation. They can use their knowledge efficiently to self-regulate their cognitive processes (Cuesta Medina 2010). More metacognitively aware students seem to act more strategically and perform better than students who are less metacognitively aware (Bandura 1977). However, teachers seldom recognize the implications – with regard to not only their students but also themselves, at least until they face actual classroom situations and the challenge of transitioning from *traditional* teacher-centred paradigms to learner-centred approaches that focus on how students personally activate, modify and maintain their learning in specific contexts (Bandura 1977).

In Colombia, the standard language teaching curriculum has been static for over a decade. However, with the advent of new technologies and more learner-inclusive teaching approaches, higher-education institutions – and especially teacher education institutions – have started to adjust curricula towards the development of critical thinking and lifelong learning, emphasizing the role of reflection as essential for one in becoming an effective teacher who can continue learning from one's own learners, tutors and peers (Fandiño 2013). Yet such changes cannot be realized if the actors involved do not know how to plan, self-regulate and evaluate, as these skills directly influence learning awareness and control. Having these skills can help students reflect critically on their own learning processes while also becoming more autonomous and efficient in decision-making scenarios where the customized use and adaptation of learning strategies play an important role.

There are many roadblocks to student-teachers' development of self-regulation, often linked to lack of relevant expertise in the field or personal reluctance to explore language teacher training (and, indeed, language learning) from perspectives that emphasize reflection and evolution. Yet the demands of an increasingly interconnected world mean teachers must foster, and students must learn, the implementation of both cognitive and metacognitive strategies and evaluate their effects on the construction of knowledge in domain-specific contexts. Successful learners can be identified by examining how they maintain control of their learning while transferring the knowledge and strategies acquired from one situation to another, modifying and extending these strategies along the way (Flavell, Miller and Miller 2002).

# Theoretical considerations

## Self-regulation and self-regulated learning

Bandura's earlier writings on self-regulation emphasize behavioural and emotional regulation; his later work on self-efficacy argues that motivation is also critical in the development of self-regulation. For Bandura, self-regulation emphasizes 'the reciprocal determinism of the environment on the person, mediated through behavior' (1977: 393), and human functioning is the interaction between person, behaviour, and environment, an understanding aligned with social learning theory, which likewise emphasizes the derivation of knowledge from the environment. SRL, understood as 'the process by which learners personally activate and sustain cognitions, affects and behaviors that are systematically oriented toward the attainment of learning goals' (Schunk and Zimmerman 2008: 6), focuses on how students personally activate, modify and maintain their learning practices in specific contexts. Significantly, 'self-regulation is not achieved by a feat of willpower: It operates through a set of subfunctions that must be developed and mobilized for self-directed change' (1977: 336).

Much SRL research has focused on learners' processes to activate and sustain behavioural conduct and cognitive and affective functioning (Boekaerts, Zeidner and Pintrich 2000; Schunk and Zimmerman 1998). Such studies have demonstrated that self-regulated learners know *how* they can become successful learners by using appropriate (meta)cognitive, motivational and affective strategies (Boekaerts 1997). They are metacognitively, motivationally and behaviourally active participants in their own learning process. In comparison to *poor self-regulators*, they are better at setting goals, implementing more effective learning strategies, monitoring and assessing progress towards goals, establishing more productive environments for learning, seeking needed assistance, expending and persisting with effort, and setting more effective goals when present ones are completed (Schunk and Zimmerman 2008).

Giving attention to motivation has been shown to have a positive and immediate impact on learning and, not surprisingly, motivation has become a key topic in SRL research. Schunk and Zimmerman (2008) have focused on sources of motivation linked to SRL and those aspects of academic learning most influenced by motivational constructs – such as initiating, guiding and maintaining students' efforts to regulate their learning – that help students build self-regulation skills. They emphasize the value of self-monitoring and feedback to sustain attention and motivation. Students can be taught to self-monitor their learning but, if they are motivationally inattentive to their feedback, their self-monitoring my falter or lose efficacy. In other words, 'students' SRL processes and motivational beliefs are reciprocally interactive' (Schunk and Zimmerman 2008: 4), since the former may influence the latter and vice versa. The development of SRL abilities is a dynamic process, with some skills and strategies developing before others (Pintrich 2000); thus it is also an *iterative* process (Barnard-Brak, Lan and Osland 2010). Prominent among the various motivators that enhance self-sources of learner motivation are self-regulatory training, the use of social resources (e.g. parental, instructor modelling, praise, rewards) and adaptive help-seeking.

## Sociocultural theory, language learning and student-teacher development

It is well understood that second language acquisition (SLA) and learning depends on cognitive processes, but the broader social context is less often taken into consideration (Cross 2010; Feryok 2013). Sociocultural theory is intimately related to Vygotsky's contention that social context is central to all communication and learning (Lantolf and Beckett 2009; Vygotsky 1978), emphasizing 'the interdependence of social and individual processes in the coconstruction of knowledge' (John-Steiner and Mahn 1996: 1). This is seen in the familiar concept of the *zone of proximal development*, where conceptual and cultural learning transpires through communication/dialogue. Thus, learning is not just conceived of but, in fact, also created through social communication by way of organized, structured dialogue (Liyanage and Bartlett 2010).

Six main concepts from sociocultural theory are particularly relevant to adult-learning educational settings (Bonk and Kim 1998):

1. zones of proximal development
2. internalization
3. scaffolding
4. intersubjectivity
5. cognitive apprenticeship
6. assisted learning

Sociocultural theory provides a 'unique understanding of SRL by its emphasis on the role of social environment and the mediational means in the development of SRL' (Yetkin Özdemir 2011: 298). Bonk and Kim (1998) observe that a key point of sociocultural theory is that as learning environments change, the available mediational tools and signs that impact cognitive functioning also change. Likewise, sociocultural theory sees knowledge as 'situated in specific cultural contexts created and developed over time to solve real-life problems that occur within that culture and society' (Eun 2010: 405). Such observations link sociocultural theory closely to SRL in the sense that student-teachers' specific contexts (in Colombia and elsewhere) play major roles in their professional development: they are accustomed to repeating the same behaviours and actions time and time again. They may be either unable or unwilling to make the efforts needed to change or adapt in accordance with their contexts, which can make it difficult for them (or their students) to deal successfully with tertiary-level programmes.

With respect to teacher professional development, research on automatic transfer of knowledge – knowledge acquired in one setting and then used in another – has seldom considered the complexities surrounding the social context of learning. These issues, critical for both formal and informal teacher-training programmes, must be analysed more thoroughly to better understand different views of teacher learning and student learning, especially with regard to the student-teacher classroom relationship, and the physical and conceptual resources, affordances and constraints within the classroom (Al-Mahdi and Al-Wadi 2015; Kelly 2006).

## Voices of Colombian teacher educators on student-teacher self-regulation challenges

As professors/coordinators in a graduate-level programme for in-service student-teachers of English (Universidad de La Sabana, Chía, Colombia) with a focus on reflective teaching, we recognize that an awareness of and capacity for self-regulation and SRL are critical for the student-teachers in it. Without indulging in a large-scale empirical investigation, we sought to uncover how self-regulation is experienced by – at this preliminary phase of the study – capturing samples from the voices of teacher educators not only in our own programme but also from a sample of teacher educators involved elsewhere in the Colombian context. We hypothesize that such voices and the challenges they identify are likewise found in many parts of the world. We surveyed forty-five teacher educators through an online questionnaire created in Google Docs. Prior to responding to the questionnaire, they received a letter of invitation to participate in the study and the information concerning the study objectives and possible outreach. These educators belonged to five different regions of Colombia and were currently involved in pre-service student-teacher education, in the capacities of either language teachers, deans, coordinators or directors of varied language departments. All questions were open-ended and the main aim of the questionnaire was to inquire about their views on their student-teachers' SRL capacities, the possible gaps/mismatches between teacher education programmes and actual practices in the field (especially with regard to SRL), and the main challenges they face as teacher educators. Thus, twenty respondents answered all required questions, and data were processed through grounded theory (Corbin and Strauss 2008). In this phase, there were no other participants called upon, since the proceeding stage of the study would cater to the voices of students, as a way to expand the scope of the data and the study itself.

Data analysis revealed that nineteen participants believed their students were not self-regulated, citing issues including strongly teacher-dependent behaviours; lack of ability to plan, monitor and assess their performance; lack of ability to manage time effectively; lack of critical and reflective thinking abilities; and lack of training to self-regulate their learning processes at earlier educational levels. Such views are typified in the following extracts from survey responses given by teacher educators:

> According to my experience of about 10 years in teaching pre-service teachers, I consider that they are not self-regulated, because in Colombia most of in-service teachers do not consider important this strategy in classroom practices. So undergraduate foreign language learners are not ready to lead their own learning process because of their lack of learning strategies, autonomy and motivation. So future foreign language teachers need to learn how to learn and at the same time they need to learn how to self-regulate their learning process. This is really evident in public universities because most teachers are not sufficiently qualified to take on such challenges in teaching a foreign language for future generations who must face the new challenges that the future society requires. (Participant 1)
>
> They do not plan their learning in terms of goals, resources, etc.; they do not monitor their process and most of the time they just expect the teachers' feedback but they do not evaluate their processes. (Participant 4)

Most of the teacher educators' views coincided with our own experiences, based on data collection and analysis of qualitative sources collected over a period of eighteen months (2014–16) from different instruments used in our programme, including documentary analysis of syllabi, classroom observation protocols, student artefacts, focus groups, committee meetings and individual interviews held with ten full- and part-time instructors in our graduate programme for in-service student-teachers of English. Among the salient results reported, we can say that few student-teachers are assertive or critical and most are uncomfortable with the idea of change in their own beliefs or practices. Thus, when comparing these findings with those noted by the pre-service teacher educators surveyed, we found noticeable parallels:

> No, they [the student-teachers] are not [self-regulated]. They are usually expecting professors to tell them what to do even when they know the program and have access to the expectations of the courses. They struggle to self-regulate. Always complain about not having time to cope with everything they have to do. (Participant 13)
>
> [The student-teachers are] Not really [self-regulated], trainees nowadays apparently do not see the benefit of planning and organizing all the aspects of teaching beforehand and do not reflect either on their practice. The lack of self-regulation for most of the tasks they have is evident in the way they understand the learning process and the autonomy they should develop to become successful. (Participant 14)
>
> No [they are not self-regulated]. They seem less able to generalize patterns, for instance, always expecting guidance in decisions for matters previously addressed, that is to say that in a way they are becoming more dependent. Students are also becoming less and less aware of their social surroundings, becoming more and more self-absorbed. These two issues, to name only a few, work against the concept of self-regulation. (Participant 19)

In the case of our graduate students, we can say that they have displayed low tolerance for either constructive criticism or failure, especially when they were challenged to reflect upon their own classroom assignments with a score below the expected average, and had to trace a course of action for further improvement. In addition, our experience highlights the numerous difficulties that candidates displayed while they were developing their research studies: (1) impediments in planning, selecting, organizing, prioritizing and postulating relationships among salient data from their in-progress research projects, and (2) difficulties in conceptualizing data, operationalizing theory and/or synthesizing information (Cuesta 2016).

Likewise, much as teacher educators from our in-service programme note that many student-teachers do not arrive prepared for the demands of work at the graduate level (lacking, for example, the cognitive skills needed to analyse or generate and support arguments effectively, or handle and process information effectively), survey responses from other teacher educators not only emphasized similar problems but also pointed towards the need to review continuously and update training-programme content as part of a coherent response:

> To be able to manage all the requirements in the initial stage as fully responsible teachers, programmes must be updated continuously, so student-teachers will have the opportunity to learn all the new techniques they need to be competitive professionals. That means, they have to get prepared for the requirements of every stage in their career, so in most cases they do not know how to do it or what to do when they face the real experience as a teacher (they need to have more than one practice). If all the programmes are in this line, the knowledge of beginning teachers will be full of experience and in that way, they will put into context their real knowledge keeping in mind the new challenges the world requires for. (Participant 2)
>
> I would add [to existing pre-service ELT teacher-training programmes] some specific courses as key components of the programme. For example, courses related to instruction or training on learning strategies, learner autonomy, and intercultural communicative competence. I also consider that it is necessary to incorporate reflective learning and teaching and professional development within the syllabi or curriculum. In some programmes there is a gap between 'teaching practicum' and 'research', so students complete these requirements or compulsory courses in an isolated and non-reflective way. (Participant 16)

Yet, a common thread in all the SRL-related problems noted by teacher educators in their survey responses – whether relating to in- or pre-service teachers, or from undergraduate or graduate teacher training programmes – is that student-teachers' difficulties in these areas ultimately result from failure to prepare them appropriately at a much younger age. Adult learners (such as at the tertiary-level) have many ingrained negative habits to unlearn, alongside new, positive habits to learn; it would have been much better if good self-regulation habits had been instilled in them from the beginning of their schooling, and extended up to their secondary and tertiary education experience. Thus, our initial claim concerning the need for articulation of a learner-centred curriculum that favours the development of critical thinking, agency and self-regulation since early childhood goes in line with the observations of those surveyed teachers insofar that they report that numerous teacher education practices are still being nurtured in traditional teacher-directed approaches.

Of course, this preliminary study has only considered the voices of teacher educators. Further research that gives greater consideration to the experiences and existing knowledge of student-teachers – and, indeed, of learners of all kinds – would help develop a more complete understanding of beliefs and practices regarding self-regulation and SRL. Though such research exceeds, in any event, the scope of this study, we plan to pursue it in future and would encourage those in other contexts to develop parallel studies in their contexts.

However, the observations already made do help point towards the kinds of strategies needed to support the development of self-regulation in not only student-teachers but all learners. Programmes must fuse theory and practice based not only on target-content discipline *savoir-faire* but also on human development competences and the so-called *soft skills*, such as self-regulation and reflective thinking, if we are to succeed in nurturing competent and competitive professionals prepared to perform (and to prepare others to perform) at the global level.

Additionally, stakeholders such as ministries of education and accreditation bodies must recognize and support the kinds of change necessary in both language teaching curricula and student-teacher education programmes. This would, first, facilitate the inclusion of a self-regulatory transversal axis within curricula to better support the development – among learners at all levels – of the skills, strategies and processes that favour (SRL) and learners. Second, it would better equip teachers to address the needs of their educational contexts from learner-centred perspectives by maximizing the use of available resources to implement pedagogical strategies that support both learners' and their own motivation and performance levels.

For such reasons, our view on the road ahead for language teacher education advocates much greater accounting for, and interdependence between, the real life of both teachers and students and educational processes and objectives, with a more humanizing perspective. This road ahead may not be straight or easily travelled, but it should be directed towards effective self-regulatory teaching and learning practices that transcend barriers, contexts and paradigms.

# Recommendations to support
# SRL among teachers and learners

There may be many reasons for the problems with learner self-regulation, though perhaps one of the chief factors is that development of SRL and associated strategies is simply not part of *traditional* educational paradigms that still dominate in much of the world. While the pace of research on SRL has accelerated since the 1970s, the impact on classroom practices and curricular objectives has been limited.

This situation is closely connected with another factor that helps perpetuate problems with learner self-regulation: many administrators and political actors as well as other stakeholders, including teachers and learners themselves, remain unaware that lack of learner self-regulation is a problem – which should not surprise us if they are themselves the products of educational systems deficient in SRL. Yet, accepting that lifelong learning skills are beneficial in virtually any contemporary professional environment, extrapolating the differences in academic success between self-regulated and non-self-regulated learners to the professional sphere suggests that a workforce deficient in SRL represents a severe drag on overall economic performance. We might hope that this realization alone might be sufficient to spur education ministers to action, though for reasons already noted this could be an overly optimistic hope.

## Strengthening SRL in teacher training contexts

In practice, the burden of strengthening SRL in teacher training contexts falls on teacher educators who are aware of the critical importance of learner self-regulation and who have the freedom to emphasize it in their programmes. Faced with a chicken-or-the-egg cycle of teachers who, lacking SRL skills themselves, predictably fail to instil them in their students, it is necessary to effect changes in both student-teachers and their own learners – with the challenge that teacher educators usually have direct access only to student-teachers.

An explicit focus on SRL within student-teacher education programmes should, of course, be part of such an effort. In our own graduate-level student-teacher education programme, coursework and evaluation procedures have been designed to help learners discover the benefits of assuming responsibility for planning and regulating their learning, as well as modifying pre-existing patterns of action. More than 90 per cent of the programme's courses focus on reflective teaching and learning in one form or another, with a comprehensive scheme of weekly student consultation sessions and personalized learning pathways that empower their learning, boost their intrinsic motivation and support their development of self-regulatory actions and self-efficacy beliefs. Student-teachers in the programme also receive formal instruction in and practice with actions intended to foster metacognitive development (Kuhn 2000). In particular, research experience can help create an environment that demands learners begin to bridge the gap between their current and needed knowledge and skills; in complement, the development of critical thinking skills through argumentation provides challenges that can be met successfully through the development of SRL. Only when learners begin to value strategic practices that demonstrate an impact on their abilities to manage their learning can they truly begin to become more aware of their own modes of thinking.

Yet it would be naïve to imagine that this kind of programme-level focus can effectively instil SRL skills and awareness in all student-teachers, given that so many are unused to being the agents of their own learning. Few postgraduate teacher training programmes exceed two years; many are much briefer, especially diploma- or certificate-level courses. Even programmes with a well-considered focus on SRL may be unable to overturn years of ingrained habits and thought patterns in the time available – and simply extending training time is unlikely to be administratively and/or politically inexpedient.

## Recommendations to strengthen SRL in primary and secondary contexts

Though a stronger focus on SRL in teacher training contexts is a critical part of any solution, given the practical challenges and time likely needed to address these more successfully, it is also necessary to develop strategies that can reach where teacher educators frequently cannot – to primary- and secondary-level students themselves. Even if student-teachers emerge from training still struggling with the concepts of SRL, it may be possible to arm them with strategies, or at least prefabricated activities and materials, designed to help foster the development of the SRL skills their learners need to reduce dependency, resistance (Deneen and Boud 2014) and frustration even in the absence of teachers well equipped to support these processes personally. Thus, though the need to instil SRL skills in student-teachers is well recognized – and unquestionably important – there is also an urgent need to research materials and activities that would serve in this additional goal. There are, nevertheless, common features in approaches to fostering SRL skills, whether in student-teachers or in their own learners with or without teacher support.

## Approaches to support SRL: Inquiry-based learning

A critical prerequisite to the development of SRL skills is self-efficacy, understood as the belief in one's capabilities to organize and execute the courses of action required to manage situations (Bandura 1995). Lack of belief that one's own efforts lead to success is related to a tendency to attribute failure to factors over which one has no control, such as insufficient teaching. However, learners who 'attribute failure to lack of effort are likely to persist and increase their efforts in the face of failure, whereas individuals who attribute failure to lack of ability are likely to give up in face of failure and avoid such tasks in the future' (Cooper and Weaver 2003: 78).

Yet, self-regulation and self-efficacy depend on both cognitive and emotional skills, and learner deficiencies in these areas cannot be addressed successfully unless both cognitive and emotional factors are addressed first. Students who are motivated to choose a task when given the opportunity show greater progress than unmotivated students. This reaffirms the importance of motivation for SRL (Schunk and Zimmerman 2008), though more research is needed on the nature of cognitive and/or emotional deficiencies, so as to then be able to identify appropriate strategies to address such deficiencies, as well as on the factors that enhance self-sources of motivation (Cuesta Medina 2014).

In terms of putting ideas into practice in the classroom, we suggest that approaches built around scaffolding, such as *inquiry-based* learning (for a freely available example intended for use with primary-level learners, see Ruiz et al. 1998), offer powerful models for fostering the growth of SRL skills. These can avoid certain dynamics of traditional teaching approaches that are hostile to SRL development – for example, the common role of teacher feedback in identifying both problems and solutions for students, thereby disconnecting identification of the problem and appropriate solutions from the learner's own cognitive processes. In contrast, in inquiry-based approaches, student questions and needs are addressed by new questions from the teacher aimed at leading the learners towards discovery of the problems they need to solve and appropriate solutions to solving those problems. Ideally, students are trained in a systematic process of self-regulation supported by continual formative assessment. Possible questions could be: *Are students getting the correct answer? How are they getting the correct answer? Or, why they are not getting the correct answer?* Student production and performance are oriented around processes of reflection on a problem, testing solutions, producing responses and sharing the resultant knowledge. Similar processes apply to the training of student-teachers themselves, as reflected in, for example, the kind of research training mentioned previously.

Among the chief challenges to implementing such learning approaches in support of SRL development is the considerable investment needed in tutoring and mentoring time. It is, after all, faster and easier for teachers to provide feedback identifying both the learner's problem and appropriate solutions than it is to entice the learner down a sequenced but non-predetermined path towards discovery and analysis. Thus, though well-designed materials and approaches can help, especially with learners at early stages, the more complicated the issues with which the learner must engage, the more complex is the scaffolding required from the teacher.

## Conclusion

Perhaps in practice, few educational systems are well prepared for the necessary investments in either teacher training time or teacher/student-scaffolding time that reorientation towards fostering SRL skills implies. Though great rewards are unlikely without great investment, practical moves towards increasing a system's emphasis on SRL may need to be made through small steps towards the distinct but aligned goals of training or retraining the teaching force and supplying learners with materials and activities that support SRL even with minimal teacher-led support. A realistic estimate might see the desired change starting to occur over the course of at least a generation – a time frame unlikely to please education ministers in search of instant sound-bites or public relations wins, but not unreasonable for educators seeking to provide current and future generations with the tools they need for lifelong learning and success.

## Questions for change

1. What strategies best support both the unlearning of *dependent learning habits* and, simultaneously, the learning of SRL skills among adults?
2. What kinds of strategies can be embedded into learning materials to help foster the development of SRL skills in younger learners even when their teachers are not personally prepared to foster these?
3. For student-teachers who are equipped with SRL skills, what kinds of strategies and materials will best help them instil such skills in their own learners?
4. What implications could sociocultural theory have for current concepts and models regarding professional development of student-teachers?
5. What is needed to better connect work on SRL with that on sociocultural theory so as to help bridge the gap between teacher education theory and student-teacher practice?

# 9

# English Language Teaching and Reflection in Higher Education

Agustin Reyes Torres

## Objectives

1. Develop the practice to become a reflective teacher of English as an L2.
2. Explore how to integrate theoretical foundations and practice in ELT.
3. Encourage students to engage in an ongoing process of active learning and critical thinking that allows them to build up their knowledge and justify their perspectives.
4. Guide students on the pursuit towards the creation of their personal philosophy of teaching.

## Introduction

The social turn in the study of learning and teaching second and foreign languages (L2) has drawn attention to the idea that language and thought are interrelated in human development and that language, as well as other cultural artefacts, are crucial in the development of knowledge and any other cognitive human activity (Block 2003; Elliot 2007; Lacorte 2015; Vygotsky 1986). Given this premise, in this chapter I will argue that the initial education of teachers of English as an L2 must aim for two main goals: in the first place, to offer them the necessary tools that foster an ability to think and reflect. As Andrew Pollard (2014: 109) points out, 'Effective teaching depends on teacher learning', so if pre-service teachers do not elaborate their own thoughts, they cannot develop their own knowledge. If there is no reflection, there is no learning. As it will be discussed, having students participate and get involved in their own education is crucial for them to understand that they need to play an active role and that any educational project is, indeed, an open and ongoing process to which they should contribute. In the second place, another important goal for teachers of English is to get acquainted with the basis of the sociocultural theory in order to apply it and be able to integrate this approach in their own lessons when teaching English as an L2 in primary schools.

This chapter is based on the experience and the work done with fourth-year students in the course *Didáctica de la lengua inglesa* (Teaching English as a Foreign Language) at the Universitat de València (Spain) over a period of five years from 2011 to 2015. To a great extent, it is the result of a gradual process of reflection on my own practice, the contents covered, its final outcomes and students' feedback. I will first present the theoretical rationale upon which the syllabus is designed and, second, how the course is organized so that students' involvement, active engagement, continuous reflection and collaborative learning constitute the axis of the subject.

## Theoretical foundations

For heterogeneous and multilingual groups of students to work together and learn, there must be a common ground in which they can meet, interact, discuss their experiences and have the opportunity to express their different perspectives. That common ground is reflection. This means that dialogue is crucial in becoming reflective. As Brockbank and McGill (2007) emphasize, 'The articulation of our ideas to others is central to the development of an open, critical perspective' (quoted in Ashwin 2015: 44). This is the key point to integrate subject contents on didactics with other specific contents related to English Language Teaching (ELT). As it will be shown, the view of the learner as an agent engaged in collaborative activity and the use of dialogue become essential in order to develop reflective teaching practices.

The theoretical foundation that informs the approach to reflective teaching stems from John Dewey's book *How to Think* (1910/1933). He defended the idea that the essentials of thinking were to carry on systematic and extended inquiry, or phrased differently, to acquire 'the attitude of suspended conclusion', which in the field of education refers to the idea of constantly reflecting on every lesson instructed. For Dewey, teachers should be committed to continuous self-appraisal and development as well as to persistent search for new materials to corroborate or to refute the first suggestions that occur.

Dewey's criteria for reflection is recapped by Carol Rodgers (2002: 845) in the following four points:

1. Reflection is a meaning-making process that moves a learner from one experience into the next with deeper understanding of its relationships and connections to other experiences and ideas. It is the thread that makes continuity of learning possible, and ensures the progress of the individual and, ultimately, society.
2. Reflection is a systematic, rigorous, disciplined way of thinking, with its roots in scientific inquiry.
3. Reflection needs to happen in community, in interaction with others.
4. Reflection requires attitudes that value the personal and intellectual growth of oneself and of others.

In this line of argument, such reflection and interactive engagement in discussion is facilitated in my course both in class and online through the Facebook group specifically created for this purpose. Some relevant advantages of using this online forum are that students not only end up conceiving reflection as part of their educational process, but also freely commit to articulate and share their opinions in an open, academic and independent way, either before or after the lecture, on a weekly basis. There are no time constraints as it may happen in class or they can dedicate as much time as they want to write down their reflections. Moreover, social influence from their peers inspires them to read the comments posted, build their knowledge and continue improving in an ongoing process of critical thinking that on a theoretical level is also in consonance with Elliot's pedagogy and principles of procedure.

According to Elliott, 'Whatever knowledge outcomes are pursued, the methods one adopts must satisfy the criteria of protecting and fostering students' ability to achieve this knowledge through their own powers of reason' (2007: 40). As educators, it is important to understand that knowledge is neither objective nor definite and it cannot be transmitted; each student has to create his or her own on the basis of what he or she already knows (Wells 1986). In this regard, two important principles established by Elliott emphasize, first, that discussion must prevail over instruction as a procedural approach to construct knowledge, and second, that the 'discussion should protect divergence of view among participants rather than attempt to achieve consensus' (Elliott 2007: 22). Thus, teachers should be receptive and welcome substantial differences among students as well as a wide variation in their understandings and critical reflections. The goal is not to have all students think the same or reach the same conclusions, but to have them engage in their own process of reflection and reach and construct their own knowledge. As Villacañas de Castro (2014b: 111) concludes:

> Only if students are allowed to express themselves along the educational process will they be able to transfer the affects which clung originally to their previous [knowledge to the new one that they are developing]. Only then may the cognitive and affective transitions take place, and learning ensue.

When students receive the right support, they gain independence and confidence to attempt to elaborate their own understandings (Ashwin 2015; Reyes Torres and Bird 2015).

On a different level, due to the fact that the social and cultural context in which each student develops as an individual plays a central and decisive role on the transformative power of human thought, Vygotsky's theory of learning that focuses on the interaction between social and cognitive aspects of language learning has gained broad attention among L2 teacher educators and researchers in the last two decades (Block 2003; Lacorte 2013, 2015). In this so-called sociocultural theory, language is viewed as a medium for the development of higher order thinking skills. Likewise, social interaction and the support of more knowledgeable peers are key factors. This process through which a teacher or other more experienced individuals work together with students and guide them to expand their critical thinking skills is what Lantolf and Thorne (2006) refer to as *mediation* and it leads to *internalization*, 'the individual's appropriation of assistance resulting in independent functioning' (Antón 2015: 11). Therefore, as Lacorte (2015: 118) points out:

> L2 teachers should be in a position to assume the role of facilitator in guiding student learning, providing ... support for their learners' autonomous progress in L2 as well as designing opportunities for interaction [and reflection] within the classroom and further with external L2 communities.

Undoubtedly, pre-service teachers should receive the necessary formation to follow this approach later in their careers. Initial English language teacher education courses must, as a result, incorporate reflective activities and practices that prepare teachers to produce and internalize their own perspectives on how to apply the sociocultural theory in their lessons. It is more likely that if they practice it as pre-service teachers, will they continue to do so as in-service teachers.

# What the learner does is more important than what the teacher does

Dewey was especially critical of the rote learning of facts in schools and argued that students should learn by experience. The old atlas complex by which many teachers felt they could transmit their wisdom and expertise through lengthy and tedious lectures is no longer acceptable. This is even more so when teaching English as an L2. As Villacañas (2014b: 96) points out, 'The characteristics of the learning process pupils undergo is far more significant than the content they should learn through it.' If students are to learn desired outcomes in a reasonably effective manner, they cannot just sit passively in the classroom. There is no doubt that the more they are involved in their learning, the more they are likely to gain from it (Ashwin 2015: 68). In this way, as Shuell (1986 quoted in Biggs 1999: 63) puts it: 'What the student does is actually more important in determining what is learned than what the teacher does.' This is the central point I introduce and highlight in my course on the very first day of class. The students' role is not to be taught and wait to receive knowledge. In fact, it is the opposite. Student engagement is directly and reciprocally related to active learning; it is about opening the mind and having the will to work and participate in class. It is about embracing a dialogic view of reflection that allows developing new thoughts and learning collaboratively as we listen to others.

In order to establish this type of dynamic in the course and facilitate students' involvement, I follow two different steps. To start with, on the first day we discuss the course schedule, objectives, expectations and assignments. Normally, there are fifteen weeks in the semester and it becomes clear to students that from week three to week nine, they are the ones in charge of leading the article discussions and presenting their thoughts on the reading assigned for that day. These presentations are done in groups and the goal is to generate a reflection on the ideas from the article that they consider the most relevant and how they can be applied to teaching English in primary schools. I prompt them to be creative, to illustrate the ideas with practical examples whenever possible and, last, to come up with a list of questions to post on the Facebook page of the class at least the day before. As we can see, the notion of engagement here emphasizes pre-service teachers' participation in their own learning both inside and outside formal educational settings.

The second step is to introduce students to the practice of reflection using their own experiences about learning. On the one hand, this allows them to start building their own knowledge and conclusions on the subject and, on the other, it allows me as an instructor to learn who they are and what their approaches to learning are. According to Ashwin, 'students make sense of their current experiences based on their previous experiences' (2015: 75). This has an impact on how they engage in their courses and how they relate to other students. Thus, for the second day of class, I post the following question on the Facebook group and I ask them to comment on it:

> Before we start the discussion of the first articles, I would like to invite you to reflect about your own experience as a student throughout the years, since you were in Primary School until now. How would you define the abstract concept of learning? What is 'learning'? How do you learn? What works for you? Take your time to think about it and share your ideas here.

The objective is not to have definite answers, but to have these pre-service teachers begin to explore how the process of reflecting is fruitful, and allowing them to elaborate and justify their perspectives. For the most part, they have a lot to say and write lengthy comments in which they make relevant points that serve to start the class discussion the following day. Some of these comments are given below:

> When I was younger I didn't like English because at school it was all about copying, colouring and singing but that didn't make sense for me, that didn't have a meaning. From my particular experience, I have to say that the more I relate what I am going to learn with my life, the more I learn. (Elena)
>
> For me, learning is doing. Unfortunately, through our academic lives only a few teachers have known how to make us learn and those teachers are the ones who we remember today. The other teachers believed that children learned exclusively from textbooks and they forgot that learning by heart is not the way to achieve effective learning. (Belén)
>
> When I was a child, I thought that learning was just doing homework, reading books and doing exams. That was what my teachers used to transmit. However, after these years at the University, I think that children truly learn when they can say: 'I can do this by myself' or 'I have many resources to solve this problem.' (Toni)

These three students are critical about their negative experiences as young students in school. Their comments are useful to raise awareness regarding what they should not do as future teachers. They realize that there is a need to change the ways that children learn English and, most importantly, that they have an important role to play in making that change possible. In addition, another significant point about the thirty-five posts made on this question is that the last ones show how students have read the previous ones and consider them when writing their own. That means that they have been engaged in reflection and that they reflect not only on their own experiences but also on the experiences of their classmates:

> After thinking about learning I want to share that for me it is creating concepts about anything in a significant way. Moreover, I agree with some comments regarding learning as a process that last forever because we can always find more knowledge about every matter. (María)
>
> It's hard to say something new or interesting after such amazing comments. For me learning is being able to apply what you 'heard' at class in your daily life. (Lorena)

Students' comments here illustrate how the processes of reflecting and learning come together. I find that it is this process that is crucial for them to understand how knowledge is constructed: as they think about their classmates' experiences and compare those with their own, they elaborate their ideas in their writing, they position themselves through their statements and they build up new knowledge and connect it to their previous one.

## Learning for teaching

In line with Ashwin's (2015) principles on effective teaching and learning in higher education, the contents of this course have been selected to engage pre-service teachers with a number of skills, concepts, ways of thinking and resources that are key for the teaching of English as an L2 in primary education. To do this, students are encouraged to develop a critical sense of the degree of effectiveness of different approaches, materials and current teaching strategies. To this aim, the course readings are organized in blocks that revolve around four particular types of knowledge and practices: (1) reflective teaching, (2) teaching English in the primary classroom, (3) the use of children's literature in the L2 class, and (4) literacy and twenty-first century skills. In this chapter, I will concentrate on the first block because it is the one directly related to the central subject of discussion.

During the first two weeks, in order to illustrate and become more acquainted with the formal practice of reflective teaching, two important models that students explore are Kolb's learning cycle (1984) and Farrell's (2015b) framework for reflecting on practice. It is noteworthy that they both help considerably to set the tone for the rest of the semester regarding the relevance and the place that reflection occupies in the course. The first model, influenced by Dewey's philosophical pragmatism, can be used as a description of the learning process in general. According to Kolb (1984: 38), 'knowledge results from the combination of grasping and transforming experience'. The second one, by Farrell (2015b: 22), consists of evidence-based reflective practice so that teachers can become more aware 'not only of their actions but also the origins, meanings and impact of such actions far beyond the classroom'.

In brief, Kolb's theory is represented by a four-stage cycle in which experience plays a central role in the learning process. The four stages, which are to be followed in sequence, are concrete experience, reflective observation, abstract conceptualization and active experimentation. The learning cycle thus provides feedback, which is the basis for new action and evaluation of the consequences of that action. In contrast, Farrell's framework consists of five levels that can be explored on their own in order to allow teachers to focus on specific aspects of their practice. Its levels are philosophy, principles, theory, practice and beyond practice. While Kolb's learning cycle focuses more directly on experience, Farrell's framework invites teachers to analyse other aspects more deeply, such as their personal profile, their assumptions and those previous experiences that may have had an influence on their teaching practice.

After discussing Kolb's model in class along with Geoff Petty's (2014) ideas on keeping a reflective journal during the first years of teaching to begin the routine of reflecting on practice, I assign the reading on Farrell's framework for the next day and I post the following question for debate on the Facebook forum:

> Compare Kolb's Learning Cycle and Farrell's framework for Reflecting on Practice. What do they have in common? How are they different? And how can they be used to complement one another?

Some significant examples of the students' comments are as follows:

> Both theories display that the only way to improve our teaching process is by reflecting. However, Kolb focuses on the practice element; that is, we're supposed to think about our practice to form our concepts from what we do in class and to test later our conclusions. On the other hand, Farrell concentrates on our ideas on teaching: our philosophy and how social and political elements may influence education. I believe that for us it is fundamental to aim at our practice in order to implement the way we work, but we should base our ideas not only on what we do in class but also on why and how we've formed these ideas so that both theories work together. (Aryah)

As my classmates already commented, it seems that Kolb's learning cycle serves us as a guide in order to be reflective about our teaching after a class, so that we can ask ourselves if the class has been successful or if it has gone as we had planned, wonder why and how we can improve it. By contrast, the Farrell's framework lets us think about our reflective practice more deeply and focus in each stage or level but it doesn't mean that we can't treat it globally. This framework tries to make teachers understand the importance of our critical reflection on our philosophy and principles which are interconnected with our beliefs, the theory that we can be put in practice (formal and not formal), and the level beyond practice which involves observation, planning and exploring critical incidents. To conclude, Farrell's framework lets us think about our teaching whenever we want to, including now that we don't have any years of experience and next semester when we are doing our student-teacher training in schools. In contrast, Kolb's learning cycle make us think only after a class. (Sofía)

The level of participation was high and students' responses demonstrate not only their engagement in reflection but also their interest in developing an understanding of the subject matter. This is what counts as good reflective practice, first, because they are constructing 'self-knowledge' based on both internal and external dialogue, and, second, because they are exercising their agency as they make judgements on the readings assigned. As Ashwin (2015) highlights, initial dialogue with oneself is essential to discuss our reflection with others. That is the case here. The Facebook forum offers the opportunity for critique and alternative explanations that can move students from personal descriptive reflections to dialogic reflection.

Likewise, the subsequent discussion in class reveals considerable agreement overall, and some insightful conclusions: Farrell's model is based on abstract concepts in order to create a theory that will guide teachers' actions. In turn, Kolb's cycle leads to an abstract conception based on concrete experiences. Additionally, the class discussion also shows that students have reached a critical realization on their own: reflection is an indispensable part of a teacher's job and it leads to self-awareness. The fact that this time it is they who verbalize the idea is particularly meaningful. They have *internalized* it. This is evident as well in their predisposition towards the *philosophy of teaching* that each of them needs to write as a final assignment by the end of the semester. At this point, they all understand that this personal reflection is a necessary step to become a teacher.

In the guidelines that students receive to write their philosophy of teaching, it states clearly that this reflection should be the product of all they have learnt throughout the years at the Faculty of Education, in the different courses and on their student-teacher practices. They are encouraged to ask themselves questions such as:

1. What kind of teacher would you like to become?
2. What are your personal beliefs about the nature of teaching and learning?
3. What have you learnt about teaching? What would you change?
4. What aspects would you like to incorporate into your own teaching and why?

According to Farrell (2015b: 25),

> When teachers write about their own lives and how they think their past experiences may have shaped the construction and development of their basic philosophy of practice, they will then be able to reflect critically on their practice because they will become more mindful and self-aware.

Put simply, the goal is to have students obtain self-knowledge and create an initial pathway on which they feel confident to embark. By way of illustration, the next excerpt constitutes an inspiring piece of a student's philosophy from Fall 2015:

> Teaching is believing in what you do, in who you are, in your aims, your talents, your ideas, your work. Teaching is believing in those who stand in front of you and need you. Teaching is realizing that you are there for them and that there are other teachers you can talk to share ideas, fears and conflicts. Teaching is being realistic and a dreamer at the same time. (Barbara)

As we can see, her attitude, her approach to working collaboratively and her creativity have certainly much to offer her learners. For a student-teacher who is at the beginning of his or her teaching career, this type of reflection can constitute a milestone in his or her developmental trajectory.

In this regard, as Petty (2014) claims, the practical implications of students' work like this one is that once we know how what we do have an impact on them, we can become far more effective as instructors. In this particular case, the participative atmosphere of the class and the eagerness with which students worked, read and sometimes replied instantly to the posts on Facebook motivated me to acknowledge that closeness and enhance it with posts that were not course related. The results were astonishing. One Sunday, for instance, I posted the video of *Learn to Fly*, a song by Foo Fighters that 1,000 musicians played together in Italy with the hope that it would compel the actual band to visit their city. My only comment was as follows: 'Some music for the background of this ongoing reflection,' and to my surprise students began to comment on the song and relate it to the world of education. Some examples are given below:

> After watching the video, I have to say that is a good way to wake up with energy on a Sunday morning. As I was watching it, the first thing that came to my mind was that the video is a perfect tool to show an example of people working together to make a beautiful song. In my opinion, it encourages us to reach our goals even if they are difficult because it is the only way to feel ourselves alive. This advice can also be applied to education. We as teachers should give opportunities to children in order to let them find their own way and encourage them to set up goals for themselves. (David)
>
> Amazing video, a real collaborative work! I have heard this song before and I think it is so motivating. It is a really really good song to drive you to do new things, make your dreams come true and wake up and say: 'Hey, I am here! I want you to know I am ready to change how things work! So, let's try to make some changes in education, let's try to give our students wings to fly freely and guide them to discover the world!' (Lola)

Needless to say, students' insightful comments exceeded my expectations. It is possible to observe the positive effect of the learning environment, the progress in their way of thinking critically and their gradual way of connecting ideas and developing their knowledge. As I see it, this interaction between knowledge and development is the product of reflection, one that leads to learning for teaching.

The approach to the other blocks in the course is the same. Students are responsible for working together in groups on different readings and presenting their ideas on how to teach the formal aspects of the English language, how to plan a lesson, the advantages of using children's literature as a didactic tool, assessment and record keeping, etc. At this point, as I already mentioned, it is they who are also in charge of posting the questions on Facebook. In this way, something remarkable is that around week five in the semester, I barely have to intervene and the interaction among students is totally fluid. The leading group would reply to individual comments and provide attentive feedback on Facebook as well as in the following class discussion.

## Literacy is thinking and organizing knowledge

The concept of literacy in the twenty-first century has evolved from a language process to an act of cognition (Kucer 2005). As I have suggested elsewhere, 'The degree to which students can make use of language to read and understand texts in all formats (books, online newspapers, pictures, videos, etc.) is a key indicator of their ability to make and communicate meaning' (Reyes Torres 2014: 42). There is no question that 'the more fluent students become as readers, writers, speakers, and listeners, the clearer, more coherent, and more flexible their thinking will become' (Roberts and Billings 2008: 33). Therefore, we should treat thinking as a fundamental literacy skill. As students learn to think, they are able to work with different disciplines and systems such as literature, math, science, online sources, etc., that contain a wide range of complex elements. Accordingly, literacy can be defined then as a dynamic and multidimensional concept that comprises a variety of abilities and types of knowledge – many literacies – which allow students to evaluate information, organize ideas and draw conclusions.

As it stands to reason, there is a certain level of literacy that all students in higher education should achieve to be able to articulate their thoughts in an effective way. However, this would also vary slightly and become more specific depending on different university degrees. Undoubtedly, the skills and the type of critical thinking pre-service teachers of English need to have will differ from that required of students in business, medicine or law.

In this line of reasoning, the design and presentation of didactic units based on picture books that pre-service teachers do in this course constitutes a reflective task and an opportunity for them to apply the literacy acquired throughout the semester and put it into practice. The objective is to have them use the advantages that children's literature offers to create lessons of English. This allows them to demonstrate both their understanding of how to plan a lesson and their ability to reflect critically on the theory covered and develop their teaching skills. In a way, what they are asked to do echoes the same pattern I follow with them, that is, to think about learning tools, materials and reflective activities that, in this case, can guide primary students to build their literacy and develop their command of English as an L2.

With this goal in mind, students follow a general outline to create a didactic unit in which among other points, they must distinguish between content and attitude goals, explain the rationale behind the teaching approach they have chosen, select a picture book and pinpoint the literacy they aim to produce from it. Some enlightening excerpts from their work that illustrate how far they have come with regard to the type of teaching they pursue are as follows:

> In our didactic unit based on the book *Each Kindness* by Jacqueline Woodson (2012), we do not only want to teach what students should be taught according to the curriculum; we want students to have a positive attitude towards the

English Language and towards learning. Finally, we want them to develop communication and critical thinking skills. (Guillermo)

In this unit, we want to develop values based on equality using the English language. The point is to teach students to become critical and responsible citizens so they can make their own decisions. (Mark)

## Conclusion

Teaching English as an L2 in primary schools is a creative and intellectually demanding job that requires a continual process of growth and learning. As I have shown, reflection in pre-service teacher education is of vital importance because it provides a vehicle for improvement, promotes active engagement and provides a better understanding of the complex world of education. Through a critical pedagogical approach based on Dewey's, Vygotsky's, and Elliot's learning theories, I have shown that equipping pre-service teachers with the literacy and practice to reflect both on their own and collaboratively brings about the production of knowledge, one that each of them develops anew and is also based on their prior personal experiences and sociocultural background. It is evident that having a high level of English is crucial but not sufficient; as I discussed, teachers must also understand how best to enable primary students to learn and, in this case, both Kolb's learning cycle and Farrell's framework for reflecting on practice constitute key models to follow. Likewise, discussing as well as exchanging ideas in class and on Facebook forums have been proven as being an effective and beneficial methodology. The ultimate goal is to engage teachers in an ongoing and active process of reflection that allows them to conceptualize learning as an attempt at meaning-making as opposed to a process of transmission of knowledge.

## Questions for change

1. To what extent is reflective teaching a sustainable current practice in higher education courses?
2. Do curricula in pre-service language teacher education discuss the impact of internal theories and reflection in trainees' practicum and future trajectories as novice teachers?
3. Do teaching strategies in higher education enable pre-service teachers to engage actively and enjoy the contents they are learning? Whose responsibility is it to learn?

# 10

# Critical Awareness in Language Teacher Development

Claudia Saraceni

## Objectives

1. Describe and discuss the interface between *teacher training* and *teacher development*.
2. Explore and inform innovative and principled techniques for enhancing teacher education development.
3. Promote critical awareness development as a tool for enhanced teacher autonomy.

## Introduction

The language classroom can take multiple forms; it is a multifaceted, complex, dynamic and, to a certain extent, unpredictable environment. It is in this context that this chapter raises the question as to whether student-teachers are suitably equipped to deal with variable, open-ended and unpredictable classroom dynamics. In this framework, we may also need to consider what can be done to make teacher education courses more beneficial in order for future teachers to deal with potentially problematic issues in the language classroom, particularly in the initial stages of their development.

More precisely, this chapter analyses the interface between *teacher training* and *teacher development* in the context of initial English language teacher education (IELTE). It therefore aims to investigate the role of critical awareness as a tool to enhance teacher development, and it explores ways of promoting a learner-centred, context-driven, research-based, experiential approach to teacher education in general.

The discussion put forward here raises a number of questions related to the above-mentioned, seemingly contrasting, issues. It specifically addresses certain views raised by teacher educators and student-teachers as its main starting point, and also those related to materials developers and, generally, applied linguists, with the aim of promoting a more insightful, research-driven approach to teacher critical development.

This chapter is structured in three main interconnected foci. An overview of different approaches to teacher education, including some of its main concepts and issues as well as its characteristics, aims and purposes, is included to provide a contextual background to the main purpose of the chapter. This is then followed by a particular emphasis on the development of critical awareness and possible suggestions for different techniques and ideas that can be used to apply this approach to practice. This represents the core element of this chapter and it is advocated particularly through a localized, context-driven approach. A discussion of proposed principles, suggestions and practices for developing critical awareness in language teacher development programmes is also offered. In its concluding section, further developments for research and data collection purposes are presented in the form of questions for change.

## From teacher training to teacher critical awareness development

In our research (Narvet, Saraceni and Sari in preparation), one of the most common issues raised by teacher trainees in reference to their learning experience can be summarized in the following point:

I would like to have more workshops on the 'do's and don'ts' of language teaching.

The above statement, found in trainees' course reviews, seems to make two basic assumptions: (1) it relates to the commonly held idea that there is a methodology of language teaching that is to be considered effective and *good* with a set of rules to follow, and therefore *correct*; and (2) it relates to the view that one of the main responsibilities of the trainer is to simply transfer those 'do's and don'ts' to the trainees in the clearest, most straightforward manner.

However, in many respects, the above view oversimplifies teaching. More specifically, the teaching of a second/foreign language is undoubtedly complex and multifaceted as it involves a number of skills, techniques, strategies and personal characteristics that should not be underestimated and need to be developed in the context of the classroom. In many ways, therefore, this chapter aims to emphasize the fundamental need for teacher trainees to *experience and experiment* their ideas and those above-mentioned teaching techniques, strategies and characteristics, through classroom practice.

Generally, there are a number of different approaches to educational pedagogy, which seem to relate to often strongly held views on what characteristics constitute a 'good language teacher' (see, for example, Gower, Phillips and Walters 2005; Harmer 2007; McDonough, Shaw and Masuhara 2013; Scrivener 2011).

## Teacher training approaches

A clear overview of teacher education approaches is summarized in Tomlinson (2003, 2013), who outlined three 'modes' of language teaching instruction: *teacher training, teacher education* and *teacher development*. Following Tomlinson's framework (Tomlinson 2003, 2013), teacher training programmes tend to provide information and guidelines for trainees to follow and put them into practice in the classroom. They mostly focus on delivering advice and guidelines and subsequently assessing specific teaching techniques, following certain preconceived frameworks and rules, based on well-established, widely accepted practices. A very common example of one of the above-mentioned techniques is the use of the so-called PPP approach to language teaching, based on a rather traditional, teacher-centred approach focusing on an extremely popular framework based on *Presentation, Practice* and *Production*. Those classroom techniques are generally learnt with the aim of applying them to classroom practice, but they are very seldom discussed, evaluated or questioned:

> In a teacher training approach teachers or trainee teachers are given procedures and advice to follow. This approach assumes a relationship of experts to novices and characterizes many pre-service courses in which the participants are trained to teach a particular textbook, methodology or curriculum. (Tomlinson 2003)

The generic rationale behind these widely accepted classroom procedures is based on the underlying idea that there is a clear distinction between *good* and *bad* teaching and that such a distinction can provide some kind of basic foundation, particularly for the relatively inexperienced teacher.

As mentioned earlier, the PPP approach to lesson planning is very often encouraged and supported in this mode of teaching, and it is generally presented as a model practice, perhaps compared with possible alternative frameworks to this specific approach. Particularly in the practical context of initial teacher training, the PPP framework focuses on widely accepted, mostly unquestioned practices: the *presentation* of language input, the subsequent *practice* and the following *production* of such input. Generally, the practice stage would also take the shape of mostly controlled practice to start with and gradually become more open-ended later on in the lesson.

This approach seems to present a number of similarities with certain teacher-centred, positivistic views of language teaching and learning approaches, which emphasize rather static, rule-governed procedures based on habit-forming, behaviourist principles, which are found on the basis of the very concept of *training*. Furthermore, the above-described teacher training approaches seem to neglect to take into account the relative unpredictability of the classroom context. They, in fact, tend to undermine the trainee's personal initiative when attempting to deal with potential problematic issues or unexpected problems that often arise in the classroom.

## Teacher education approaches

This mode represents, in many ways, a further development of the above-described teacher training approaches, as it provides the opportunity for teacher trainees to develop their knowledge about pedagogical approaches to language teaching and learning and also discover different techniques for themselves, thus enhancing teacher autonomy.

The above-described approaches based on teacher training are most commonly found in various practical courses, which are considered particularly valid in relation to the distinction between initial teacher training of relatively inexperienced teachers – perhaps following a programme at a certificate level (typically a Certificate in English Language Teaching or CELTA courses) – and those more advanced trainees following a programme at postgraduate or diploma level, who are often associated with a teacher education mode. Richards and Rodgers note the following:

> Teacher education courses reflect a variety of different positions concerning the role they attribute to the study of teaching approaches and methods. Some of

these differences reflect whether the course has a 'teacher-training' approach and is intended for pre-service teachers or a 'teacher-development' perspective and is aimed at experienced teachers completing more advanced courses, perhaps at the MA level. (Richards and Rodgers 2014: 355)

The above relates to the view that, at initial stages, trainees need to be given specific procedures and guidance. As they progress and become more advanced and experienced, they are also thought to become better able to understand teaching methodologies in order to apply them in the classroom. Such progression is seen as a similar process to what may be involved when helping a toddler learn how to stand and, subsequently, walk and run.

## Teacher development approaches

What happens when things do not go as planned in the classroom? Teacher development represents a first attempt to answer this question as it takes the approaches mentioned above further and aims to promote critical understanding through gaining a better insight and awareness of the techniques and strategies used in classroom practice. In his article, Tomlinson (2003) describes these approaches emphasizing the following focus and aim:

In the best type of teacher development course the teachers are helped to decide what to think and do for themselves and are encouraged to develop novel approaches themselves. (Tomlinson 2003)

A number of different practical techniques have been put forward to enhance teacher development. McDonough, Shaw and Masuhara (2013), for example, have proposed teaching observation as a tool to achieve teacher development, whereas Saraceni (2013) and Tomlinson (2013) propose to achieve this through materials development and adaptation. The key element that seems to make this approach more distinctive and potentially more impactful is based on a process of systematic self-reflection through self-evaluation and self-assessment, with classroom experience as a starting point (Ghaye 2011). Promoting self-assessment techniques in teacher development approaches also relates to what Green (2014) refers to as *potential beneficial consequences of assessment*. This can be achieved, for example, by involving the trainees in evaluating their own work and progress in their classroom practice.

Teacher development differs from the other modes described here, as it aims at enabling trainees to develop confidence and insight in classroom dynamics, to deal with a variety of different teaching and learning scenarios as well as potentially problematic issues, and to use their own initiative without over-relying on their trainer. Perhaps in different ways, the need for teacher development has been emphasized in a variety of papers with different views and foci (Andrews 2007; Harmer 2007; Scrivener 2011; Sugrue and Day 2002).

## Critical awareness development approaches

Critical awareness principles and techniques represent one of the developments that originated from approaches and principles based on language awareness (see Arndt, Harvey and Nuttall 2000; Bolitho 2003; Bolitho et al. 2003; Gebhard and Oprandy 1999; Wright and Bolitho 1993).

In many ways, critical awareness development approaches also relate to the core principles and practices of teacher development described above and represent a further possible application of such mode. More specifically, in the context of this chapter, the *critical* element of this approach is based on the skill of evaluating and questioning. A parallel with *critical language awareness* may also offer a possible definition to conceptualize this element. Fairclough highlights the importance of critical consciousness in the following point:

> People cannot be effective citizens in a democratic society if their education cuts them off from critical consciousness of key elements within their physical or social environment. (Fairclough 1992 as reported in Pennycook 2001: 95)

Similarly, the above comment can be considered valid also for teachers in training who are encouraged to experience and critically evaluate their classroom work and to question their choices to ultimately develop their *critical consciousness*. Therefore, this mode opens opportunities for discussion, evaluation, reflection, questioning and, eventually, gradually forming one's own views, perceptions and possible applications to classroom practice.

### The role of context

Perhaps one of the most significant elements of this approach can be found in its emphasis on the role context can play in developing a more learner-centred, localized approach to the language classroom. Bax (2003a, 2003b) emphasizes this approach to language teaching and learning rather effectively, and he places its main focus on learners and their language learning needs and purposes, as well as their cultural backgrounds and characteristics:

> The first priority is the learning context and the first step is to identify key aspects of that context before deciding what and how to teach in any given class. This will include an understanding of individual students and their learning needs, wants, styles and strategies … as well as the classroom culture, school culture and national culture. (Bax 2003a: 285)

Some of the main characteristic features of critical awareness development and a more context-driven approach are also embedded in the use of action research, particularly in its cyclical nature and its potential applications to the language classroom. As research generally poses questions as its starting point, the use of action research also seems a suitable and appropriate tool in this framework, as it emphasizes the skill of questioning and, consequently, taking action in the classroom

Nunan (2005) provides a clear definition of action research, which is also significant in the context of this chapter:

> The three defining characteristics of action research are that it is carried out by practitioners …; secondly, that it is collaborative; and thirdly, that it is aimed at changing things. (Nunan 2005: 17)

Kemmis and McTaggart (1988) have also suggested that

> those affected by planned changes have the primary responsibility for deciding on courses of critically informed action which seem likely to lead to improvement, and for evaluating the results of strategies tried out in practice. (Kemmis and McTaggart 1988: 6)

The aforementioned cycle is depicted in Figure 10.1, which emphasizes some of the main characteristics of a context-driven approach, promoted through critical awareness development and the use of action research, whereby self-reflection and self-assessment are used as tools for the purposes of developing a rationale, which in turn informs context-based language teaching.

Very often research is considered a separate entity from teaching and vice versa. Therefore, there seem to be two parallel categories of practitioners: researchers and teachers and, perhaps paradoxically, the two very seldom meet.

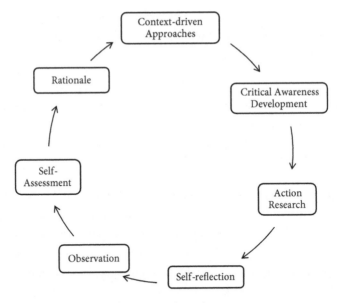

**Figure 10.1** Critical awareness cycle in teacher education.

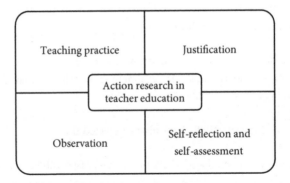

**Figure 10.2** Action research as a tool for teacher education.

However, within this approach, practitioners take the role of researchers, as also noted by Tomlinson (2013) in the following:

> In the process of developing awareness and skills, teachers can also develop the ability to theorize their practice (Schon, 1987) to question their procedures, to check their hypotheses and to find answers to their questions about the processes of language learning and teaching. (Tomlinson 2013: 482)

In this context, adopting action research therefore necessarily involves the use of teaching practice as an essential part of teacher development programmes as well as self-reflection (Figure 10.2).

# A personal view

Considering the above discussion, perhaps student-teachers should most effectively be given the opportunity to progress from a more controlled teacher training perspective to one based on critical awareness development, gradually moving from a teacher-centred approach to a more learner-centred, autonomous role. This may be especially true for inexperienced teachers in their initial stages of teacher development, and it may also reflect what a number of teacher educators and student-teachers would consider to be most appropriate.

However, according to Narvet, Saraceni and Sari (in preparation), more experienced trainees very often recognize the difficulty they find when they start questioning their teaching approaches and try to move away from those classroom habits they have developed for many years in their practice. As a result of their training, they, in fact, may come to understand the potential limits of their practice and aim to move towards what they realize can be innovative and more effective techniques in their teaching context. Yet, they often find it hard to apply those new ideas to practice. On the other hand, from this perspective, those at initial stages of their training often find this transition easier to implement, perhaps paradoxically, as they are relatively new to teaching and somewhat better prepared to question what may seem established, commonly accepted practices.

It is in this context that the use of a more teacher-controlled type of training, particularly in the first stages of their development, may inevitably influence the trainees' experience, and consequently determine the approach they use to teaching and learning later on in their career, and possibly delay their autonomous development. Therefore, new trainees should not be denied the opportunity to use their initiative and experiment classroom work as a tool to also develop their critical awareness in the initial stages of their development. This would be most beneficial in terms of enhancing their experience through questioning different techniques and approaches, and perhaps facilitating their independent learning through learner empowerment and self-confidence.

Teacher critical development approaches, therefore, can promote trainee teachers' personal initiative and autonomy through the development of a rationale that aims to support their choices in the language teaching and learning classroom, as well as some of its underlining principles, which can be advantageous at all stages of development.

The approach described above, however, may be received with some resistance from teacher trainers and also from the point of view of teacher trainees. Both may find this approach rather uncomfortable and challenging due to its seeming lack of teacher control. In my experience in a multicultural context, such as what is most commonly found in the UK classroom, there may be a great variety of expectations, perceptions and responses to this approach. However, generally, both trainers and trainees from different cultural backgrounds understand the potential benefits of this approach, but may still need time to apply its principles to the practice of their own classroom teaching.

The following section offers possible ways of applying critical awareness development, as it emphasizes certain aspects embedded in the type of context-driven approach promoted in this chapter. More specifically, it takes into account the role of teaching practice, the significance of writing a rationale and of self-reflection and self-assessment, as well as the role of observation.

## The role of teaching practice (TP)

In many ways, a parallel can be drawn between learning teaching and learning how to drive a car, which to a certain extent may be considered similar processes. When learning how to drive, studying the theory manual provides useful knowledge and information but does not necessarily facilitate learning what to do when in the driver's seat; learning to drive necessarily involves actual driving. Similarly, experiencing actual classroom teaching is the most effective way to learn how to teach. As mentioned earlier in this chapter, this emphasizes the validity of teaching practice as an essential element of teacher training and development programmes. This is particularly evident, especially for IELTE, as teaching practice can help initial, inexperienced teachers move away from a relatively passive role when receiving information, to a more engaged, active role when taking control and responsibility for the dynamics of the classroom. For the above reasons, this type of experience takes initial teachers out of their comfort zone in what may be one of the most challenging, but also beneficial and perhaps rewarding, elements of their development (Narvet, Saraceni and Sari in preparation).

In summary of the above discussion, despite the fact that teaching practice can be generally a stressful and rather sensitive and vulnerable experience (perhaps for the majority of trainees and trainers), it can also represent the core element of teacher development programmes at all levels, and can provide the most impactful and beneficial learning curve experienced by both teacher trainees and trainers.

## Writing a rationale

Teaching practice should be accompanied by the process of writing a rationale, which is equally valuable and significant, as it facilitates the type of research-driven, systematic, more objective and principled approach to teaching advocated in this chapter. The main focus of this exercise outlines the purposes and objectives behind the choices made in lesson planning, and justifies those choices in relation to the trainees' teaching and learning context, their learners' needs and their reading. A rationale, therefore, encourages trainees to reflect upon their lesson planning and delivery, and it may also originate from group/class discussions carried out through focus group meetings and teamwork in general. This would encourage trainees to rationalize the process of planning teaching and learning, taking it beyond the trainees' experience, impressions and intuition, as it aims to justify and substantiate their teaching from existing research.

## Self-reflection and self-assessment

As also mentioned earlier in this chapter, critical awareness development is further reinforced and emphasized by enabling trainee teachers to contribute to the assessment of teaching practice and therefore play a significant role in feedback sessions. Feedback is generally provided in written and/or oral form mostly in a *one-way* direction: from the trainer to the trainee. However, there are a number of ways of making feedback sessions more beneficial for trainee teachers by involving them in a more active role where the trainer and the whole teaching practice team contribute to the actual TP assessment (as also noted by Narvet, Saraceni and Sari in preparation).

Contributions to feedback sessions can also be combined with other sessions such as discussions carried out in focus group meetings and in teamwork meetings to be conducted independently of the trainer. This gives trainees an opportunity to reflect upon different issues related to their teaching more freely and perhaps more constructively. This also presents an added value related to the fact that encouraging trainees to work in a team with such a mindset would also resemble what actually happens in a potential workplace context.

## Observation

Observation is often part of the requirements of teacher training programmes and it is commonly imposed on trainees as a compulsory part of their course.

This is, as a result, often seen as something to be done in the quickest and easiest possible way, without necessarily appreciating its purposes and aims and therefore failing to take advantage of its potential benefits.

In this framework, however, this practice is considered beyond the limitations of simple classroom observation whereby trainees observe a professional teacher and take notes following a pre-prepared form provided by their trainer or their institution. Observation needs to be seen as part of research and, in this case, part of action research (see also Dörnyei 2007; Nunan 2005). It is for these purposes that observation here can take a multifaceted form in terms of classroom experimentation in peer teaching scenarios, where trainees take more control of classroom dynamics and prepare and use a variety of different activities on the basis of a task provided by their trainer. This can also be achieved with the use of materials evaluation and adaptation as an additional tool for similar purposes and objectives (see also Saraceni 2013; Tomlinson 2013). Therefore, observation can become a starting point for reflection, discussion and depth of understanding.

All the examples and suggestions above do not represent an exhaustive list of possible techniques that can be used to develop trainees' critical awareness. However, they do represent a few possible methods that may be used with the aim of encouraging independent learning and promoting autonomous critical thinking as a way of empowering trainees to take a more active role in the classroom and eventually enable them to claim ownership of a more in-depth awareness of their own progress.

## Conclusion

In an attempt to provide an overview of some of the main approaches to teacher education, this chapter offered a description and evaluation of some of the most distinctive features, principles and practices between *teacher training* and *teacher development*. Furthermore, this chapter also put forward an approach based on critical awareness development as a tool for promoting learner empowerment and autonomy in the context of initial teacher education, mostly through a more learner-centred, localized context-based approach (Table 10.1).

McDonough, Shaw and Masuhara (2013) and Canagarajah (2005) highlight the distinctive nature of teaching and learning and teacher education, particularly

**Table 10.1** Three views on teacher education

| Teacher training | Teacher education | Critical awareness development |
|---|---|---|
| Teacher-centred | Learner-centred | Learner autonomy development |
| Classroom procedures provided | Knowledge focused | Trainee's personal initiative |
| Emphasis on good/ bad practices | Focus on different options | Localized context-driven |

in its variety of different characteristics, its open-endedness and, therefore, its relative unpredictability:

> The sheer number of variables involved in teaching will probably mean that identifying the characteristics of a good language teacher remains an impossible task, especially when we consider the sheer diversity of teaching contexts around the globe. (McDonough, Shaw and Masuhara 2013: 299)

Within the context of such an open-ended field, in this concluding section it is probably most appropriate to offer questions for further discussion, evaluation and analysis, rather than providing possible answers to the issues presented here. Nevertheless, perhaps the most obvious concluding point that can be made relates to a rather noticeable need for more research in this field in order to inform a more principled approach to teacher education in general and to initial teacher development in particular. The following questions may also lead to a proposal for possible further developments and research.

## Questions for change

1. How can we reconcile a context-driven approach to teacher critical awareness development with the necessity for assessment and also for grading?
2. To what extent can we combine critical awareness development with cultural awareness in the context of teacher development?
3. To what extent can critical awareness development be suitable for initial language teacher education?

# 11

# Emancipating EFL Student-teachers through Audiovisual Identity Texts

Luis S. Villacañas de Castro

## Objectives

1. Identify oppressive practices embedded in standard EFL education in Spain.
2. Formulate ways of applying critical pedagogical orientations for university EFL student-teachers to emancipate themselves from their previous and oppressive learner experiences.
3. Describe a workshop on audiovisual identity texts that allowed EFL student-teachers to express their cultures and identities and identify those components that could potentially enrich their EFL teaching practice in the near future.

## Oppressive images of EFL learning

Generally, the EFL classes involved working through a couple of pages of a textbook, once again translating everything to Spanish, with no deviation from the contents. There were rushed grammar instructions worked into the process and then homework assigned from the workbook and a date set for an exam on the unit. ... The teacher ignored his students for the most part, when he did speak to them it was generally to interrupt or shout at them. In class he never showed any personal interest, caring or sense of humor. ... Most students were completely disconnected and understandably so. (Eoghan, student-teacher)

This quote from an EFL Irish student-teacher (ST) directed to me and another six of his peers describes his experience in the EFL lessons he attended during his practicum placement in a public school in Valencia (Spain). Just as disturbing as the situation he described was the fact that his peers agreed with him: yes, they too had witnessed similar episodes during their training periods. Yet none of them seemed too appalled by this, since this episode simply brought their own school experiences as EFL learners back to them. As Noelia, another ST, wrote in the final report on her practicum placement:

> When I try to recall my EFL classes back in school, I remember a boring textbook with foreign students in the pictures that did not look like us (for example, they were wearing very posh uniforms and studied in well-equipped schools, they would eat food we did not eat, or live in houses which did not exist in Spain); I remember doing many exercises but with very little variety among them (most were fill-in-the-gaps), writing some artificial text with no purpose (like writing to an imaginary friend about an imaginary journey we never made); I remember struggling when we were requested to memorize the list of irregular verbs and their past simple and past participle versions – I was used to learning by *understanding*, and memorizing things was something I simply could not do. … With these experiences as an EFL learner, I wonder how I managed to learn and master the English language. (Noelia, ST)

Testimonies like these, and many more that I have encountered in the course of my research and lecturing on EFL at the University of Valencia, led me to the following thought: Spanish students who generally had the chance to connect to education in other school contexts, and who were not necessarily oppressed from a socio-economic angle, were being forced to feel like foreigners in the EFL classroom, migrants in their own school, even *colonized* subjects (López-Gopar and Sughrua 2014), oppressed and alienated from their own realities. This could be the reason why a claim originally formulated by Meyer (2007: 217) in relation to the English education received by immigrant students in mainstream classrooms of the United States seemed to apply so well to the experience of many EFL learners in Spain, for in both cases 'students' learning opportunities, and ultimately their life potentials, [were] wasted by instructional activities and teaching strategies that reveal[ed] the low expectations teachers h[e]ld for them'.

Indeed, in far too many cases, inadequate pedagogical decisions such as placing excessive emphasis on linguistic, native-like competence (of teachers and learners alike) (Tarnopolsky 2008); or top-down, narrow and scripted curricula (Banegas, Pavese, Velázquez and Vélez 2013); or developing meaningless, unchallenging and de-contextualized classroom practices with a close focus on decoding, drills, fill-in-the-gaps and so on, and not on meaning and context (Lorenzo 2014; Reyes Torres and Bird 2015); or opting for sanitized international textbooks that not only idealize Western English-speaking countries (their forms of life and their language) but offering no possibility whatsoever for learners to showcase their own cultural and linguistic heritage (Moirano 2012), led Spanish EFL teachers to reproduce in their classrooms the same negative educational effects that, in other circumstances, were created by profound socio-economic factors (Bourne, 2007).

## Emancipating EFL teachers and learners

Hence I decided to initiate a general research project, starting in the 2014–15 academic year, aimed specifically at emancipating teachers and learners involved in EFL education in Spain. My method was the following: I first became acquainted with those critical pedagogies that had already proved capable of addressing the effects of socio-economic, ethnic and cultural marginalization of immigrant and minority language learners in a wide range of local contexts, such as participatory action research (Cammarota and Romero 2011), learning communities (Pérez Gómez, Sola Fernández, Soto Gómez and Murillo Mas 2013), or funds of knowledge and identity (Esteban-Guitart and Saubich 2013). Next, I applied some of these models to my EFL educational context to assess their emancipatory potential, especially with EFL STs registered in my university courses. Persuaded as I was by the idea that we EFL teachers must emancipate ourselves from oppressive forms of EFL teaching, which have become the standard, before we can actually emancipate our own learners intellectually, I organized tasks that combined theory with practice, action with pedagogical reflection, aimed at giving these STs the chance to experience (as learners) critical forms of EFL education that contrasted sharply with those they had been exposed to in the past and which had shaped their inherited educational common sense. At the same time, these activities encouraged the STs to take a teacher stand and analyse the guiding principles that underpinned the critical pedagogy I put forward – a first step to translate these practices in the future into emancipatory tasks for their primary EFL classes by intervening directly in curricular matters in ways that allowed teachers and learners to show their best possible version of themselves.

## Identity texts

The pedagogical strategy explored in this chapter – *identity texts* – did not arise directly from the field of critical pedagogy but from the realm of ELT research and practice. It did so, however, as a result of a serious effort to open this discipline to wider, transformative contributions to critical literacy (Cummins, Hu, Markus and Montero 2015). Originally conceived by Cummins as the pedagogical follow-up of his theory of cross-language transfer (Cummins 2005), identity texts are

> the products of students' creative work or performances carried out within the pedagogical space orchestrated by the classroom teachers. Students invest their identities in the creation of these texts which can be written, spoken, visual, musical, dramatic, or combinations of multimodal form. The identity text then holds a mirror up to students in which their identities are reflected back in a positive light. … Although not always an essential component, technology acts as an amplifier to enhance the process of identity text production and dissemination. (Cummins and Early 2011: 3)

Within Cummins' pedagogical framework, identity texts encourage cross-language transfer precisely because they provide learners with an educational experience that is the exact opposite of what prevalent ELT approaches tend to offer; that is, one that allows learners to channel their cognitive, linguistic, experiential and affective wealth from their native language to the process of EFL learning, and leads them to produce texts they can feel proud of. Not only are they capable, then, of identifying lexical items that are common to, or similar, in both languages but, more importantly, they also become English learners who feel intelligent and thus more capable of learning more, unlike what ELT teachers and textbooks usually expect and demand from them (Cummins, Hu, Markus and Montero 2015). Because of this, identity texts share a clear emancipatory intention that *lies* in agreement with the general orientation of this research. While their use has often been restricted to research on language learner identity – identity texts do not yet belong in the mainstream of language teacher identity research (Varghese, Morgan, Johnston and Johnson 2005) – they have also been used in IELTE programmes in non-core countries, precisely to boost confidence among non-native STs who felt that their pedagogical and linguistic capital was being debased by prevalent native-speaker educational paradigms. Those paradigms showed total disregard for their cultural identities, in accordance with a neocolonial stance that seems both ideologically and pedagogically inadequate (López-Gopar 2011).

## A participatory workshop on teacher identity

The workshop I describe below lasted for a month and a half (from mid-February to the end of March 2015) and was developed during ten two-hour lessons. It consisted of the creation of video identity texts by fifty-one STs in the third year of their Degree in Elementary EFL education. It was conducted entirely in English and in the context of the subject *Culture in EFL education*, which I taught, and whose main goal was to provide future elementary EFL teachers with the theoretical and practical knowledge necessary to handle the cultural variables in their EFL classroom in ways that were conducive to meaningful learning. The subject included two additional workshops, which will not be analysed in this chapter but which also adopted a participatory and critical orientation: a photovoice that addressed what culture was for each of them, and a final project aimed at developing their intercultural awareness by researching the black history of the United States and writing a poem based on any one of its remarkable struggles. Eighty-seven per cent of the STs who took part in this subject were female, 80 per cent under twenty-three years old, and all of them from middle- and upper-class SES backgrounds (which testifies to the growing difficulties that students from less advantageous SES face to access university). They were also overwhelmingly white, except for one student who had a Latin American origin. Apart from having a certified B2 level in English (Council of Europe, no date), the STs were bilingual speakers of Spanish and Catalan, since both are official languages in the Valencia region. Their privileged socio-economic background, however, had not spared them oppressive experiences in the EFL classroom, as was soon revealed by their identity texts.

The double teacher and learner identities of the participants opened up methodological possibilities for conducting research along participatory lines, and I worked hard to realize them. Videos were the outcome of a collective process that proceeded along pedagogical paths similar to those followed by participatory action research projects, in which certain collectives research subject matters that are inherently connected to their own lives (Van Sluys 2010). To make this possible, the workshop covered the following methodological phases: First, the participants became acquainted with the conceptual and educational underpinnings of identity texts (especially in relation to literacy education) through my own explanations, readings and collective discussions of key articles and case studies on this matter. After this, the STs explored (first in small groups, then by sharing their ideas through brainstorming) the many different levels that identity might consist of: familial, ethnic, racial, economic, ideological, cultural, linguistic, genre (male vs. female), sexual, professional, educational, physical, etc. All of these dimensions could give rise to conflicts and struggles, the negotiation of which would become the backbone of their own identity texts. Still in small groups, they recalled any first-hand critical incident or experience belonging to any of these levels that had impacted or contributed to shaping their present identity. Taking this as a point of departure for their written work, each ST then produced a text in English that made an explicit connection between this critical incident and at least one of the identity planes already identified. They also had to reflect on how their identity included traits that could prove helpful and enriching from a teacher perspective. This written text became the raw material that was transformed once the STs started to search for images (photos, drawings), sound (music, voice) or even other videos they would use to complete and improve their audiovisual identity texts. The final videos were thus a collage of textual, visual and aural elements that were mostly of their own making, and which the STs produced by using any one computer program they felt comfortable with (PhotoStory3, Windows MovieMaker, Prezi and Windows PowerPoint all served their purpose). The videos were shared and discussed during a couple of sessions, and the successes or failures of the workshop were assessed by analysing the extent to which the texts had been able to bring together and expand different planes of their identities.

In this regard, different kinds of conversations were maintained through which the workshop was explicitly analysed in a participatory and collective way. For example, the STs and I had a collective assessment session in class in which we discussed the strengths and weaknesses of the workshop in relation to their identity and cognitive engagement, as well as the interest and quality of the resulting texts. In addition, I held individual interviews and focus groups (three to five people) in my office with STs who volunteered to comment on the workshop. All three sources of evidence – the collective assessment session, interviews and focus groups – were sound-recorded. Unlike the phases of the workshop (which was held entirely in English), the interviews and focus groups were conducted in Spanish and were semi-structured around questions that dealt with the STs' identity and cognitive investment, the changes (if any) experienced in their pedagogical knowledge, and their expectations towards their future EFL teaching.

# Evidence of intellectual, linguistic and pedagogical developments

'This is not the kind of work we are normally asked to do at university. Normally we only have to study some contents or write reflections about external issues,' Yussel said during her focus group, 'but never think about ourselves, our past, what we have done or failed to do to be the way we are.' 'Never before had I reflected on what has made me the way I am – something I had never even considered thinking about,' added Pilar. As these quotes make clear, during the assessment session, interviews and focus groups, the STs took advantage of the opportunity to emphasize how demanding it had been for them to carry out their identity texts, linguistically and, especially, cognitively speaking. Since this was the case, it was understandable that some common discomforts arose during the initial phases: fear, shyness, misunderstanding, lack of confidence at what seemed a breach of their own intimacy, but especially the feeling of anguish at having to pinpoint the most relevant aspects of their own life and identity and justifying them in an academic piece of work. 'At first you felt ashamed, afraid, thought that your work was going to be shabby or inadequate,' said Eva during her focus group. 'I thought my life was boring and that nothing special happened to me,' commented María. 'It is so monotonous: just going to the university and back home'.

Despite these initial uncertainties, all the STs completed their identity texts. And it became clear, while observing them, that they had successfully accomplished two parallel cognitive developments. The workshop clearly succeeded in unblocking the STs' intelligence as well as in helping them improve and amplify their pedagogical knowledge. Independently of the identity traits that each of them had chosen to analyse in their videos – which dwelt on many different realities, and often did so on more than one at the same time: familial, professional, educational, cultural or more personal ones connected to specific life choices, key experiences, past relationships, passage to maturity, etc. as shown in Table 11.1. – all the STs had succeeded in connecting their selected identity traits with teaching by emphasizing the pedagogical potential that lay dormant in them. In other words, their exploration of identity in general (first line of analysis) had simultaneously strengthened and expanded their specific identity as teachers (second line of analysis).

Let me give some examples of this. Álvaro based his video on how enriching it had been for him to belong to a band and a scouts organization in his town and concluded by saying that 'with my previous knowledge of music, scouts, and art

**Table 11.1** Identity planes present in the identity texts

| Identity planes | No. of identity texts including each identity plane |
| --- | --- |
| Family | 24 |
| Professional choice | 17 |
| Educational experiences (EFL or general) at school, high-school or university levels | 17 |
| Hobbies and interests: journeys, sports, nature, and animals | 14 |
| Cultural interests: reading, writing, art, languages, music or technology | 13 |
| Love or friendship | 11 |
| Place of birth, location and traditions | 10 |
| Socio-economic level | 5 |
| Socialization inside institutions | 5 |
| Multicultural experiences | 2 |
| Womanhood | 2 |
| Vegetarianism | 1 |

(but that's another story) and my university degree, I can become a good teacher since I have lots of resources to teach wonderful lessons'. And Ana, who made her video as if she were introducing someone else, ended it by saying that 'Ana wanted to be the kind of person who creates, discusses and flies around the world. So she decided to change the world through education', hence presenting teaching as a successful synthesis of her previous and diverse interests and identities.

This synthesis was a hard one to accomplish, however. Due to the STs' assumptions about EFL teaching (which assimilated it with a strict adherence to ELT course books and materials), they found it extremely difficult to reconcile their teacher identity with the rest of their identity traits, some of which embodied the most interesting and valuable dimensions of their personalities. Many of these STs experienced this separation as an internal contradiction that led to paralysis or even painful feelings, two phenomena that I interpreted as detrimental consequences of the oppressive nature of mainstream EFL teaching weighing down on them. For example, at the time of deciding which university degree to study, Mar had had to choose between arts or education. 'It was the saddest day in my whole life,' she recalled in her video. She finally opted for education, but the problem was that she did so convinced that she had thereby relinquished her artistic talents forever. Only during the making of her video did she become aware of how much of her love of painting and photography she could still transfer to EFL lessons, for instance, by designing visual resources or by guiding her future learners through artistic tasks that would enrich the EFL

**Figure 11.1** Slide from Álvaro's identity text.

classroom. 'I will encourage creativity in the classroom for students to acquire language in a more natural way,' she said.

This workshop was based on the hypothesis that analysing the STs' wider identity would be liberating and beneficial for their development as EFL teachers. Fortunately, this hypothesis was borne out during the process. The workshop not only succeeded in encouraging the STs to use all their wealth of interests, abilities, experiences and cultural resources in making their videos, but also persuaded them to insist on this synthesis in their future EFL teaching, presenting it as an instrumental move to enrich their own lessons. This point is worth stressing. Rather than demanding that they invent and innovate in a vacuum, as is often done in teacher training programmes, the workshop conveyed the idea that teaching innovations could be an organic expression of their drawing on and integrating other cultural and experiential dimensions included in their lives and personalities (not necessarily academic ones) (Figure 11.1). In line with this thought, those STs who had an interest in the visual arts, as Mar and Ana did (Figure 11.2), drew illustrations for their videos; those who enjoyed playing music, like Álvaro (Figure 11.3), Celia and Cristina, included footage from their own performances; those who practised sports at a professional level, like Marta, shared their self-discipline, failures and successes with the rest of students; and those whose identity was defined by a variety of languages and cultures, like Consol, opted for multilingual videos in which this linguistic capital was harmoniously conveyed. And all of them expressed a desire to explore ways for these identity traits, interests or practices to form

**Figure 11.2** Slide showing Ana's drawings.

**Figure 11.3** Slide showing Álvaro playing the clarinet.

part of their own EFL teaching. As a result, the workshop fulfilled its original, emancipatory intention, precisely by making the STs realize that they did not have to sacrifice any of their present interests, cultures and experiences in order to become the efficient EFL teachers that the standard ELT common sense told them to be, since the multiple dimensions of their identity could be harmonized and originally embedded in their teaching in the same way as in making their videos. 'The final objective of this project', as Eva aptly formulated during the collective assessment session, 'was for us to get to know ourselves better and learn also how to better apply all that we have lived to our future EFL lessons.'

Not surprisingly, pride (both in their videos and in themselves) soon replaced the uncertainties that the STs had initially expressed towards the cognitive and linguistic dimensions of the workshop. María, who had voiced her fear that her life was too boring to be reflected on, concluded that many 'simple things' had shaped her own identity, but that this video helped her 'to acknowledge their worth and importance'. 'Good *and* bad,' she said, 'they form part of my past and have made me the way I am.' Violeta derived a similar sense of pride from the proficiency in English that she displayed during this workshop. She was pleasantly surprised: 'You feel good after this kind of task, not only because you know that you can do beautiful and profound things, but especially because you are capable of doing them in English, which was a challenge for all of us. It gives you a sense of self-confidence,' she concluded, 'which in turn encourages you to take on further risks in English.'

## New images of EFL teaching

As suggested above, the production of these identity texts triggered changes in the way the fifty-one STs articulated their identities as teachers, their identities as EFL learners and other components of their identities. But it did more than this, since the change brought about within these dynamics led to a corresponding transformation in the way they conceived of EFL teaching. This change translated itself into a series of positive images of EFL teaching that emerged in the videos and during the following conversations held during the interviews and focus groups. Indeed, they afforded key examples of the STs' pedagogical development, which they were eager to actualize in the near future.

For instance, several STs described the paths they had followed as language learners, ones that had led them to become EFL teachers themselves. Paz's video was representative in this regard, since it took the form of a third-person narrative that she planned to show to her elementary EFL learners in the future as a model to do their own simplified versions. Her video consisted of drawings she had done herself, illustrating situations that ranged from her early disappointment at school when she discovered that 'learning English could also be boring', to a final slide that showed her proudly presenting this identity video, while her voice said:

Now that Paz is specializing in English, she is so happy. For her, English is more than a subject; it is more than a language. It forms part of her identity. Through it, she has met amazing people; she has discovered new experiences, and cultures, and finally she has discovered that through identity texts (Figure 11.4) she can make students love English as much as she does.

**Figure 11.4** Final slide from Paz's identity text.

In a similar manner, Violeta recalled during her interview a negative anecdote from her practicum placement at a primary school the previous year. This memory not only illustrated the oppressive dynamics that unluckily continue to plague EFL educators today (which cause many to end up inattentively distorting their own teaching practice), but more than this, it also offered by contrast a vivid image of what an emancipated EFL teacher might look like some day. Her anecdote involved an elementary EFL teacher whose identity orbited too tightly around her native-like English, to the point that it had become counterproductive for her teaching since it separated her from her students. 'This teacher,' Violeta recalled,

> liked to show off in front of her students, especially when I was around, as if she needed to prove her English in front of me and make her students responsible for their own lack of learning. It was as if she needed to say, 'Look how much English *I* know – how come you can't learn anything?' I think we need to avoid these attitudes, which betray a deeper insecurity. If you believe that your own or your learners' English level is the only important element in EFL education, then the chances are that you are going to insist too much on it. ...[On the other hand] when you are finally able to free yourself from this burden, when you are able to tell yourself: 'Ok, maybe I don't know all the English in the world, but that doesn't mean I must be a bad teacher; my English level is not bad, and on top of this I know how to do wonderful things with my students' – then you can start to show your best teaching. (Violeta, ST)

As illustrated by Violeta above, the STs accessed an essential understanding from engaging in this participatory identity workshop. In the same way as it was unfair for them to be assessed as EFL teachers only on the grounds of native-English proficiency which they would never be able to attain, EFL teachers' placing too much emphasis on English language in the classroom often oppressed their learners by evaluating them only on the grounds of what they lacked and not of what they could already contribute to the educational process. This workshop, by contrast, helped the STs rediscover their diverse identity components by reflecting on the full range of cultural interests, experiences and funds of knowledge that they already possessed (Safford and Kelly 2010), and that – even more important from a pedagogical point of view – they could more easily share with their future EFL learners. These shared identity traits could give way to future innovative strategies to help them bridge the gap that the restricted focus on the English language usually opens up in the EFL classroom, separating students and teachers from themselves and from each other, oppressing both of them alike. By the end of this workshop, the participants were firmly committed to realizing this emancipatory goal in the future.

## Conclusion

Unfortunately, the way the Primary Education Programme is organized in my university did not allow me to develop this workshop at the same time as the STs carried out their practicum placements in schools of the region, which would have made it easier for me to trace the practical effects that derived from this experience. Only now, as I am finishing this chapter (a year after the experience took place) are the STs who participated in the study starting to visit schools to develop their final practical training period, which will last for three months. While I cannot make their audiovisual identity texts responsible for whatever pedagogical know-how they reveal during this coming training period, some facts already suggest that the processes ignited by this memorable experience continue to shed light on the STs' perspectives. Paz, for example, has already contacted me and asked for my guidance for organizing an identity text workshop in the primary EFL class that she is going to visit, and she still plans to show her video in class as an example for her primary students to create their own. Likewise, Ana and Violeta have decided to carry out their placements in a destitute, urban school with whose EFL staff I have just started to collaborate, and they plan to use identity texts to engage the local, multicultural students in an EFL subject that they still find too distant from their lives, cultures and interests. Unplanned or accidental as these facts may seem, they certainly hold a promise that the emancipatory effects of this workshop will continue to resonate in the near future. Other questions, of course, will surely emerge in this new phase. But I am certain that the first-hand experience of having their voices and identities heard, respected and transformed into something they could feel proud of in the EFL classroom will guide these STs towards making the correct pedagogical decisions, whatever the problems they encounter along the way.

## Questions for change

1. How can critical teacher educators expand the emancipatory effects of STs' identity texts by strengthening the connection between the STs' latent cultural capital and their emerging EFL teacher identity?
2. What can critical teacher educators do to translate the effects of STs' engagement in identity texts into innovative and emancipatory curriculum proposals for the EFL classroom?

### Funding

This work was supported by the Conselleria d'Educació, Culturai Esport of the Generalitat Valenciana (Spain) [grant number GV/2015/050] and the Vicerrectorat de Polítiques de Formació i Qualitat Educativa of the Universitat de València (Spain) [grant number UV-SFPIE_RMD15–314975].

# 12

# Globalization, Superdiversity, Language Learning and Teacher Education in Brazil

Fernanda Coelho Liberali

## Objectives

1. Discuss processes of globalization, superdiversity and multilingualism and their implications for language teaching.
2. Present the *Multicultural Education Project*.
3. Describe how play contributes to the development of a multilingual educational context.
4. Argue about the importance of critical collaboration as a tool for teacher development.

## Introduction

This chapter aims to discuss the relationship between globalization, superdiversity, multilingualism and teacher education in a Brazilian context. It displays the context created by globalization and superdiversity (Blommaert 2010; Vertovec 2007) that sustains the interest in the area of multilingualism (Martin-Jones, Blackledge and Creese 2012). After describing the extramural-research project, *Multicultural Education*, it presents the importance of play as central to the creation of an imaginary possibility for recreating realities. Finally, it argues in favour of the development of critical collaborative contexts for teacher education. These discussions are permeated by descriptions of situations related to the project, which aims at pre-service and in-service teacher education.

## Globalization, superdiversity and multilingualism and language teaching in Brazil

The flux we call globalization could be seen as a complex of processes, at 'different scale-levels, with differences in scope, speed and intensity' (Blommaert, 2010: 25). As stated by Burbules and Torres (2004), the devastating impact of global economic processes as well as the emergence of new cultural forms, global media and communication technologies seem to have intensified how people see themselves and with whom they interact. These lead to what Vertovec (2007) termed superdiversity, which is characterized as the mixture and interweaving of diversities, in terms of an assortment of significant variables that affect where, how and with whom people live.

Our understanding of superdiversity is taken as the recognition and perception of a myriad of diverse forms of being and acting in the world in complementary, contradictory, different ways that are interwoven not only in certain space-time but also within the subjects. These diversities are expanded by the interactions, which allow for the development of mobility of people within space-time.

In this regard, language could be understood as intrinsically connected to processes of globalization (Blommaert 2010). It would be viewed in terms of the mobility created by multimodal resources (Kress 2010) that subjects are required to develop as repertoires, resources and skills prior to the synchronic deployment. These repertoires provide the potential to play certain social roles, producing certain identities and inhibiting others.

This leads to an increase in the yield for multilingualism (Martin-Jones, Blackledge and Creese 2012) and, at the same time, to the fact that some languages acquire a larger number of functions and centrality in different societies, such as the one achieved by the English language (Calvet 2006). The imperialist thesis, which was used to explain the diffusion of English in the globalized world, is not pertinent anymore (Assis-Peterson and Cox 2013). English is now understood as a world language (Ortiz 2006; Rajagopalan 2008). That is, it is seen as a commodity, which was initially spread with an Anglo-Saxon tradition, but is now deterritorialized, manipulated and changed by participants from different parts of the world. Not knowing English could mean being illiterate in a globalized world, because any individual, regardless of his or her origin, has to have the opportunity and the right to manipulate and recreate it in his/her own way, generating a diversity of ways for creating meaning through English.

It would never be viewed as decontextualized from social practices and this could help language teachers and learners to move beyond the model concept of native speaker to sketch the language they are working with, without fear of ridicule (Assis-Peterson and Cox 2013). This would direct to a view of learning in a superdiverse globalized world as dynamic processes that could be comprehensive, permanent, specialized, minimal and/or ephemeral (Blommaert and Backus 2012). These different possible processes could enhance the movement of people with language resources through different social arenas, creating ways of constructing meaning together.

In Brazil, the growth of elite multilingual education together with foreign language education has become evident. Although it is a rather recent phenomenon, it has had a pivotal impact on schools. Two important issues have developed: an increase in the number of elite bilingual schools and the inclusion of foreign language teaching in the early years of both private and public schools (preschool and primary levels).

Nevertheless, according to federal legislation, all schools in the country, bilingual or monolingual, must follow the same curriculum guidelines, proposed by the Ministry of Education of Brazil, and focus on foreign language education, starting in middle school (*Ensino Fundamental 2*). Apart from that, there is almost no movement, in the teacher education programmes at the universities, to provide training in the area of bilingual education or early childhood foreign language learning. Therefore, there is no pre-service preparation for this task, and, in some cases, not even in-service ones.

Moreover, most English teachers in Brazil seem to have difficulties in disentangling from 'the seriousness, the stiffness, the austerity and the weight of the formal teaching and learning of Standard English' (Assis-Peterson and Cox 2013: 164). They are constrained by the idea that they must master and teach the four skills with the same degree of proficiency of an American or a Britisher. Many of them do not see themselves as proficient enough to use the language as a means to produce meaning with others, but see the language simply as a standardized goal to be achieved.

This attitude of teachers is infused in and reinforced by students. The episode described below exemplifies this discussion and calls for an understanding of the impacts of globalization, superdiversity and multilingualism on the processes of language teaching in Brazil. In the moment of the interaction, two middle school female students, one from a private and the other from a public school, were involved in presenting their projects in a research forum. When the public school girl visited the poster presented by the girl from the private school, the following situation took place:

> Two girls observed a poster in English at a small forum at a Brazilian university. They were both poster presenters. One was white, blond haired and dressed in very fancy clothes. The other one was black, had black straightened hair and was dressed in her school uniform. The black girl asked, in Portuguese, to the white one: 'What is written there?' in relation to the white girl's English written poster. Immediately and very confidently, the white girl started presenting her poster in English. The black girl listened attentively. When the white girl concluded her presentation, the black girl asked, in Portuguese: 'But what does it mean?' The white girl was surprised and, after a short while, started explaining everything again in Portuguese. When she finished again, the black girl looked the white one in the eyes and said: 'You speak English beautifully. You do not study at a public school, do you?' And the white girl answered: 'No, I do not.' The black girl replied: 'I was certain about that. I always wished I could learn to speak English but in public schools this is not possible.' (Report extract from the 2016 Forum LACE)

In this excerpt, both girls were involved with their poster presentations; however, issues of power were clearly marked not only in the colour of their skin, in the type of their hair, in the clothes they wore, but also in the possibility of their making meaning together.

First, while the white rich blonde girl from a private bilingual school was using English as a way to convey meaning and produce ideas about her poster, the black girl was creating views of herself as an improper user of this language and about her school as inferior to the white girl's. On the other hand, the blonde white girl could not perceive the context she was in and the social demands of the context she was participating in. She did not have a perception of the reality and its demands for a different form of interaction. She reproduced the school activity of presenting her poster in English without attending to the context of enunciation and realizing the adjustments necessary to the event she was in.

Similarly, the black girl did not feel entitled to create meaning with the repertoires built with the different trajectories she has certainly had with English in her everyday and school life. In this way, their silent moments seem to reveal trajectories as language learners that do not take into account that language is a lived experience, that observing the contexts is essential for the construction of meaning, and that there are important shifts to be made in order to develop mobility in different circumstances.

When people realize they are part of a superdiverse reality, they start to understand that the patterns of participation generally accepted as normal and determined can be learnt and, most importantly, can be transformed. Their ways of participation in reality can then be reenacted if individuals develop mobility (Blommaert, 2010) to act intensely in various activities of life, overcoming the boundaries of spaces and roles usually pre-established for each of them.

## The *Multicultural Education Project*

In order to deal with situations such as the one presented above, a group of undergraduate, master and doctoral researchers from the Language in activities in school contexts research group (LACE, from the Portuguese title: *Linguagem em Atividades do Contexto Escolar*) created the extramural and research project *Multicultural Education,* the focus of our discussion. The project started in 2008 as part of a larger programme *Acting as Citizens,* which integrated the postgraduate programme in Applied Linguistics and Language Studies at the Pontifical Catholic University of São Paulo. The programme comprised empirical studies that worked with educators' and students' development in a critical-collaborative-creative way. In the beginning, it focused only on preschool, but, in 2009, it expanded to older children, teenagers and adults.

The *Multicultural Education Project* works with English and French pre-service multilingual teacher education and is organized as a network of activities involving planning, conducting and evaluating teaching-learning activities in a multilingual perspective. All activities are conducted by the group of researchers who voluntarily assume the roles of student-teachers, teacher educators and project coordinator.

This project was conducted in two different places: an after-school institution and a nursery school, both subsidized by the city of São Paulo. These two institutions gathered people from very deprived communities of São Paulo. Since 2014, the project has not had the same type of development due to the reduced number of participants who have enrolled in the undergraduate courses for teacher education at the university.

In a critical collaborative perspective, the project presupposes that all participants (children, teenagers, student-teachers and teacher educators):

1. Become socially integrated in the additional language[1] that is being learnt.
2. Deal with scientific concepts in order to find ways for the transformation of their contexts.
3. Work cross-disciplinarily in school-like contexts.
4. Use the additional language as a tool for understanding and searching for ways to deal with the different contexts of reality.

5. Work creatively with the specific contents of different area subjects relating everyday and scientific knowledge in the additional language.
6. Produce citizenship participation for the whole community through the development, management, dissemination and discussion of knowledge with other members of the community.
7. Develop teaching-learning contexts as places for identity construction.

The project is organized in four essential activities:

1. Monthly meetings with the project coordinator, teacher educators and student-teachers, for the theoretical-practical discussion of the central themes and of the steps to be taken in the project.
2. Weekly meetings with the teacher educators and student-teachers, as co-responsible partners for a specific group of students, to plan the weekly activities in the institution where the project takes place.
3. Weekly one- to two-hour lessons for specific groups, taught in tandem by the teacher educator and/or student-teachers.
4. Participation in virtual space with e-mail messages for the planning and discussion of essential issues under development.

The relevance of the project relies on its innovative critical collaborative (Liberali 2013b; Magalhães 2010) perspective for teacher education, which understands that participants are active in the construction of their professional skills in the sense that they do not simply talk about teaching and teaching practices but engage in activities that are present in school contexts. In other words, they learn to cope with new situations and new needs in inventive ways, creating modes of acting that were never thought of before, but are closely connected with the possibilities presented by reality.

## Play/performance for creating new possibilities

Play, or performance as suggested by Newman and Holzman (2013), based on Vygotsky (1933/2002), leads people beyond their immediate possibilities and triggers critical, reflexive and self-conscious development. It involves considering how the subjects participate, appropriate and create the culture of a particular social group. According to Holzman (2009), performing is being simultaneously who you are and other than who you are. It works for both children and adults, onstage and offstage.

Performing is group-oriented, cooperative and creative without privileging cognition over emotion. This creates opportunities for collaborative and meaningful connections among people, who see themselves and others as an ensemble. When play occurs in school, the role of the teacher, as stated by Van Oers (2013), is to adjust, deepen and broaden the activity.

In this context, agency depends on the participants' abilities to break away from a given frame of action and on taking initiatives to transform it (Engeström 2005). Such a process is expanded here as one that allows the broadening of the participants' action horizons beyond the functions and duties currently assigned to them, creating the foundation for the development of mobility. According to Blommaert (2015), based on Bakhtin's concept of chronotope, mobility involves using the experiences of a space-temporal context as a basis for the construction of new possibilities of acting and producing meanings in new and/or different sociocultural and historical contexts. This perspective of agency considers the range of discourses used by the participants individually, taking into account different degrees of power, authority and validity.

In the *Multicultural Education Project*, the interplay between performance and further discussion about it creates spaces for participants to be better involved in the process of acting and reflecting by combining experiencing and discussing their performance (Liberali 2013a). In this process, participants simultaneously live two roles: the one of the performer and the one of the person reflecting about it. Their ideas and ways of acting are transformed and this transformation changes the way they understand and act in different activities. These new creative and challenging activities allow facing new situations and new needs in an inventive way, generating new solutions.

Therefore, by engaging in the performance of everyday social activities in a different language than the one they are used to, students are provided with a repertoire for constructing new ways of being and acting in the world within the scope of this additional language. The main aim as in the excerpt presented below is not the use of the additional language with focus on a native-like perspective. On the contrary, students are invited to play various situations through active engagement in the additional language.

This way, a cognitive-emotional experience is lived. Through performance, students live new ways of acting in the world, incorporating scientific knowledge, taking on positions and creating repertoires for future possible contacts. They see films, read stories, engage with different roles and, by doing so, grasp multimodal resources that can be activated in order to play the activities. They are permanently challenged to go beyond, and try more and different, possibilities. They discuss and evaluate their ways of becoming through the play situations.

In the preschool context of English teaching-learning in 2013, teacher educators, student-teachers and two- to four-year-old children experimented with the social activity of *going to bed*. In order to do that, educators planned some possible topics that could compose the performances they would work with. For instance, they selected some bedtime songs and some children's stories in which the situation of going to bed was emphasized. They also listed most common actions for bedtime in different communities and contexts (reading a story, praying, brushing the teeth, taking a shower, watching TV, singing lullabies). Besides, they thought of the multimodal resources that could be included in the play activities they planned to have with the children and which they would use as possible repertoires to be lived by the children.

Many times, some of these resources were common neither to the educators nor to the children. Therefore, engaging in the performances of the social activity of going to bed involved a challenge to all the participants. They had to learn new songs, new ways of using linguistic resources, their gestures, their ways of reading aloud, their ways of looking and kissing a child good night. They also had to study and reflect about the similarities and differences between ways people go to bed and their implications. They had to think about the context of the children they worked with – kids belonging to impoverished communities, whose houses did not even have a bedroom for the family to sleep in.

Considering people to be constituted socio-historically and culturally in relation to other people in the world, the performance of social activities such as this provided the participants with opportunities to reconstruct themselves and become agents in the world, acting and making possibilities for new future histories. They built new forms of participating and interacting in a different language and in *imaginary different worlds*. These types of performances offered them access to varied contexts that, as depicted in the third excerpt below, were never imagined before.

In 2012, W was a sixteen-year-old teenager in the second year of high school. He lived in a favela in the city of São Paulo and participated in the *Multicultural Education Project* in the after-school programme. As part of the project, students were invited to make performative presentations (All Stars) at a research group symposium. This is his report about participating in the event:

> Bro, it was very interesting because, in my view, you called us to go there only
> to sing and come back. Then you put us in there. I saw that little girl speaking in

French singing in French. ... Your daughter already used to it. ... Then I wondered, like: if the little girl is talking like this so I'll try to talk too. I will try to speak, I want to speak. Because the people, only because we had gone and tried to sing ... people said 'thank you for coming'. ... They were ... well ... were not saying: you made mistakes and that. ... In many places you see that people try to do things and some people put you down ... 'you made this mistake'.

Then I went there and started singing ... at the end only my voice appeared there. ... Then I said ah: at least we learned more. ... (It was) very worthy. ...

From there I went to my godmother's home. ... It was the birthday of my mother and my godfather together. ... Then it was full of relatives. ... Everyone was wondering where I was. ... I had to keep saying all the time, I was there: at: SIAC. I was there at the All Stars ... doing things in French. ... Oh, my godmother did not know I was studying French. ... 'French? Ah then when we go to France you'll be asking people things for me. ... Then we go to the mall there and everything is in French ... so you ask people things for me'. ... Then my godmother ... everyone was amazed when I told these things. ... She said she wanted to have this opportunity ... everyone wanted it and was talking about it. My godmother and my godfather wanted to have an opportunity like this to be able to speak other languages. ... To my family I'm quite ... I'm very proud of my family and my family is quite proud of me too.[2]

In this excerpt, W created possibilities of reconstructing his identities and creating new forms of agency for himself. W described his surprise for being thanked because he accepted to participate in the performative presentation of All Stars/Multiple Worlds. He was also very taken aback because people were supportive and did not correct or point out his mistakes. His astonishment over these reactions and his enthusiasm in becoming a French spokesperson for his family in a possible future history transformed the way he saw himself and emphasized his and his family's pride: 'I'm very proud of my family and my family is quite proud of me too.'

Differently from the first excerpt above in which the black girl felt disqualified by her lack of understanding in English and lack of possibilities to learn it in a public school, in this example, the student from the same background could build his agency and his trajectory for more possibilities of engaging in future situations.

Using performance as a means to create transformation is a way to go beyond the restrictions imposed by lived histories of these participants, creating new mobility. In 2012, the theme of the Multicultural Project was *making choices and taking decisions*. The group understood it as organizing practices in order to develop intentional and conscious movements that presuppose listening, discussing and negotiating alternatives, considering their impact on oneself, on each other, and on the general context, to, then, decide transformative ways on how to act. In order to work with this theme and bearing in my mind that there were going to be elections for mayor in Brazil, the group of educators and researchers decided to work with the social activity of *participating in the election process* with a group of students composed of caretakers and cleaning staff of the nursery school and the bilingual school that were part of the project.

The students were supposed to learn how to participate in the election process, by taking the roles of politicians and voters, reflecting and acting as both. However, these students had no previous background with using the English language as a means for acting in society. Some of them had tremendous difficulties with reading and writing in Portuguese. One of them reported that her coworkers had questioned her about her reasons for joining the class, since, according to them, she was so stupid and could never learn a foreign language.

The challenge for the educators was how to work with the language necessary for participating in an election process with these real beginners. In the classes, students were invited to learn how to be a candidate by using four essential genres: the very quick TV introduction, the slogan, the jingle and the campaign discourse that are very common in Brazil during election time. All students had the chance to observe different examples, in both Portuguese and English, of each of these genres (from the candidates running for mayor and city councillor in São Paulo and candidates running for president in the United States in that year). Examples of their participation, which were video recorded as part of their campaigns showed their deep involvement with the project:

1. Very quick TV introduction: 'My name is Susan Dias, I am from Guaianases, My number is 10.'
2. Slogan: 'I am Michael Jackson. Think in the children!' (pointing to the camera) 'Vote for me!' (pointing to himself)
3. Jingles: 'Trust meee, vote for meeee. I am the best candidate for youuuu, for youuuuu!' (singing). 'Michael is the future, future, future! Vote for me!' (singing and dancing like a rapper)
4. Campaign discourse: 'Good night, my people!!!' (standing on a chair, opens his arms when saying 'people'). 'My people, my people' (two followers stand next to him, dancing and cheering). 'My name is Michael, my party is PDR'. (points to his heart). 'My number is two, four' (shows the numbers with his fingers – 24). 'I will end corruption, I will write a law for public health. Vote for me!'

At the end of the year, soon after elections, both in the class and in the city, students reported on how they learnt to pay closer attention to candidates, their platforms, their ways of expressing fake interest in the people. According to one of the students, she had never seen the campaign videos before or studied about the candidates. During her classes, she said she learnt how to speak a bit of English and, simultaneously, to be more attentive to candidates she had to choose.

This was very similar to some other groups who stated learning the importance of reading the newspaper and watching the news critically after participating/performing the social activity of *following the news*. Students' engagement in the social activities through play/performance creates a repertoire of forms of participating in the world. As stated by Freire (1970), learning to read and act in the world was essential for the construction of who they could be. The way of planning the classes in this section is not a simple one for the educators. It happens as a result of a process of teacher education in which critical collaboration has an essential role.

## Critical collaboration for teacher education

Departing from a socio-historical-cultural tradition, based on ideas developed by Vygotsky and followers, the LACE research group relies on collaboration as a process of participation in the collective construction of living. As stated by Magalhães (2006), the founder of LACE, collaboration does not mean there will be no conflict, only that there are means of resolving it or of focusing on it to enhance learning and development.

Collaboration, in the critical perspective we adopt, is understood as a process of creating, sharing, designing, evaluating ideas. It involves deliberately making joint decisions (Magalhães 2011) through a process of critically reflecting on social-cultural-historical and political issues, interweaving the social and individual processes through language. In this perspective, conflicts and different positions are valued and creating common notions is a means for strengthening everybody's power of acting (Liberali 2013b).

In this type of research, the role of critical collaboration emphasizes the process of participation in the construction of new possibilities of becoming (Newman and Holzman 2013). It implies understanding, completing, expanding and contradicting others as well as being understood, completed, and contradicted by others (Liberali 2013b).

In 2013, this project was conducted by members of the LACE group in a preschool subsidized by the city council and located in the centre of São Paulo, which had children (0–4 years old), coming from socio-economically disadvantaged backgrounds. In the excerpt, a group formed by two experienced English teacher educators, a teacher-student and a project coordinator discussed a lesson seen on video. This was part of the monthly teacher education programme for development and monitoring of the teaching-learning activities. At this meeting, the critical discussion and the joint review of the lessons were the object of discussion. The focus was on how to create involvement of children in the play activities during class.

The meeting was held as a long sequence in which a class is seen on video and interrupted by comments by the teachers and coordinators. At one point, when the children seemed especially dispersed, the coordinator stopped the film and asked the group of teachers what was going on. As usual, the group discussed the problem situation, sought explanations and practical-theoretical understandings, tried to find ways to overcome the situation and suggested new possible tasks for the following classes.

One of the experienced teachers, however, expressed her difficulty in finding a way to deal with the fact that there were many students with attitudinal problems. She stated that while teachers were playing with a few, there were always many others who just scattered around the class. The other two teachers agreed and also provided comments on the topic. In response to this, the coordinator stood up, went to the front of the group and began to act out the situation displayed in the video. In the play activity they observed, children were visiting a zoo, so the coordinator enacted ways of participating in the situation as follows: she clapped her hands very loudly, called children's attention to imaginary animals, pretending to be in fear of them or showing surprise when she saw an imaginary lion. Besides, she used different voices, pointing to the *animals* and calling the 'children' to look and comment. The teachers laughed at this performance.

After a few minutes, the coordinator stopped the performance and one of the teacher educators said: 'I see what you mean but I do not know if I have the courage to do it' and added, 'this is not me'. The teacher-student agreed and said she thought it was very nice but she would be ashamed of acting like that. The coordinator questioned their statements and replied that they should remember that when they were in the classroom, they were just like actors on a stage. She also reminded them about a Vygotskian text they had read about the role of the actor. She asked them what the role of the actor was. After some answers, the coordinator pointed out: 'We cannot think of shame. The important thing is the experience it creates for students and how they will learn from it.' After that, a teacher educator referred to other readings and discussions similar to this one and explained how it can contribute to the students' learning. Teachers began to think about possible changes that they could introduce in their classes. However, they were still not very sure about how they felt in relation to this.

At the following meeting, the teachers reported about their classes and described the fundamental importance of the performance of the coordinator, and there was further discussion about the zoo class. They reported how it had influenced their understanding of possible ways to create interaction with the children. According to the teachers, their new combination of gestures, movements, facial expressions, tone of voice, word choice used, as if in an actor's role, transformed the way children participated in the class. They also expressed that difficulty and shame permeated the first moments of the class. However, these were quickly overcome when children's responses were so intense.

The observation of the difficult situation faced by the group started a process of reflection on possibilities that were not created by the imposition of 'what should be', but by the questioning and the performance of multiple representational forms. The observation of the video was the first factor to trigger the controversy and to generate questions for reflection. This prompted both the immersion of participants in the reality and the attempt to critical immersion. This process was not conducted by a coordinator's centralized directions, determining what the teachers should do. In fact, the performance, the exposed personal feelings and the theoretical connections with the situation set the basis for addressing the issue.

In the critical process of collaboration, the performance was a counterpoint to the problematic situations reported. It created a new perspective to see the reality and to engage participants with each other's doubts and possibilities. Teachers were taken from their immediate comfort zone. In the example, it was the attempt to collaboratively produce new possibilities of understanding the reality and of creating something unheard of, yet very valid for both the teachers and the students (Freire 1970).

## Conclusion

In this chapter, the discussion about processes of globalization, superdiversity and multilingualism was considered in relation to the implications they had for language teaching. These processes are not a choice in our lives. They are part of them. Our choice is to be critical about them and try to recreate the realities we live in a non-oppressed perspective – a Pedagogy of Freedom, such as the one suggested by Freire (1970).

It seems more difficult than we imagine because we have learnt to be oppressed. Our roles as teachers and teacher educators are to contribute to the development of a multilingual education in a superdiverse perspective, which goes against the oppressive restrictions of our present reality. We need to learn how to play with new possibilities of being and becoming. In order to do that, we must understand our roles as those of critical collaborators in the creation of new types of relationships, which can trigger new forms of development for teachers, students and the collectivity. Hopefully, the ideas presented here may serve as attempts to ignite this discussion.

## Questions for change

1. In a society marked by processes of globalization, superdiversity and multilingualism, why would language teaching and teacher education be viewed in a playful, critical and collaborative perspective?
2. How important is play in the creation of repertoires for possible ways to have mobility through possible life experiences?
3. How can teacher education overcome the traditional patterns of a presentation of a set of pre-established norms on ways of acting?
4. How can the ideas presented in this chapter contribute to teachers who want to work together in trying to go beyond their immediate possibilities?
5. How did the examples and the theoretical ideas discussed suggest possibilities for dealing with new realities with creative tools?

## Acknowledgements

I would like to thank all the participants involved in the *Multicultural Education Project* and CNPq (a Brazilian Funding Agency) for contributing to this research. I also would like to specifically thank Darío Luis Banegas, Antonieta Megale and Airton Pretini Junior for their comments and contributions for this chapter.

# Notes

1   According to Garcez and Schlatter (2012), the term 'additional languages'
    contributes to the recognition that these languages are used for transnational
    communication, that is, for the dialogue between individuals of different
    sociocultural backgrounds and nationalities. In this perspective, languages are part
    of the resources needed for contemporary citizenship.

2   This excerpt was part of the interviews conducted by Amarante for her Master
    thesis: Amarante, G. B. M. F. (2010). 'Conhecer, vivenciar, desejar: 'Perejivanie' no
    ensino em francês. Dissertação (Mestrado em Linguística Aplicada e Estudos da
    Linguagem) – LAEL, Pontifícia Universidade Católica, São Paulo.'

# Conclusion

## Darío Luis Banegas

We have reached the end of our journey. Geographically speaking, this journey finishes in the city of Esquel, in southern Argentina, where I wrote this concluding chapter. In our journey, we have read twelve different stories set in South America, Europe, Africa and Asia. They all capture the voices of those teacher educators and student-teachers who are engaged in IELTE. Such voices have been incorporated as a result of teacher research (all the authors are teacher educators examining their own programmes) or reflective formative activities such as mentoring. The chapters have illustrated ways in which IELTE can be enacted and researched at the intersection of curriculum and practice.

## Enacting IELTE

It has now become clear that meaningful IELTE programmes need to travel back in time to the days when student-teachers were primary and secondary school learners. As outlined in the introduction to this book, the IELTE knowledge base materialized in an IELTE curriculum and practices should thoroughly include those student-teachers' trajectories as learners. Their personal and shared experiences after so many years of formal (and informal!) education have imprinted powerful marks in their, what I shall call, pedagogical DNA, and innovative practices in IELTE include them in varying degrees (Edge and Mann 2013). They come armed with internal theories of learning and teaching, with stories of success and stories of failure or frustration. Some student-teachers enter and go through a course with suspicions about external theories, particularly when their observation and professional practice modules invite them to analyse and reflect on the curricula they see enacted in everyday classrooms.

In this book, Hannington et al. (Chapter 3) describe a programme specifically aimed at improving teacher preparation for primary education with a focus on literacy in a Singaporean context. In addition, we have seen how Kiai and Kioko (Chapter 4) emphasize the necessity to strengthen the alignment between IELTE curricula and secondary school curricula in Kenya. Last, Coelho Liberali (Chapter 12) suggests that alignment of theories and practices can be overcome by providing student-teachers with tools for developing their professional skills through collaborative ways of teacher research in their school contexts. These chapters remind us of the fact that IELTE programmes need to prepare future teachers for the levels of education where they are needed the most as ELT provision expands, but it should be one that is context-responsive.

Concerns about alignment between teacher preparation and practice may be the product of dissonances between theory and practice. Korthagen (2010: 99) wonders:

> Isn't this somewhat confusing, though? Many of us have frequently had the experience of learning a lot from an inspiring teacher or teacher educator, whose lectures on theory opened our eyes, who helped us understand phenomena not understood before, or at least not so deeply. We may even remember a specific book that strongly boosted our own learning and changed our worldviews. How can we reconcile such experiences with the notions of situated learning and communities of practice?

As mentioned above, Korthagen (2011) believes that one of the reasons for the gap between theory and practice in teacher education is caused by the relatively little attention given to student-teachers' prior experiences. Even when IELTE programmes take them into account, there is still the underlying assumption that effective teaching is the result of applying theories into practice and waiting for the results to emerge. They do emerge, but not in the way we think. Therefore, he suggests that we should work towards 'realistic teacher education', which places the student-teacher at the heart of the programmes, and assume a bottom-up process built around situated learning, interaction, reflection and integration of several disciplines.

Such a view emphasizes something that we all know: we do not become teachers overnight. We do not become teachers in a vacuum. We walk this path with others in context, a context we wish to understand, reflect on and transform. In terms of IELTE programme development and implementation, this undoubtedly calls for a pedagogy of language teacher education that integrates sociocultural theory, as shown through most of the chapters in this book, constructivism (see Phipps 2015), cognitive views and criticality.

An integrative position in IELTE offers countless opportunities of realization. For example, one dimension that strongly emerges from this book is that of student-teacher engagement. Engagement may have multiple causes and occur in different forms. For example, student-teachers can become engaged in curriculum reform by discussing their perceptions regarding the knowledge base in IELTE with teacher educators, as shown by Amez and Dobboletta (Chapter 1). In so doing, their engagement is channelled through active and critical participation in the delineation of their and others' pre-service development. Engagement through participation is also central in Yan's contribution (Chapter 2). Not only did student-teachers have a say in coursework development for autonomy but they also participated in action research led by their teacher educators.

In addition, engagement can be promoted through self-regulated learning. Drawing on the experiences discussed by Cuesta Medina et al. (Chapter 8), by developing our student-teachers' sense of self-regulated learning, we can empower them to assume greater participation and more democratic forms of engagement with their own formation as teachers. Reyes Torres (Chapter 10) adds that engagement could also be the result of reflection on student-teachers' own trajectories, practices and collaborative work for the development of new knowledge.

Another dimension that emerges forcefully from this book is that of identity. Identity formation, Pennington and Richards (2016: 7) observe, 'is a major aspect of growing and maturing as a human being and of defining one's place in society'. In teaching, identity refers to our positioning as professionals in the complex settings we inhabit (see Trent, Gao and Gu 2014). In the current landscape, the identity of future teachers in IELTE goes beyond the confinements of a classroom; it also includes their positioning and selves in online communities. In this book, Manzur and Zemborain (Chapter 7) have shown how student-teachers in an online environment narrate their stories in complex forms. From a critical perspective, Villacañas de Castro (Chapter 11) has underlined that exploratory work on identity formation can help future teachers emancipate and transform fossilized concepts in EFL teaching.

A third dimension that responds to an integrative approach in IELTE is that of teacher educators' development. In a recent article, Hadar and Brody (2016) observe that teacher educators have unique learning needs and that, for example, talk about student learning among teacher educators helps them become aware of their own practices, professional learning and impact on the wider community.

From a general perspective on teacher education, Saraceni's reflections (Chapter 10) have convincingly shown that moving from teacher training to teacher development requires the implementation of strategies that integrate reflection, teacher research and critical awareness of the teaching practice and observation periods and how we provide feedback to future teachers. With reference to feedback, Ma's contribution (Chapter 5) has stressed that teacher educators need to reflect and investigate their own practices as regards post-observation feedback so that their interventions and guidance can help future teachers maximize their experience in the field. In line with these interests, a recent article (Kleinknecht and Gröschner 2016) has shown that video-based self-reflection programmes can help student-teachers reflect more deeply.

If feedback plays a central role in IELTE, then teacher education can be seen as a dialogue rather than one-way instruction. Based on the experiences reported by Saraceni and Ma, we should agree with Chick (2015: 306) when he concludes:

> Despite the challenges inherent in creating dialogic spaces on courses that require formal assessment, viewing the feedback discussion as reflective conversation, can nevertheless assist in alerting learner teachers to the importance of socio-contextual factors, to an appreciation of what learners bring to a classroom, and to the fact that the path to language teaching expertise is a lifelong endeavour.

Last, Chapter 6 authored by Diaz Maggioli refers to teacher educators as ToTs. In this chapter, he has suggested that online IELTE demands the development of different formative practices. Face-to-face practices in IELTE cannot be directly translated into online spaces. Therefore, he has put forward a framework of online pedagogies that combine conceptual understanding with experiential learning mostly focused on lesson planning and implementation.

## Researching IELTE

With reference to IELTE research in a study carried out in Norway, Munthe and Rogne (2015: 23) observe:

> If a main goal for teacher education is to qualify teachers who can learn systematically, who can identify relevant literature and be critical of new research, who can use inquiry methods, and can develop knowledge necessary to improve teaching and learning for future generations of children, then we must take a closer look at how research and inquiry are addressed in the teacher education programs.

Behind such a powerful quote, we may ask ourselves at least two questions: (1) How is research taught in IELTE programmes? and (2) How do teacher educators engage in and with research?

Following the chapters included in this book, particularly Chapters 2 and 12, it may be concluded that one way of teaching research in IELTE programmes is through student-teachers' inclusion in collaborative action research projects. This hinges on the need to articulate theory and practice because research is not transmitted as declarative knowledge. On the contrary, research is explored in action as student-teachers learn about research by doing research. The effect of such an approach to research in IELTE is fruitful as Yan (Chapter 2) explains:

> The collaborative research project was commonly deemed as more effective learning than lectures. It demystified the research process to apply theory into practice, and enhanced the participants' research ability and collaborative spirit.

Similarly, Coelho Liberali (Chapter 12) has pointed out that by including student-teachers in a research team allows them to witness and be part of the process, tensions, affordances and outcomes of research carried out in the field with a direct impact on the participants and the wider community where research takes place. Such an experience should remind us that educational research, even when it is assessed as small-scale and even 'too local', should have an impact on those who are part of it regardless of their roles, as well as on the context where the research takes place. Research activities such as interviewing people or classroom observations generate expectations and concerns, anxiety even, and therefore it is ethically necessary that those who enter our research universe communicate the results of our undertakings together with the possible implications they may have in practice.

Regarding the second question posited above, we may conclude that IELTE teacher educators engage with research through the following features:

1. They do teacher research. They have researched their own institutions, their own classrooms, their own student-teachers.
2. They follow a qualitative paradigm. They engage, in different degrees, in descriptive-exploratory studies, phenomenological approaches, thick descriptions of their context, narrative approaches, grounded theory and reflection.
3. Their participants include themselves, student-teachers as well as other teacher educators.
4. Their preferred data collection instruments are interviews (individual and focus groups), journals (digital and paper-based), observations (e.g. lessons

or feedback sessions), surveys with closed and open-ended questions and student-teachers' own assignments or activities such as forum participation.
5. They favour collaborative action research.

In my Patagonian context, I often complain that research carried out by tertiary teacher education institutions usually has other levels of the education system as its target. In other words, TE-based research shows a tendency to examine what teachers and learners do in primary or secondary schools. However, the features listed above show that other roads are also possible. Teacher educators in IELTE programmes can also investigate their own practices. Their research appears to be embedded in their own practices and responsibilities. They wish to understand, reflect and transform. Their research practices are not isolated from their teaching practices. In fact, it is the outcome of such practices that informs and constitutes their research endeavours. Thus, they analyse their student-teachers' practices. This practice is less stressful and more integrative. It is less stressful because there is no need to collect 'other data'. What happens in the classroom is what becomes data, and the need to collect data elsewhere is reduced. The stress of arranging interviews, meetings, observations and other complex forms of data collection diminishes. In this regard, teacher educators' own teaching is researched; research becomes integrative and the notion of theorizing practice becomes not only possible but also tangible. Teacher educators and student-teachers examine their realities and discuss ways in which they can be enhanced, improved and recreated. The authors' questions for change at the end of each chapter are an invitation to systematize our concerns as teacher educators.

## Future directions

In the sections above, I have condensed what the authors of the twelve chapters in this book have shared with us. They show where we come from and where we are. Yet, we may also speculate about the future, what is in store for us in IELTE.

If we wish to improve IELTE programmes, then we need to overcome the division I made above. Therefore, enacting IELTE through curriculum development and formative practices should be integrated with research. As McDonald, Kazemi and Schneider Kavanagh (2013: 379) suggest, 'To realize this vision we must reimagine not only the curriculum for learning to teach but also the pedagogy of teacher education.' Such reimagining cannot be done in isolation;

we need to strengthen aspects such as collaboration and interdisciplinarity, and, above all, agency.

One area that can help us achieve the three aspects mentioned above is that of IELTE curriculum innovation and implementation. Governments and institutions around the world are under pressure to revitalize and update their IELTE programmes. As I have stated elsewhere (Banegas 2015), innovation and change should be embraced and operationalized in ways in which IELTE programmes can become sustainable, context-responsive and critical of mainstream or dominant forms of English language teacher education (see Banegas and Villacañas de Castro 2016).

The implementation of IELTE curriculum reforms should be accompanied by programme evaluation and research. Our professional community deserves to investigate, share and read more publications that answer questions such as the following: Who is in charge of curricular reforms at the levels of design and implementation? On what grounds are IELTE programmes revised? To what extent are new IELTE programmes based on in-house studies that examine aspects such as impact of the knowledge base, the transition into the first years of teaching, teacher educators' perceptions, student-teachers' perceptions and performance, and assessment practices, among others? Do teacher educators change their practices as they move from one curriculum to another? What gets changed in practice? How can we promote the professional development of teacher educators? What changes are seen in what we may call the observed curriculum in IELTE? What is the impact of each area of the knowledge base on teachers during the practicum and in their first years of teaching?

To answer these and other questions, we must work across disciplines. As the *2016 FAAPI Conference* in Argentina has recently illustrated (Banegas, Lopez Barrios, Porto and Soto 2016), we must engage in collaboration and strengthen the links within programmes, academic fields and other levels of our educational systems. Teacher education programmes cannot ignore what happens at schools. IELTE programmes then need to be built around a knowledge base that, without losing touch with a wider landscape, responds to local needs and opportunities. In a similar vein, ToTs' pedagogies should maintain an in-context dialogic relationship so that concepts such as appropriate learner-centred pedagogies, emotions, mindful teaching (see Johnson and Golombek 2016), telecollaboration (see Dooly and Sadler 2013), inclusivity, diversity, interculturality, creativity and empowerment, among others are not simply talked about but experienced first-hand. Such key concepts together with others we may add should be offered as a cohesive and synergic experience so that a sense of community of practice and shared language is lived inside and outside educational institutions. In the same way that we promote project-based learning with EFL learners of all ages, we could also organize collaborative projects at institutions that offer IELTE programmes. Furthermore, collaborative research projects can also be carried out between pre-service and in-service teachers through the support of technology (see Schmid and Hegelheimer 2014).

In relation to IELTE pedagogies, we usually equate IELTE programmes to face-to-face opportunities. Most publications in our field refer to research in classroom settings. However, issues around accessibility, mobility and time constraints are pushing in the direction of online or blended-learning IELTE programmes. The experiences reported by Diaz Maggioli (Chapter 6) and Manzur and Zemborain (Chapter 7) show two roads 'under construction': (1) we need to work towards configuring online IELTE pedagogies, and (2) we need to start researching online IELTE. It goes without saying that both should be condensed into one through, for example, collaborative action research, and also studies that combine mixed methods and offer an ethnographic view of what is happening around the world.

Such roads have implications at two macro levels. At a pedagogical level, both roads require that administrators, policymakers and other stakeholders move away from static paradigms and create the necessary working and administrative conditions that will allow institutions to provide quality online IELTE courses. Drawing on recent publications (e.g. Bolldén 2016; Kissau 2015), the delineation and implementation of online IELTE also demands not only the education of ToTs for virtual spaces but also the development of student-teachers' language practices through, for example, awareness (Mok 2013). In this fluid territory, pedagogies and supporting materials now acquire new meanings and affordances as multimodal and multi-/pluriliteracy practices (see Burnett, Davies, Merchant and Rowsell 2014; Jewitt, Bezemer and O'Halloran 2016). Imbricated in wider changes, these practices irradiate new ways of creating and engaging with knowledge generation.

At a research level, necessarily interwoven with the pedagogical level, researching online IELTE demands new skills and offers new opportunities to understand how language as situated practice, interaction and teacher education are e-constructed.

In relation to language online, Barton and Lee (2013) have suggested three approaches to the study of language online and the concomitant changes noticed in literacy and the fluidity of texts: (1) structural features of computer-mediated communication, (2) social variation of computer-mediated discourse and (3) language ideologies and meta-language. In relation to IELTE, the area of language online is critical as it provides course designers and materials writers with ways in which online language practices are appropriated and texts as physical entities can be manipulated by their users.

As for researching online IELTE, we will find no physical classrooms to observe (though recorded lessons as resources can be uploaded for analysis). However, we can navigate VLE and examine instructional materials, student-teachers' assignment and forum participations (both written and spoken), teacher educators' feedback and support, peer support, features of webinars and multimodal texts, types of tasks student-teachers engage in, self-regulation, and synchronous and asynchronous interaction among other areas. Researching online IELTE demands the deployment of online research techniques and instruments that accompany the process of pulling down walls to build fluid and hyper-dynamic realities across the globe. Such a demand affects teacher educators as they need to become acquainted with e-research (see Hine 2000).

# Envoi

I would like to close this edited book with another dialogue between Lourdes and me. The context of the situation was my showing her the manuscript of this book on my laptop:

> Lourdes: 'I can understand only a few words. And some words are similar to Spanish; those are easier.'
> Darío: 'Well, that's something positive.'
> Lourdes: (after a few minutes) 'Uncle, do all teachers who teach to teach write books or chapters?'
> Darío: 'Some do. It's not easy. You need a lot of time. But it's not impossible.'
> Lourdes: 'Imagine if more teachers could write books or tell people I did this and I did that. Maybe I can have better teachers. I'd love to have teachers that write and teach me better.'

# References

Al-Mahdi, O. and H. Al-Wadi (2015), 'Towards a Sociocultural Approach on Teachers' Professional Development in Bahrain', *Journal of Teaching and Teacher Education*, 3 (1): 89–100.

Alsup, J. (2006), *Teacher Identity Discourses. Negotiating Personal and Professional Spaces*, New Jersey: Lawrence Erlbaum Associates.

Álvarez Valencia, J. (2009), 'An Exploration of Colombian EFL teachers' Knowledge Base through Teachers' Reflection', *Revista Linguagem & Ensino*, 12 (1): 73–108.

Amez, M. (2015), '*Desire* to End Violence: Human Rights and Intercultural Citizenship in Teacher Education', *Argentinian Journal of Applied Linguistics*, 3 (2): 104–24.

Anderson, J. (2015), 'Initial Teacher Training Courses and Non-native Speaker Teachers', *ELT Journal*, 70 (3): 261–74.

Andrews, S. (2007), *Teacher Language Awareness*, Cambridge: Cambridge University Press.

Antón, M. (2015), 'Sociocultural Perspectives', in M. Lacorte (ed.), *The Routledge Handbook of Hispanic Applied Linguistics*, 9–24, New York: Routledge.

Arndt, V., P. Harvey and J. Nuttall (2000), *Alive to Language: Perspectives on Language Awareness for English Language Teachers*, Cambridge: Cambridge University Press.

Arnold, E. (2006), 'Assessing the Quality of Mentoring: Sinking or Learning to Swim?' *ELT Journal*, 60 (1): 117–24.

Ashwin, P. (2015), *Reflective Teaching in Higher Education*, London: Bloomsbury.

Assis-Peterson, A. A. and M. I. P. Cox (2013), 'Standard English & World English: entre o siso e o riso', *Calidoscópio*, 11 (2): 153–66.

Bailey, K. (2006), *Language Teacher Supervision: A Case-Based Approach*, Cambridge: Cambridge University Press.

Bailey, K. M., A. Curtis and D. Nunan (2001), *Pursuing Professional Development: The Self as Source*, Boston: Heinle & Heinle.

Baker, L. and A. Brown (1984), 'Handbook of Research in Reading', in P. Pearson, M. Kamil, R. Barr and P. Mosenthal (eds), *Handbook of Research in Reading*, 353–95, New York, NY: Longman.

Bandura, A. (1977), *Social Learning Theory*, Englewood Cliffs, NJ: Prentice-Hall.

Bandura, A. (1995), *Self-Efficacy in Changing Societies*, Cambridge: Cambridge University Press.

Banegas, D. L. (2009), 'Content Knowledge in Teacher Education: Where Professionalisation Lies', *ELTED Journal*, 12: 44–51.

Banegas, D. L. (2014), 'Initial English Language Teacher Education: Processes and Tensions towards a Unifying Curriculum in an Argentinian Province', *English Teaching: Practice and Critique*, 13 (1): 224–37.

Banegas, D. L. (2015), 'Innovation from/for the New Millennium: Where do Argentinian Universities stand?', in L. Anglada, N. Sapag, D. L. Banegas and A. Soto (eds), *EFL Classrooms in the New Millennium: Selected Papers from the 40th FAAPI Conference*, 120–31, Córdoba: ACPI.

Banegas, D. L. (2016), 'Exploring Perceptions of Curriculum Change in Initial English Language Teacher Education: A Case in Argentina', *Estudios sobre Educación*, 31: 71–93.

Banegas, D. L. and A. Velázquez (2014), 'Enacting a People-centered Curriculum in ELT with Teenage Learners', *Profile*, 16 (2): 199–205.

Banegas, D. L. and G. Manzur Busleimán (2014), 'Motivating Factors in Online Language Teacher Education in Southern Argentina', *Computers & Education*, 76 (1): 131–42.

Banegas, D. L. and L. S. Villacañas de Castro (2016), 'Criticality', *ELT Journal*, doi:10.1093/elt/ccw048

Banegas, D. L., A. Pavese, A. Velázquez and S. M. Vélez (2013), 'Teacher Professional Development through Collaborative Action Research: Impact on Foreign English Language Teaching and Learning', *Educational Action Research*, 21 (2): 185–201.

Banegas, D. L., M. López-Barrios, M. Porto and M. A. Soto, eds. (2016), *ELT as a Multidisciplinary Endeavour: Growing through Collaboration. Selected Papers from the 41st FAAPI Conference*, San Juan: ASJPI.

Banfi, C. (2013), 'The Landscape of English Language Teaching: Roots, Routes and Ramifications', in L. Renart and D. L. Banegas (eds), *Roots and Routes in Language Education: Bi-multi-plurilingualism, Interculturality and Identity. Selected Papers from the 38th FAAPI Conference*, 198–209, Buenos Aires: APIBA.

Barab, S. A. and T. Duffy (2012), 'From Practice Fields to Communities of Practice', in D. Jonassen and S. Land (eds), *Theoretical Foundations of Learning Environments*, 2nd edn, 30–65, New York: Routledge.

Barahona, M. (2016), *English Language Teacher Education in Chile: A Cultural Historical Activity Theory Perspective*, London/New York: Routledge.

Barnard-Brak, L., W. Lan and V. Osland (2010), 'Profiles in Self-Regulated Learning in the Online Learning Environment', *The International Review of Research in Open and Distributed Learning*, 11 (1): 61–80.

Barton, D. and C. Lee (2013), *Language Online: Investigating Digital Texts and Practices*, Abingdon/New York: Routledge.

Bax. S. (2002), 'The Social and Cultural Dimensions of Trainer Training', *Journal of Education for Teaching*, 28 (2): 165–78.

Bax, S. (2003a), 'The End of CLT: A Context Approach to Language Teaching', *ELT Journal*, 57 (3): 278–87.

Bax. S. (2003b), 'Bringing Context and Methodology Together', *ELT Journal*, 15 (3): 295–6.

Bedacarratx, V. (2009), *Futuros Maestros: Búsqueda y Construcción de una Identidad Profesional. Una mirada Psicosocial a los Procesos Subjetivos que se Juegan en los Trayectos de Práctica*, Buenos Aires: Biblos.

Benesch, S. (2001), *Critical English for Academic Purposes: Theory, Politics and Practice*, Mahwah, NJ: Lawrence Erlbaum.

Bevitt, S. (2015), 'Assessment Innovation and Student Experience: A New Assessment Challenge and Call for a Multi-perspective Approach to Assessment Research', *Assessment and Evaluation in Higher Education*, 40 (1): 103–19.

Biggs, J. (1999), 'What the Student Does: Teaching for Enhanced Learning', *Higher Education Research and Development*, 18 (1): 57–75.

Billett, S. (1996), 'Situated Learning: Bridging Sociocultural and Cognitive Theorising', *Learning and Instruction*, 6 (3): 262–80.

Block, D. (2003), *The Social Turn in Second Language Acquisition*, Edinburgh: Edinburgh University Press.

Block, D. (2015), 'Researching Language and Identity', in B. Paltridge and A. Phack (eds), *Methods in Applied Linguistics*, 527–40, London: Bloomsbury.

Blommaert, J. (2010), *The Sociolinguistics of Globalization*, Cambridge: Cambridge University Press.

Blommaert, J. (2015), 'Chronotopes, Scales and Complexity in the Study of Language in Society', *Annual Review of Anthropology*, 10: 1–24.

Blommaert, J. and A. Backus (2012), 'Superdiverse Repertoires and the Individual', *Tilbur Papers in Culture Studies*, paper 24.

Boekaerts, M. (1997), 'Self-Regulated Learning: A New Concept Embraced by Researchers, Policy Makers, Educators, Teachers, and Students', *Learning and Instruction*, 7 (2): 161–86.

Boekaerts, M., M. Zeidner and P. Pintrich (2000), *Handbook of Self Regulation*, San Diego, CA: Academic Press.

Bolitho, R. (2003), 'Materials for Language Awareness', in B. Tomlinson (ed.), *Developing Materials for Language Teaching*, 422–5, London, New York: Continuum.

Bolitho, R., R. Carter, R. Hughes, R. Ivanic, H. Masuhara and B. Tomlinson (2003), 'Ten Questions about Language Awareness', *ELT Journal*, 57 (3): 251–9.

Bolldén, K. (2016), 'Teachers' Embodied Presence in Online Teaching Practices', *Studies in Continuing Education*, 38 (1): 1–15.

Bonadeo, F. (2013), 'Using a Virtual Classroom in the Practicum: Innovations and Enhanced Practices', *Argentinian Journal of Applied Linguistics*, 1 (2): 79–87.

Bonk, C. J. and Kim K. A. (1998), 'Extending Sociocultural Theory to Adult Learning', in M. C. Smith and T. Pourchot (eds), *Adult Learning and Development: Perspectives from Educational Psychology*, 67–88, Mahwah, NJ: Erlbaum.

Borg, S. (2006a), 'The Distinctive Characteristics of Foreign Language Teachers', *Language Teaching Research*, 10 (1): 331.

Borg, S. (2006b), *Teacher Cognition and Language Education: Research and Practice*, London: Continuum.

Borg, S. (2009), 'Language Teacher Cognition', in A. Burns and J. C. Richards (eds), *The Cambridge Guide to Second Language Teacher Education*, 163–71, New York: Cambridge University Press.

Borg, S. (2010), 'Contemporary Themes in Language Teacher Education', *Foreign Language Pedagogies in China*, 7 (4): 84–9.

Borg, S., M. Birello, I. Civera and T. Zanatta (2015), *The Impact of Teacher Education on Pre-service Primary English Language Teachers*, London: The British Council.

Bourne, J. (2007), 'Focus on Literacy: ELT and Educational Attainment in England', In J. Cummins and C. Davison (eds), *International Handbook of English Language Teaching. Part I*, 199–210, New York: Springer Science + Business Media.

Brandt, C. (2006), 'Allowing for Practice: A Critical Issue in TESOL Teacher Preparation', *ELT Journal*, 60 (4): 355–64.

Brandt, C. (2008), 'Integrating feedback and reflection in teacher preparation', *ELT Journal*, 62 (1): 37–46.

Bray, T. M. and Lykins C. R. (2012), 'Shadow Education: Private Supplementary Tutoring and Its Implications for Policy Makers in Asia', *Metro Manila*, Philippines: Asian Development Bank. Available online: http://hdl.handle.net/10722/161051 (accessed 4 April 2016).

Building Capacity through Quality Teacher Preparation (2014). Available online: http://cuseinkenya.syr.edu/wp-content/uploads/2014/08/Policy-Brief-on-Mentoring-in-Teacher-Education.pdf

Burbules, N. C. and C. A. Torres (2004), 'Globalização e Educação: Uma Introdução', in N. C. Burbules and C. A. Torres (eds), *Globalização e Educação – Perspectivas Críticas*, Porto Alegre: Artmed Editora.

Burnett, C., J. Davies, G. Merchant and J. Rowsell, eds. (2014), *New Literacies around the Globe: Policy and Pedagogy*, Abingdon/New York: Routledge.

Burns, A. and J. C. Richards, eds. (2009), *Cambridge Guide to Second Language Teacher Education*, Cambridge: Cambridge University Press.

Calvet, L.-J. (2006), *Towards an Ecology of World Languages*, Malden MA: Polity.

Cammarota, J. and R. Romero (2011), 'Participatory Action Research for High School Students: Transforming Policy, Practice, and the Personal with Social Justice Education', *Educational Policy*, 25 (3): 488–506.

Canagarajah, S., ed. (2005), *Reclaiming the Local in Language Policy and Practice*, Mahwah, NJ: Lawrence Erlbaum.

Çapan, S. (2014), 'Pre-Service English as a Foreign Language Teachers' Belief Development about Grammar Instruction', *Australian Journal of Teacher Education*, 39 (12): 131–52.

Carless, D. (2011), *From Testing to Productive Student Learning: Implementing Formative Assessment in Confucian-Heritage Settings*, New York: Routledge.

Carless, D. and J. M. Zhou (2015), 'Starting Small in Assessment Change: Short In-class Written Responses', *Assessment and Evaluation in Higher Education*, doi:10.1080/02602938.2015.1068272.

Carr, R., S. Palmer, and P. Hagel (2015), 'Active Learning: The Importance of Developing a Comprehensive Measure', *Active Learning in Higher Education*, 16 (3): 173–86.

Carr, W. and S. Kemmis (1986), *Becoming Critical: Education, Knowledge and Action Research*, Lewes: Falmer.

Castro Garcés, A. Y. and L. Martínez Granada (2016), 'The Role of Collaborative Action Research in Teachers' Professional Development', *PROFILE Issues in Teachers' Professional Development*, 18 (1): 39–54.

Chick, M. (2015), 'The Education of Language Teachers: Instruction or Conversation?' *ELT Journal*, 69 (3): 297–307.

Clandinin, D. J. and F. M. Connelly (2000), *Narrative Inquiry: Experience and Story in Qualitative Research*, San Francisco, CA: Jossey Bass.

Clark, H. (1990), 'Clinical Supervision and the Alternatives', *Journal of Teaching Practice*, 10 (1): 39–58.

Clarke, M. (2008), *Language Teacher Identities. Co-constructing Discourse and Community*, Clevedon: Multilingual Matters.

Coady, M. R., C. Harper and E. J. De Jong (2015), 'Aiming for Equity: Preparing Mainstream Teachers for Inclusion or Inclusive Classrooms?' *TESOL Quarterly*, doi:10.1002/tesq.223

Cohen, L., L. Manion and K. Morrison (2000), *Research Methods in Education*, London: Routledge.

Conway, P. F., R. Murphy and A. Rath (2009), *Learning to Teach and its Implications for the Continuum of Teacher Education: A nine-country cross-national study*, Report commissioned and published online by the Teaching Council of Ireland. Available online: http://www.teachingcouncil.ie/en/Publications/Research/Documents/Learning-to-Teach-and-its-Implications-for-the-Continuum-of-Teacher-Education.pdf (accessed 8 April 2016).

Cooper, J. and K. Weaver (2003), *Gender and Computers: Understanding the Digital Divide*, Mahwah, NJ: Erlbaum.

Copland, F. (2010), 'Causes of Tension in Post-observation Feedback in Pre-service Teacher Education: An Alternative View', *Teaching and Teacher Education Journal*, 26, 466–72.

Copland, F., G. Ma and S. Mann (2009), Reflecting on and in Post-observation Feedback in Initial Teacher Education on Certificate Courses', *English Language Teacher Education and Development Journal*, 12: 14–22.

Corbin, J. and A. Strauss (2008), *Basics of Qualitative Research: Techniques and Procedures for Developing Grounded Theory*, 3rd edn, Thousand Oaks, CA: Sage.

Council of Europe (2001), *Common European Framework of Reference: Learning, Teaching and Assessment*, Cambridge: Cambridge University Press.

Council of Europe (n.d.), *Common European Framework of Reference for Languages: Learning, Teaching and Assessment*. Strasbourg: Language Policy Unit.

Crawford-Garrett, K., S. Anderson, A. Grayson and C. Suter (2015), 'Transformational Practice: Critical Teacher Research in Pre-service Teacher Education', *Educational Action Research*, 23 (4): 479–96.

Cross, N. (2011), *Design Thinking: Understanding how Designers Think and Work*, London: Berg.

Cross, R. (2010), 'Language Teaching as Sociocultural Activity: Rethinking Language Teacher Practice', *Modern Language Journal*, 94 (3): 434–52.

Cuesta Medina, L. (2010), 'Metacognitive Instructional Strategies: A Study of E-Learners' Self Regulation', in A. Aerts, J. Colpaert and M. Oberhofer (eds), *Motivation and Beyond: Proceedings of the Fourteenth International CALL Conference, Linguapolis, 18-20 August 2010*, 20–4, Antwerp, Belgium: Universiteit Antwerpen.

Cuesta Medina, L. (2014), 'The Role of Scaffolding in Fostering Self-Regulation in English Language Blended Learning Environments', Unpublished PhD dissertation, Universidad Nacional de Educación a Distancia, Madrid, Spain.

Cuesta Medina, L. M. (March 2016), 'From Deficiencies and Shortcomings to Bumpy Paths: Undertaking Research in Graduate Education', Paper presented at the XI Encuentro de Universidades Formadoras de Licenciados en Idiomas y II ELT Conference, Escuela de Ciencias del Lenguaje, Universidad del Valle, Cali, Colombia. Retrieved from http://universidadesidiomas-elt-english.weebly.com/

Cullen, J. G. (2011), 'The Writing Skills Course as an Introduction to Critical Practice for Larger Business Undergraduate Classes', *International Journal of Management Education*, 9 (4): 25–38.

Cummins, J. (2005), 'La hipótesis de interdependencia 25 años después [The interdependence hypothesis 25 years later: Current research and implications for bilingual education]', in D. Lasagabaster and J. Sierra (eds), *Multilingüismo y Multiculturalismo en la Escuela* [Multilingualism and multiculturalism in school], 113–32, Barcelona: ICE-Horsori/University of Barcelona.

Cummins, J. and M. Early (2011), 'Introduction', in J. Cummins and M. Early (eds), *Identity Texts: The Collaborative Creation of Power in Multilingual Schools*, 1–11, Stoke-on-Trent, England: Trentham Books.

Cummins, J., S. Hu, P. Markus and M. K. Montero (2015), 'Identity Texts and Academic Achievement: Connecting the Dots in Multilingual School Contexts', *TESOL Quarterly*, 49 (3): 555–81.

Davey, R. (2013), *The Professional Identity of Teacher Educators. Career on the Cusp?* London: Routledge.

Davie, S. (2016), 'PSLE Grading System Set To Change Amid Broad Reforms', *The Straits Times*, 9 April. Available online: http://www.straitstimes.com/singapore/psle-grading-system-set-to-change-amid-broad-reforms?xtor=CS3-18 (accessed 9 April 2016).

Debreli, E. (2012), 'Change in Beliefs of Pre-service Teachers about Teaching and Learning English as a Foreign Language throughout an Undergraduate Pre-service Teacher Training Program', *Procedia – Social and Behavioral Sciences*, 46: 367–73.

Demirbilek, M. (2015), 'Social Media and Peer Feedback: What do Students Really Think about Using Wiki and Facebook as Platforms for Peer Feedback?' *Active Learning in Higher Education*, 16 (3): 211–24.

Deneen, C. and D. Boud (2014), 'Patterns of Resistance in Managing Assessment Change', *Assessment and Evaluation in Higher Education*, 39 (5): 577–91.

Deng, Z. (2004), 'The Role of Theory in Teacher Preparation: An Analysis of the Concept of Theory Application', *Asia-Pacific Journal of Teacher Education*, 32 (2): 143–57.

Dewey, J. (1933), *How We Think: A Restatement of the Relations of Reflective Thinking to the Educative Process*, Chicago: Henry Regnery.

Diaz Maggioli, G. (2012), *Teaching Language Teachers: Scaffolding Professional Learning*, Lanham: Rowman and Littlefield Education.

Diaz Maggioli, G. (2013), 'Of Metaphors and Literalization: Reconceptualizing Scaffolding in Language Teaching', *Encounters/Encontres/Encuentros on Education*, 14: 133–50.

Diaz Maggioli, G. (2014), 'Mentor–Mentee Interactions in the Practicum: Whose/Who's Learning?' *Argentinian Journal of Applied Linguistics*, 2 (2): 23–41.

Diaz Maggioli, G. and L. Painter-Farrell (2013), 'Virtually There: Thoughts for a Principled Online Pedagogy', in M. De Castro (ed.), *Proceedings of the Fifth Modern Foreign Languages Forum*, 209–21. Montevideo: ANEP.

Dick, L. (2013), 'Top Tips: A Model for Participant-led, Shared Learning', in J. Edge and S. Mann (eds), *Innovations in Pre-Service Education and Training for English Language Teachers*, 133–46, London: British Council.

Doberti, J. and J. Rigal (2014), *Las Juntas de Clasificación. Características y Funcionamiento*. Serie La Educación en Debate N° 14, Buenos Aires: Dirección Nacional de Información y Evaluación de la Calidad Educativa. Ministerio de Educación de la Nación.

Dooly, M. and R. Sadler (2013), 'Filling in the Gaps: Linking Theory and Practice through Telecollaboration in Teacher Education', *ReCALL Journal*, 25 (1): 4–29.

Dörnyei, Z. (2007), *Research Methods in Applied Linguistics*, Oxford: Oxford University Press.

Dörnyei, Z. and E. Ushioda (2013), *Teaching and Researching Motivation*, 2nd edn, Harlow: Pearson.

Dorst, K. (2015), *Frame Innovation: Create New Thinking by Design*, Cambridge: The MIT Press.

Edge, J. and Mann, S. eds. (2013), *Innovations in Pre-service Education and Training for English Language Teachers*, London: British Council.

Elliot, J. (2007), *Reflecting Where the Action is. The Selected Works of John Elliott*, London: Routledge.

Ellis, R. (2010), 'Second Language Acquisition, Teacher Education and Language Pedagogy', *Language Teaching*, 43 (2): 182–201.

Engeström, Y. (2000), 'Activity Theory as a Framework for Analyzing and Redesigning Work', *Ergonomics*, 43 (7): 960–74.

Engeström, Y. (2005), 'Collaborative Intentionality Papital: Object-oriented Interageny in Multiorganizational Fields', http://www.edu.helsinki.fi/activity/people/engestro/files/Collaborative_intentionality.pdf (last accessed 13 May 2016).

England, L., ed. (2012), *Online Language Teacher Education: TESOL Perspectives*, New York/Abingdon: Routledge.

Erten, I. H. (2015), 'Listening to Practising Teachers: Implications for Teacher Training Programs', *Procedia - Social and Behavioral Sciences*, 199: 581–8.

Esau, O. (2013), 'Preparing Pre-service Teachers as Emancipatory and Participatory Action Researchers in a Teacher Education Programme', *South African Journal of Education*, 33 (4): 1–10.

Esteban-Guitart, M. and X. Saubich (2013), 'La Práctica Educativa desde la Perspectiva de los Fondos de Conocimiento e Identidad [Educational practice based on the funds of knowledge]', *Teoría de la Educación*, 25 (2): 189–211.

Eun, B. (2010), 'From Learning to Development: A Sociocultural Approach to Instruction', *Cambridge Journal of Education*, 40 (4): 401–18.

Faez, F. and A. Valeo (2012), 'TESOL Teacher Education: Novice Teachers' Perceptions of their Preparedness and Efficacy in the Classroom', *TESOL Quarterly*, 46 (3): 450–71.

Fairclough, N. (1992), *Discourse and Social Change*, Cambridge: Polity.

Fandiño, Y. (2013), 'Knowledge Base and EFL Teacher Education Programs: A Colombian Perspective', *Íkala, Revista de Lenguaje y Cultura*, 18 (1): 83–95.

Farr, F. (2011), *The Discourse of Teaching Practice Feedback: A Corpus-Based Investigation of Spoken and Written Modes*, Oxon: Routledge.

Farrell, T. S. C. (2009), 'The Novice Teacher', in A. Burns and J. C. Richards (eds), *The Cambridge Guide to Language Teacher Education*, 182–9, New York: Cambridge University Press.

Farrell, T. S. C. (2012), 'Novice-Service Language Teacher Development: Bridging the Gap between Preservice and In-Service Education and Development', *TESOL Quarterly*, 46 (3): 435–49.

Farrell, T. S. C. (2015a), 'Second Language Teacher Education: A Reality Check', in T. S. C. Farrell (ed.), *International Perspectives on English Language Teacher Education: Innovations from the field*, Kindle edn, London/New York: Palgrave Macmillan.

Farrell, T. S. C. (2015b), *Promoting Teacher Reflection in Second Language Education*, New York: Routledge.

Farrell, T. S. C., ed. (2015c), *International Perspectives on English Language Teacher Education: Innovations from the Field*, Basingstoke: Palgrave.

Feiman-Nemser, S. (2001), 'From Preparation to Practice: Designing a Continuum to Strengthen and Sustain Teaching', *Teachers College Record*, 103 (6): 1013–55.

Feryok, A. (2013), 'Teaching for Learner Autonomy: The Teacher's Role and Sociocultural Theory', *Innovation in Language Learning and Teaching*, 7 (3): 213–25.

Flavell, J., P. Miller and S. Miller (2002), *Cognitive Development*, 4th edn, Upper Saddle River NJ: Prentice-Hall.

Foucault, M. (1980), *Power/Knowledge: Selected Interviews and Other Writings, 1972–1977*, New York: Pantheon.

Franson, G. and A. Holliday (2009), 'Social and Cultural Perspectives', in A. Burns and J. C. Richards (eds), *The Cambridge Guide to Second Language Teacher Education*, 40–6, Cambridge: Cambridge University Press.

Freeman, D. (2007), 'Redefining the Relationship between Research and What Teachers Know', in K. Bailey and D. Nunan (eds), *Voices from the Language Classroom*, 88–115, Cambridge: Cambridge University Press.

Freeman, D. (2013), 'Teacher Thinking, Learning and Identity in the Process of Educational Change', in K. Hyland and L. L. C. Wong (eds), *Innovation and Change in English Language Education*, 123–36, London, UK: Routledge.

Freeman, D. and K. E. Johnson (1998), 'Reconceptualizing the Knowledge-base of Language Teacher Education', *TESOL Quarterly*, 32 (3): 397–417.

Freiburg, H. and H. Waxman (1990), 'Alternative Feedback Approaches for Improving Student Teachers' Classroom Instruction', *Journal of Teacher Education*, 39 (4): 8–14.

Freire, P. (1970), *Pedagogia do Oprimido*, Rio de Janeiro: Paz e Terra.

Garcez, P. M and M. Schlatter (2012), *Línguas Adicionais na Escola: Aprendizagens Colaborativas em Inglês*, São Paulo: Edelbra.

Gardiner, C. M. (2015), 'From Certificate Chasing to Genuine Engagement: The Contribution of Curriculum Design to Students' Career Intent in a Subfield', *Australian Journal of Career Development*, 24 (1): 53–63.

Gebhard, J. (1990), 'Models of Supervision: Choices,' in J. C. Richards and D. Nunan (eds), *Second Language Teacher Education*, 156–66, Cambridge: Cambridge University Press.

Gebhard, J. G. and R. Oprandy (1999), *Language Teaching Awareness: A Guide to Exploring Beliefs and Practices*, Cambridge: Cambridge Language Education.

Geitz, G., D. J. Desirée Joosten-ten Brinke and P. A. Kirschner (2016), 'Changing Learning Behaviour: Self-efficacy and Goal Orientation in PBL Groups in Higher Education', *International Journal of Educational Research*, 75: 146–58.

Ghaye, T. (2011), *Teaching and Learning through Reflective practice: A Practical Guide for Positive Action*, London: Routledge.

Gibbs, G. (2006), 'How Assessment Frames Student Learning', in C. Bryan and K. Clegg (eds), *Innovative Assessment in Higher Education*, 23–36, London: Routledge.

Gimenez, T., A. Ferreira, R. A. Alves Basso and R. Carvalho Cruvinel (2016), 'Policies for English Language Teacher Education in Brazil Today: Preliminary Remarks', *PROFILE Issues in Teachers' Professional Development*, 18 (1): 219–34.

Goh, C. T. (1997), 'Shaping Our Future: Thinking Schools, Learning Nation', Speech by Prime Minister Goh Chok Tong at the opening of the 7th International Conference on Thinking, 2 June. Available online: https://www.moe.gov.sg/media/speeches/1997/020697.htm (accessed 4 April 2016).

Golombek, P. and P. Klager (2015), 'Play and Imagination in Developing Language Teacher Identity-in-activity', *Ilha do Desterro*, 68 (1): 17–32.

Golombek, P. R. (2015), 'Redrawing the Boundaries of Language Teacher Cognition: Language Teacher Educators' Emotion, Cognition, and Activity', *The Modern Language Journal*, 99 (3): 470–84.

Gower, R., D. Phillips and S. Walters (2005), *Teaching Practice: A Guide for Teachers in Training*, Oxford: Macmillan.

Graves, K. (2009), 'The Curriculum of Second Language Teacher Education', in A. Burns and J. C. Richards (eds), *The Cambridge Guide to Second Language Teacher Education*, 115–24, New York: Cambridge University Press.

Green, A. (2014), *Exploring Language Assessment and Testing: Language in Action*, London/New York: Routledge.

Güngör, M. N. (2016), 'Turkish Pre-service Teachers' Reflective Practices in Teaching English to Young Learners', *Australian Journal of Teacher Education*, 41 (2): 137–51.

Guskey, T. (2002), 'Professional Development and Teacher Change', *Teachers and Teaching*, 8 (3): 381–91.

Hadar, L. L. and D. L. Brody (2016), 'Talk about Student Learning: Promoting Professional Growth among Teacher Educators', *Teaching and Teacher Education*, 59: 101–14.

Harmer, J. (2005), *The Practice of English Language Teaching*, 3rd edn, Essex: Pearson Education Limited.

Harmer, J. (2007), *The Practice of English Language Teaching*, Harlow, Pearson.

Hashim, N. H. and M. L. Jones (2007), 'Activity Theory: A Framework for Qualitative Analysis', Faculty of Commerce – Papers. University of Wollongong. Retrieved 7 October 2014 from http://works.bepress.com/michael_jones3/24

Hattie, J. and H. Timperley (2007), 'The Power of Feedback', *Review of Educational Research*, 77 (1): 81–112.

Hawkins, M. and B. Norton (2009), 'Critical Language Teacher Education', in A. Burns and J. C. Richards (eds), *Cambridge Guide to Second Language Teacher Education*, 30–9, Cambridge: Cambridge University Press.

Head, K. and P. Taylor (1997), *Readings in Teacher Development*, Oxford: Heinemann ELT.

Heaslip, G., P. Donovan and J. G. Cullen (2014), 'Student Response Systems and Learner Engagement in Large Classes', *Active Learning in Higher Education*, 15 (1): 11–24.

Higuita Lopera, M. and A. E. Díaz Monsalve (2015), 'Docentes Noveles de Inglés en Shock: ¿Qué Factores lo Generan?' *Íkala, Revista de Lenguaje y Cultura*, 20 (2): 173–85.

Hine, C. (2000), *Virtual Ethnography*, London/Thousand Oaks, CA: Sage.

Holdaway, D. (1979), '*The Foundations of Literacy*', Sydney: Ashton Scholastic.

Holliday, A. (2007), *Doing and Writing Qualitative Research*, 2nd edn, London: Sage Publications.

Holzman, L. (2009), *Vygotsky at Work and Play*, Routledge: New York and London.

Hospel, V. and B. Galand (2015), 'Are Both Classroom Autonomy Support and Structure Equally Important for Students' Engagement? A Multilevel Analysis', *Learning and Instruction*, 41: 1–10.

Ibáñez, M. S. and R. Lothringer (2013), 'The Future Teacher of English in Argentina: The Roles of the Humanities, of Research and of Collaboration in the New Curricula', in L. Renart and D. L. Banegas (eds), *Roots and Routes in Language Education: Bi-multi-plurilingualism, Interculturality and Identity. Selected papers from the 38th FAAPI Conference*, 198–209, Buenos Aires, Argentina: APIBA.

Iswaran, S. (2009), 'Crossing Cultures, Bridging Minds: A Role for Singapore's Languages and Literatures', Opening Address by Mr S. Iswaran, Senior Minister for Trade and Industry and Education at the SIM *University Public Forum*, 15 August. Available online: http://www.moe.gov.sg/media/speeches/2009/08/15/opening-address-by-mr-s-iswara.php (accessed 4 April 2016).

Jewitt, C., J. Bezemer and K. O'Halloran (2016), *Introducing Multimodality*, Abingdon/New York: Routledge.

Johnson, K. E. (2009), *Second Language Teacher Education: A Sociocultural Perspective*, London/New York: Routledge.

Johnson, K. E. (2013), 'Innovation through Teacher Education Programs', in K. Hyland and L. C. Wong (eds), *Innovation and Change in English Language Education*, 79–89, London/New York: Routledge.

Johnson, K. E. (2015), 'Reclaiming the Relevance of L2 Teacher Education', *The Modern Language Journal*, 99 (3): 515–28.

Johnson, K. E. and P. R. Golombek (2016), *Mindful L2 Teacher Education: A Sociocultural Perspective on Cultivating Teachers' Professional Development*, London/New York: Routledge.

Johnson, K. E. and P. R. Golombek, eds. (2011), *Research on Second Language Teacher Education: A Sociocultural Perspective on Professional Development*, London/New York: Routledge.

John-Steiner, V. and H. Mahn (1996), 'Sociocultural Approaches to Learning and Development: A Vygotskian Framework', *Educational Psychologist*, 31 (3): 191–206.

K. I. E. (2002), *Secondary Education Syllabus. Volume One.* Nairobi: Government Printers.

Kanno, Y. and C. Stuart (2011), 'Learning to Become a Second Language Teacher: Identity in Practice', *The Modern Journal*, 95: 236–52.

Kaptelenin, V. and B. A. Nardi (2009), *Acting with Technology: Activity Theory and Interaction Design*, Cambridge: The MIT Press.

Kelly, P. (2006), 'What Is Teacher Learning? A Socio⊠cultural Perspective', *Oxford Review of Education*, 32 (4): 505–19.

Kemmis, S. and R. McTaggart, (1988), *The Action Research Planner*, 3rd edn, Victoria: Deakin.

Keogh, J., S. Dole and E. Hudson (2006), 'Supervisor or mentor? Questioning the quality of pre-service teacher practicum experiences', Proceedings of Australian Association for Research in Education International Education Research Conference, Adelaide: SA AARE Inc.

Kiai, A. W. (2013), 'Am I a Robot? Teachers on Teachers' Guides', *Argentinian Journal of Applied Linguistics*, 1 (2): 23–46.

K. I. E. (2002), *Secondary Education Syllabus, Volume One*, Nairobi: Government Printers.

Kioko, A. N. (2015), 'The Integrated English Syllabus in Kenya: Perceptions and Misconceptions', Paper presented at the *English for Effective Communication; Challenges and Opportunities in East Africa Conference* at Strathmore University, 16th to 17th April 2015.

Kioko, A. N. and M.J. Muthwii, (2001), 'The Demands of a Changing Society: English in Education in Kenya Today', *Language, Culture and Curriculum*, 14 (3): 201–13.

Kirkland, K. and D. Sutch (2009), Overcoming the Barriers to Educational Innovation. A Literature Review. Futurelab. Available online: https://www.nfer.ac.uk/publications/FUTL61/FUTL61.pdf (accessed 8 April 2016).

Kissau, S. (2015), 'Type of Instructional Delivery and Second Language Teacher Candidate Performance: Online versus Face-to-face', *Computer Assisted Language Learning*, 28 (6): 513–31.

Kleinknecht, M. and A. Gröschner (2016), 'Fostering Preservice Teachers' Noticing with Structured Video Feedback: Results of an Online- and Video-based Intervention Study', *Teaching and Teacher Education*, 59: 45–56.

KNBS (2015), *Facts and Figures 2015*, Kenya National Bureau of Statistics.

Kolb, D. A. (1984), *Experiential Learning: Experience as the Source of Learning and Development*, New Englewood Cliffs NJ: Prentice-Hall.

Kolb, D. A. (2015), *Experiential Learning: Experience as the Source of Learning and Development*, 2nd edn, Upper Saddle River: Pearson.

Korthagen, F. A. J. (2010), 'Situated Learning Theory and the Pedagogy of Teacher Education: Towards an Integrative View of Teacher Behavior and Teacher Learning', *Teaching and Teacher Education*, 26: 98–106.

Korthagen, F. A. J. (2011), 'Making Teacher Education Relevant for Practice: The Pedagogy of Realistic Teacher Education', *Orbis Scholae*, 5 (2): 31–50.

Kramsch, C. (2008), 'Ecological Perspectives on Foreign Language Education', *Language Teaching*, 41 (3): 389–408.

Kress, G. (2010), *Multimodality: A Social Semiotic Approach to Contemporary Communication*, London: Routledge.

Kubanyiova, M. (2014), 'Motivating Language Teachers: Inspiring Vision', in D. Lasagabaster, A. Doiz and J. M. Sierra (eds), *Motivation and Foreign Language Learning: From Theory to Practice*, 71–89, Amsterdam: John Benjamins.

Kubanyiova, M. and M. Feryok (2015), 'Language Teacher Cognition in Applied Linguistics Research: Revisiting the Territory, Redrawing the Boundaries, Reclaiming the Relevance', *The Modern Language Journal*, 99 (3): 435–49.

Kucer, S. B. (2005), *Dimensions of Literacy. A Conceptual Base for Teaching Reading and Writing in School Settings*, London: Lawrence Erlbaum Associates.

Kuhn, D. (2000), 'Metacognitive Development', *Current Directions in Psychological Science*, 9 (5): 178–81.

Kumazawa, M. (2013), 'Four Novice EFL Teachers' Self-concept and Motivation', *Teaching and Teacher Education*, 33 (1): 45–55.

Kurtoglu Eken, D. (2010), 'Principles and Practice in Trainer Education and Supervision', *IATEFL TTED SIG Newsletter*, 1: 5–12.

Kwan, F. (2011), Formative Assessment: 'The One-minute Paper vs. The Daily Quiz', *Journal of Instructional Pedagogies*, 5: 1–8.

Lacorte, M. (2013), 'Planteamientos ecológicos para la metodología del español como L2,' *Miríada Hispánica*, 6: 21–36.

Lacorte, M. (2015), 'Methodological Approaches and Realities,' in M. Lacorte (ed.), *The Routledge Handbook of Hispanic Applied Linguistics*, 99–116, New York: Routledge.

Lantolf, J. P. and M. E. Poehner (2014), Sociocultural Theory and the Pedagogical Imperative in L2 Education: Vygotskian Praxis and the Research/Practice Divide, London/New York: Routledge.

Lantolf, J. P. and S. L. Thorne (2007), *Sociocultural Theory and the Genesis of Second Language Development*, Oxford: Oxford University Press.

Lantolf, J. P. and T. G. Beckett (2009), 'Sociocultural Theory and Second Language Acquisition', *Language Teaching*, 42 (4): 459–75.

Laurillard, D. (2012), *Teaching as a Design Science: Building Pedagogical Patterns for Learning and Technology*, London: Routledge.

Lave J. and E. Wenger (1991), *Situated Learning: Legitimate Peripheral Participation*, Cambridge: Cambridge University Press.

Lee, H. L. (2013), 'Prime Minister Lee Hsien Loong's National Day Rally 2013', Speech by Prime Minister Lee Hsien Loong, 18 August. Available online: http://www.pmo. gov.sg/mediacentre/prime-minister-lee-hsien-loongs-national-day-rally-2013-speech-english (accessed 4 April 2016).

Lee, I. (2015), 'Student Teachers' Changing Beliefs on a Pre-service Teacher Education Course in Hong Kong', in T. Wright and M. Beaumont (eds), *Experiences of Second Language Teacher Education*, 15–41, Basingstoke: Palgrave.

Lee, P. (2016), 'English Most Common Home Language in Singapore, Bilingualism Also Up: Government Survey', *The Straits Times*, 10 March. Available online: http://www. straitstimes.com/singapore/english-most-common-home-language-in-singapore-bilingualism-also-up-government-survey (accessed4 April 2016).

Lee, S-S. and D. Hung (2016), 'A Socio-cultural Perspective to Teacher Adaptivity: The Spreading of Curricular Innovations in Singapore Schools', *Learning: Research and Practice*, 2 (1): 64–84.

Leontiev, A. (1978), *Activity, Consciousness and Personality*, Englewood Cliffs: Prentice-Hall.

Liberali, F. C. (2013a), Student-teachers and Teacher-educators Experience New Roles in Pre-service Bilingual Teacher Education in Brazil', in C. Abello-Contesse, P. M. Chandler, M. D. López-Jiménez and R. Chacón-Beltrán (eds), *Bilingual and Multilingual Education in the 21st Century*, 1st edn, 231–55, Bristol: Multilingual Matters.

Liberali, F. C. (2013b), *Argumentação em Contexto Escolar*, Campinas-SP: Pontes Editora.

Liyanage, I. and B. J. Bartlett (2010), 'From Autopsy to Biopsy: A Metacognitive View of Lesson Planning and Teacher Trainees in ELT,' *Teaching and Teacher Education*, 26 (7): 1362–71.

López-Gopar, M. E. (2011), '"I Am Becoming More Intelligent Every Day": Non-native Student-teachers Liberating Identity Texts', in J. Cummins and M. Early (eds), *Identity Texts: The Collaborative Creation of Power in Multilingual Schools*, 45–57, London: Trentham/Institute of Education Press.

López-Gopar, M. E. and W. Sughrua (2014), 'Social Class in English Language Education in Oaxaca, México', *Journal of Language, Identity, and Education*, 13: 104–10.

Lorenzo, F. (2014), 'Motivation Meets Milingual Models: Goal-oriented Behavior in the CLIL Classroom', in D. Lasagabaster, A. Doiz and J. M. Sierra (eds), *Motivation and Foreign Language Learning. From Theory to Practice*, 139–58, Amsterdam/Philadelphia: John Benjamins.

Lortie, D. (1975), *Schoolteacher*, Chicago: The University of Chicago Press.

Low, E. L., S. K. Lim, A. Ch'ng, and K. C. Goh (2011), 'Pre-service Teachers' Reasons for Choosing Teaching as a Career in Singapore', *Asia Pacific Journal of Education*, 31 (2): 195–210.

Ma, G. (2009), An Enquiry into the Discourse of Post-observation Feedback on the TESOL Course at WLS. Unpublished MA dissertation, University of Warwick, United Kingdom.

Ma, G. (in progress), Supporting Post-observation Feedback in the EFL Teaching Practicum: A case study of a professional development intervention. Unpublished PhD thesis, University of the Witwatersrand, South Africa.

Macharia, A. N. (2011), 'Teachers' Strategies for Managing Challenges of Integrated English in Secondary Schools in Kiambu East region, Kiambu County, Kenya', Unpublished Master of Education Dissertation, Kenyatta University.

Magalhães, M. C. C. (2006), 'Ação Colaborativa na Formação do Professor como Pesquisador', in S. S. Fidalgo and A. S. Shimoura (eds), *Pesquisa Crítica de Colaboração: Um Percurso da Formação Docente*. São Paulo: Doctor.

Magalhães, M. C. C. (2010), 'Pesquisa Crítica de Colaboração: Uma Pesquisa de Intervenção no Contexto Escolar', in l. S. P. Silva and J. J. M. Lopes (eds), *Diálogos de Pesquisas sobre Crianças e Infâncias*, 20–40, Niterói, RJ: Editora da UFF.

Magalhães, M. C. C. (2011), 'Pesquisa Crítica de Colaboração: Escolhas Epistemo-metodológicas na Organização e Condução de Pesquisas de Intervenção no Contexto Escolar', in M. C. C. Magalhães and S. S. Fidalgo (eds), *Questões de Método e de Linguagem na Formação Docente*, 13–40, São Paulo: Mercado de Letras.

Malderez, A. and C. Bodóczky (1999), *Mentor Courses: A Resource Book for Trainer-Trainers*, Cambridge: Cambridge University Press.

Malderez, A. and M. Wedell (2007), *Teaching Language Teachers*, London: Continuum.

Mann, S. and A. Robinson (2009), 'Boredom in the Lecture Theatre: an Investigation into the Contributors, Moderators and Outcomes of Boredom amongst University Students', *British Educational Research Journal*, 35 (2): 243–58.

Mann, S. and E. H. H. Tang (2012), 'The Role of Mentoring in Supporting Novice English Language Teachers in Hong Kong', *TESOL Quarterly*, 46 (3): 472–95.

Mann, S., and J. Edge (2013), 'Overview – Innovation as Action New-in-context: An Introduction to the PRESETT Collection', in J. Edge and S. Mann (eds), *Innovations in Pre-service Education and Training for English Language Teachers*, 5–13, London: British Council.

Manyasi, N. B. (2014), 'Integrated Approach in Teaching English Language: The Practice in Kenya', *International Journal of Education and Research*, 2 (4): 253–64.

Martin, J. R. and P. R. R. White (2005), *The Language of Evaluation. Appraisal in English*, New York: Palgrave Macmillan.

Martin-Jones, M., A. Blackledge and A. Creese, eds. (2012), *The Routledge Handbook of Multilingualism*, New York: Routledge.

Massi, M. P., Z. Risso, M.A. Verdú, and P. Scilipoti (2012), 'Tagging Facebook in the ELT Picture: Developing Student Motivation with Social Networks', in L. Anglada and D. L. Banegas (eds), *Views on Motivation and Autonomy in ELT: Selected Papers from the XXXVII FAAPI Conference*, 64–9, San Martín de los Andes: APIZALS.

McCune, V. (2009), 'Final Year Biosciences Students' Willingness to Engage: Teaching–learning Environments, Authentic Learning Experiences and Identities', *Studies in Higher Education*, 34 (3): 347–61.

McDonald, M., E. Kazemi and S. Schneider Kavanagh (2013), Core Practices and Pedagogies of Teacher Education: A Call for a Common Language and Collective Activity', *Journal of Teacher Education*, 64 (5): 378–86.

McDonough, J., C. Shaw and H. Masuhara (2013), *Materials and Methods in ELT. A Teacher's Guide*, 3rd edn, Oxford: Wiley-Blackwell.

McFarlane, K. J. (2016), 'Tutoring the Tutors: Supporting Effective Personal Tutoring', *Active Learning in Higher Education*, doi: 1469787415616720.

McNiff, J. (2010), *Action Research for Professional Development: Concise Advice for New (and Experienced) Action Researchers*, Dorset: September Books.

McNiff, J., P. Lomax and J. Whitehead (1996), *You and Your Action Research Project*, London: Routledge.

McThige, J. and G. Wiggins (2007), *Understanding by Design*, 2nd edn, Alexandria, VA: ASCD.

Menard-Warwick, J. (2014), *English Language Teachers on the Discursive Faultlines. Identities, Ideologies and Pedagogies*, Clevedon: Multilingual Matters.

Meyer, L. M. (2007), 'Methods, Meanings and Education Policy in the United States', In J. Cummins and C. Davison (eds), *International Handbook of English Language Teaching*, 211–28, New York: Springer.

Ministry of Education. (2010), 'English Language Syllabus 2010', *Ministry of Education, Singapore*. Available online: http://www.moe.gove.sg/docs/defaultsource/document/education/syllabuses/english-language-and-literature/files/english-primary-secondary-express-noraml-academic.pdf (accessed 4 April 2016).

Ministry of Education. (2016), 'Desired Outcomes of Education', Ministry of Education, Singapore. Available online: https://www.moe.gov.sg/education/education-system/desired-outcomes-of-education (accessed 4 April 2016).

Moirano, M. C. (2012), 'Teaching the Students and not the Book: Addressing the Problem of Culture in Teaching in EFL in Argentina', *Gist Education and Learning Research Journal*, 6: 71–96.

Mok, J. (2013), 'A Case Study of Developing Student-teachers' Language Awareness through Online Discussion Forums', *Language Awareness*, 22 (2): 161–75.

Mol, S. E., A. G. Bus, M. T. de Jong and D. J. H. Smeets (2008), 'Added Value of Dialogic Parent-Child Book Readings: A Meta-Analysis', *Early Education and Development*, 19 (1): 7–26.

Morrow, L. M. (2012), *Literacy Development in the Early years: Helping Children Read and Write*, 7th edn, Boston: Pearson.

Motteram, G. (2013), 'Developing and Extending our Understanding of Language Learning and Technology', in G. Motteram (ed.), *Innovations in Learning Technologies for English Language Teaching*, 177–91, London: British Council.

Mugford, G. (2015), 'Participative Investigation: Narratives in Critical Research in the EFL Classroom', in S. Borg and H. S. Sanchez (eds), *International Perspectives on Teacher Research*, 87–97, Basingstoke: Palgrave.

Munthe, E. and M. Rogne (2015), 'Research Based Teacher Education', *Teaching and Teacher Education*, 46: 17–24.

Muscará, F. (2013), 'Problems and Challenges of Educational Policies in Latin America. The Argentina Viewpoint', *New Approaches in Educational Research*, 2 (2): 109–16.

Musfirah, H. A. K. (2016), 'Primary School Teachers to Specialise in Two Subjects: MOE', *Channel News Asia*, 20 February. Available online: http://www.channelnewsasia.com/news/singapore/primary-school- teachers/2533332.html (accessed 4 April 2016).

Muthwii, M. J. and A. N. Kioko (2002), 'Whose English in Kenyan Schools? A Case for a Nativized Variety', *CHEMICHEMI: International Journal of the School of Humanities and Social Sciences*, 2 (1): 78–86.

Narvet, K., C. Saraceni and I. Sari (in preparation), 'Ways of Assessing Teaching Practice'.

Newman, F. and L. Holzman (2013), *Lev Vygotsky: Revolutionary Scientist*, New York: Psychology Press.

Newton, C. and T. Tarrant (1992), *Managing Change in Schools*, New York: Routledge.

Ng, S. M. and C. Sullivan (2001), 'The Singapore Reading and English Acquisition Program', International *Journal of Educational Research*, 35 (2): 157–67.

Ngo, T. and L. Unsworth (2015), 'Reworking the Appraisal Framework in ESL Research: Refining Attitude Resources', *Functional Linguistics*, 2 (1). Available online: http://functionallinguistics.springeropen.com/articles/10.1186/s40554-015-0013-x

Nguyen, L. T. and M. Ikeda (2015), 'The Effects of ePortfolio-based Learning Model on Student Self-regulated Learning', *Active Learning in Higher Education*, 16 (3): 197–209.

Nguyen, M. (2013), 'The Curriculum for English Language Teacher Education in Australian and Vietnamese Universities', *Australian Journal of Teacher Education*, 38 (11): 33–53.

Njagi, M. W., C. K. Muriuni and C. A. Peter (2014), 'Effectiveness of Professional Development of English and Literature Teachers in Selected Schools in Tharaka-Nithi and Meru County, Kenya', *American International Journal of Contemporary Research*, 4 (8): 142–8.

Northcote, M. and C. P. Lim (2009), 'The State of Pre-service Teacher Education in the Asia-Pacific Region', in C. P. Lim, K. Cock, and C. Brook (eds), *Innovative Practices in Pre-service Teacher Education: An Asia-Pacific Perspective*, 23–38, Rotterdam, Netherlands: Sense Publishers.

Norton, B. (2013), *Identity and Language Learning, Extending the Conversation*, 2nd edn, Clevedon: Multilingual Matters.

Norton, B. and K. Toohey (2011), 'Identity, Language Learning, and Social Change', *Language Teaching*, 44 (4): 412–46.

Nunan, D. (2005), *Research Methods in Language Learning*, Cambridge: Cambridge University Press.

Nunan. D. and K. M. Bailey (2009), *Exploring Second Language Classroom Research: A Comprehensive Guide*, Boston: Heinle-Cengage Learning.

Ochieng' Ong'ondo, C. and S. Borg (2011), '"We Teach Plastic Lessons to Please Them": The Influence of Supervision on the Practice of English Language Student Teachers in Kenya', *Language Teaching Research*, 15 (4): 509–28.

Ong'ondo, C. O. (2009), 'Pedagogical Practice and Support of English Language Student-teachers During the Practicum in Kenya', Unpublished PhD thesis, Leeds University.

Ongong'a, J. O., M. O. Okwara and K. N. Nyangara (2010), 'Using Integrated Approach in Teaching and Learning at the Secondary School Level in Kenya', *International Research Journals: Educational Research*, 1 (11): 618–23.

Ortiz, R. (2006), *Cultura Brasileira e Identidade Nacional*. São Paulo: Brasiliense.

Otto, T. and R. C. Smith (2013), 'Design Anthropology: A Distinct Style of Knowing', in W. Gunn, T. Otto and R. C. Smith (eds), *Design Anthropology: Theory and Practice*, London: Bloomsbury.

Palfreyman, D. (2006), 'Social Context and Resources for Language Learning', *System*, 34 (3): 352–70.

Pang, E. S., F. V. Lim, K. C. Choe, C. Peters and L. C. Chua (2015), 'System Scaling in Singapore: The STELLAR Story', in C. K. Looi and L.W. Teh, (eds), *Scaling Educational Innovations*, 105–22, Singapore: Springer.

Pennington, M. C. and J. C. Richards (2016), 'Teacher Identity in Language Teaching: Integrating Personal, Contextual, and Professional Factors', *RELC Journal*, 47 (1): 15–23.

Pennycook, A. (2001), *Critical Applied Linguistics: A Critical Introduction*, Mahwah, NJ/London: Lawrence Erlbaum Associates Publishers.

Pérez Gómez, A. I., M. Sola Fernández, E. Soto Gómez and J. F. Murillo Mas (2013), 'The Impact of Action Research in the Spanish Schools in the Post-Franco Era', in S. Noffke and B. Somekh (eds), *The SAGE Handbook of Educational Action Research*, 481–94, Los Angeles: SAGE.

Petty, G. (2014). *Teaching Today: A Practical Guide*, 5th edn, Oxford: Oxford University Press.

Phipps, S. (2015), 'Constructivist Language Teacher Education: An Example from Turkey', in T. S. C. Farrell (ed.), *International Perspectives on English Language Teacher Education*, 16–35, Basingstoke: Palgrave.

Pinahs-Schultz, P. and B. Beck (2015), 'Development and Assessment of Signature Assignments to Increase Student Engagement in Undergraduate Public Health', *Pedagogy in Health Promotion*, doi: 2373379915606454.

Pintrich, P. R. (2000), 'The Role of Goal Orientation in Self-Regulated Learning', in M. Boekaerts, P. Pintrich and M. Zeidner (eds), *Handbook of Self-Regulation*, 451–502, San Diego, CA: Academic Press.

Pollard, A. (2014), *Reflective Teaching in Schools*, London: Bloomsbury.

Porto, M. (2010), 'Culturally Responsive L2 Education: an Awareness-raising Proposal', *ELT Journal*, 64 (1): 45–53.

Porto, M. (2015), 'Concluding Remarks. Beyond Foreign Language Teaching: Intercultural Citizenship and Human Rights Education in Practice', *Argentinian Journal of Applied Linguistics*, 3 (2): 139–47.

Porto, M., A. Montemayor-Borsinger and M. López-Barrios (2016), 'Research on English Language Teaching and Learning in Argentina (2007–2013)', *Language Teaching*, 49 (3): 356–89.

Rajagopalan, K. (2008), 'Política Linguística e a Política da Linguística', in D. Simões and C. C. Henriques (eds), *Língua Portuguesa, Educação & Mudança*, 11–22, Rio de Janeiro, Ed. Europa.

Randall, M. and B. Thornton (2001), *Advising and Supporting Teachers*, Cambridge: Cambridge University Press.

Reyes Torres, A. (2014), 'Literacy Education: The First Step towards Literary Competence', in A. Reyes Torres, L. S. Villacañas-de-Castro and B. Soler-Pardo (eds), *Thinking Through Children's Literature in the Classroom*, 42–52, Cambridge: Cambridge Scholar Publishing.

Reyes Torres, A. and A. R. Bird (2015), 'Reshaping Curriculum to Enhance the Relevance of Literary Competence in Children's Education', *Childhood Education*, 91 (1): 9–15.

Richards, J. C. (2010), 'Competence and-Performance in Language Teaching', *RELC Journal*, 41 (2): 101–22.

Richards, J. C. (2015), *Key Issues in Language Teaching*, Cambridge: Cambridge University Press.

Richards, J. C. and T. Rodgers (2014), *Approaches and Methods in Language Teaching*, 3rd edn, New York, NY: Cambridge University Press.

Rixon, S. (2015), 'Primary English and Critical Issues: A Worldwide Perspective', in J. Bland (ed.), *Teaching English to Young Learners. Critical Issues in Language Teaching with 3-12 Year Olds*, 31–50, London/New York: Bloomsbury Academic.

Roberts, T. and L. Billings. (2008), 'Thinking is Literacy, Literacy Thinking', *Educational Leadership*, 65 (5): 32–36.

Rodgers, C. (2002), 'Defining Reflection: Another Look at John Dewey and Reflective Thinking', *Teachers College Record*, 104 (4): 842–66.

Ruegg, R. (2015), 'Differences in the uptake of Peer and Teacher Feedback', *RELC Journal*, 46 (2): 131–45.

Ruiz, M. C. and S. Schoo (2014), 'La Obligatoriedad de la Educación Secundaria en América Latina. Convergencias y Divergencias en Cinco Países', *Foro de Educación*, 12 (16): 71–98.

Ruiz, T., E. Mandel, C. Jones, T. Grotzer and C. E. Anderson (1998), 'Everyday Classroom Tools: Observing the World around Us: An Inquiry-Based Science Curriculum for Kindergarten through Sixth Grade', *Harvard-Smithsonian Center for Astrophysics*, Cambridge, MA: Smithsonian Astrophysical Observatory/NASA's Learning Technologies Project.

Safford, K. and A. Kelly (2010), 'Linguistic Capital of Trainee Teachers: Knowledge Worth Knowing', *Language and Education*, 24 (5): 401–14.

Sambell, K., L. McDowell and C. Montgomery (2013), *Assessment for Learning in Higher Education*, London: Routledge.

Sanchez, H. S. (2010), 'An Investigation into the Relationships among Experience, Teacher Cognition, Context, and Classroom Practice in EFL Grammar Teaching in Argentina', Unpublished PhD thesis, University of Warwick, UK.

Saraceni, C. (2013), 'Adapting Courses: A Personal View', in Tomlinson, B. (ed.), *Developing Materials for Language Teaching*, 2nd edn, 49–62, London, New York: Bloomsbury

Sarasa, M. (2013), 'Narrative Inquiry within Argentinean EFLTE: Crafting Professional Identities and Knowledge through Students' Narratives', in L. Renart and D. L. Banegas (eds), *Roots and Routes in Language Education. Bi/Multi/Plurilingualism, Interculturality and Identity: Selected Papers from the 38th FAAPI Conference*, 44–55, Buenos Aires: APIBA.

Schmid, E. C. and V. Hegelheimer (2014), 'Collaborative Research Projects in the Technology-enhanced Language Classroom: Pre-service and In-service Teachers Exchange Knowledge about Technology', *ReCALL Journal*, 26 (3): 315–32.

Schon, D. (1987), *Educating the Reflective Practitioner*, San Francisco: Jossey-Bass.

Schunk, D. and B. Zimmerman (1998), *Self-Regulated Learning: From Teaching to Self-Reflective Practice*, New York, NY: Guilford Press.

Schunk, D. and B. Zimmerman (2008), *Motivation and Self-Regulated Learning: Theory, Research, and Applications*, New Jersey: Erlbaum.

Scrivener, J. (2011), *Learning Teaching: The Essential Guide to English Language Teaching*, 3rd edn, London: Macmillan.

Sharma, B. R. and P. K. Bhaumik (2013), 'Student Engagement and its Predictors: An Exploratory Study in an Indian Business School', *Global Business Review*, 14 (1): 25–42.

Shulman, L. (1983), 'Autonomy and Obligation: The Remote Control of Teaching', in L. Shulman and G. Sykes (eds), *Handbook of Teaching and Policy*, 484–504, New York: Longman.

Shulman, L. (1986), 'Those Who Understand: Knowledge Growth in Teaching',
   *Educational Researcher*, 15 (2): 4–14.

Shulman, L. (1987), 'Knowledge and Teaching: Foundations of the New Reform',
   *Harvard Educational Review*, 57 (1): 1–22.

Simon, H. A. (1986), *The Sciences of the Artificial*, Cambridge: Massachusetts Institute
   of Technology.

Singapore Department of Statistics (2015), 'Population Trends', Department of Statistics
   Singapore. Available online: http://www.singstat.gov.sg/publications/publications-
   and-papers/population-and-population-structure/population-trends (accessed
   4 April 2016).

Singh, A. K. and S. Srivastava (2014), 'Development and Validation of Student
   Engagement Scale in the Indian Context', *Global Business Review*, 15 (3): 505–15.

Smolcic, E. (2011), 'Becoming a Culturally Responsive Teacher: Personal
   Transformation and Shifting Identities during an Immersion Experience Abroad', in
   K. Johnson and P. Golombek (eds), *Research on Second language Teaching Education.
   A Sociocultural Perspective on Professional Development*, 15–30, Abingdon:
   Routledge.

Sugrue, C. and C. Day, eds. (2002) *Developing Teachers and Teaching Practice: Internal
   Research Perspectives*, London and New York: Routledge Falmer.

Swain, M., P. Kinnear and L. Steinman (2011), *Sociocultural Theory in Second Language
   Education: An Introduction through Narratives*, Bristol: Multilingual Matters.

Swain, M., P. Kinnear and L. Steinman (2015), *Sociocultural Theory in Second Language
   Education: An Introduction through Narratives*, 2nd edn, Bristol: Multilingual Matters.

Tam, K. Y., M. A. Heng and G. H. Jiang (2009), What Undergraduate Students in China
   say about their Professors' Teaching', *Teaching in Higher Education*, 14 (2): 147–59.

Tarnopolsky, O. (2008), 'Nonnative Speaking Teachers of English as a Foreign
   Language', in N. Van Deusen-Scholl and N. H. Hornberger (eds), *Encyclopedia of
   Language and Education*, 2nd edn, 309–21, Philadelphia: Springer.

Tarone, E. and D. Allwright (2005), 'Second Language Teacher Learning and Student
   Second Language Learning: Shaping the Knowledge Base', in D. Tedick (ed.), *Second
   Language Teacher Education*, 5–24, Mahwah, NJ: Erlbaum.

Taylor, S. A., G. L. Hunter, H. Melton and S. A. Goodwin (2011), 'Student Engagement
   and Marketing Classes', *Journal of Marketing Education*, 33 (1): 73–92.

Terigi, F. (2009), 'La Formación Inicial de Profesores de Educación Secundaria:
   Necesidades de Mejora, Reconocimiento de sus Límites', *Revista de Educación*, 350:
   123–44.

Tharman, S. (2004), 'MOE Work Plan Seminar Speech 2004', Speech by Minister of
   Education Tharman Shanmugaratnam, 29 September. Available online: https://www.
   moe.gov.sg/media/speeches/2004/sp20040929.htm (accessed 4 April 2016).

Thornton, M. and I. Reid (2001a), 'Primary School Teaching as A Career: The Views of
   the Successfully Recruited', *Journal of Education for Teaching*, 27 (1): 111–12.

Thornton, M. and I. Reid (2001b), 'Primary Teacher Recruitment: Careers Guidance and Advice', *Education 3–13*, 29 (2): 49–54.

Thornton, M., P. Bricheno and I. Reid (2002), 'Students Reasons For Wanting to Teach in Primary School', *Research in Education*, 67: 33–43.

Timperley, H. (2001), 'Mentoring Conversations Designed to Promote Student Teacher Learning', *Asia Pacific Journal of Teacher Education*, 29 (2): 111–23.

Tomlinson, B. (2003), 'Developing Materials to Develop Yourself', *Humanising Language Teaching*, 5 (4). Available online: http://www.hltmag.co.uk/jul03/mart1.htm

Tomlinson, B., ed. (2013), *Developing Materials for Language Teaching*, 2nd edn, London, New York: Bloomsbury.

Tormey, R. and D. Henchy (2008), 'Re-imagining the Traditional Lecture: An Action Research Approach to Teaching Student Teachers to "Do" Philosophy', *Teaching in Higher Education*, 13: 303–14.

Trent, J., X. Gao and M. Gu (2014), *Language Teacher Education in a Multilingual Context: Experiences from Hong Kong*, London/New York: Springer.

Tsui, A. and M. Ng (2000), 'Do Secondary L2 Writers Benefit from Peer Comments?' *Journal of Second Language Writing*, 9: 147–70.

Tyler, R. W. (1949), *Basic Principles of Curriculum and Instruction*, Chicago: The University of Chicago Press.

Ulvik, M. and H. Riese (2016), 'Action Research in Pre-service Teacher Education – A Never-ending Story Promoting Professional Development', *Professional Development in Education*, 42 (3): 441–57.

Ushioda, E. (2009), 'A Person-in-context Relational View of Emergent Motivation, Self and Identity', in Z. Dörnyei and E. Ushioda (eds), *Motivation, Language and the L2 Self*, 215–28, Clevedon: Multilingual Matters.

Ushioda, E. (2011), 'Motivating Learners to Speak as Themselves', in G. Murray, G. Xuesong and T. Lamb (eds), *Identity, Motivation and Autonomy in Language Learning*, 11–24, Clevedon: Multilingual Matters.

Van Oers, B. (2013), 'Is it Play? Towards a Reconceptualization of Role-play from an Activity Theory Perspective', *European Early Childhood Education Research Journal*, 21 (2): 185–98.

Van Sluys, K. (2010), 'Trying On and Trying Out: Participatory Action Research as a Tool for Literacy and Identity Work in Middle Grades Classrooms', *American Journal of Psychology*, 46: 139–51.

Varghese, M., B. Morgan, B. Johnston and K. A. Johnson (2005), 'Theorizing Language Teacher Identity: Three Perspectives and Beyond', *Journal of Language, Identity & Education*, 4 (1): 21–44.

Vertovec, S. (2007), 'Super-diversity and its Implications', *Ethnic and Racial Studies*, 30 (6): 1024–54.

Villacañas de Castro, L. S. (2014a), 'Meta-action Research with Preservice Teachers: a Case Study', *Educational Action Research*, 22 (4): 534–51.

Villacañas de Castro, L. S. (2014b), 'Epistemology and Pedagogy Re-examined. The Unsuspected Potential of John Elliott's "Liberal" Pedagogy for Teaching Content-Goals in the Social and Human Sciences,' *Teoría de la Educación*, 26 (2): 93–113.

Villacañas de Castro, L. S. (2015), '"Why Should I Study English If I'm Never Going to Leave This Town?" Developing Alternative Orientations to Culture in the EFL Classroom through CAR,' *Review of Education, Pedagogy, and Cultural Studies*, 37 (4): 289–307.

Vitanova, G. (2010), *Authoring the Dialogic Self: Gender, Agency and Language Practices*, Amsterdam/Philadelphia: John Benjamins.

Vygotsky, L. (1978), *Mind in Society. The Development of Higher Psychological Processes*, Cambridge: Harvard University Press.

Vygotsky, L. S. (1933/2002), 'Play and its Role in the Mental Development of the Child', http://www.marx.org/archive/vygotsky/works/1933/play.htm (last accessed 13 May 2016).

Vygotsky, L. S. (1986), *Thought and Language*, Cambridge: The MIT Press.

Wach, A. (2015), 'Promoting Pre-Service Teachers' Reflections through a Cross-Cultural Keypal Project', *Language Learning & Technology*, 19 (1): 34–45.

Wajnryb, R. (1994), The Pragmatics of Feedback: A Study of Mitigation in the Supervisory Discourse of TESOL Teacher Educators. Unpublished doctoral dissertation, Macquarie University, Sydney, Australia.

Wallace, M. (1991), *Education Foreign Language Teachers*, Cambridge: Cambridge University Press.

Wang, J. (2001), 'Contexts of Mentoring and Opportunities for Learning How to Teach: A Comparative Study of Mentoring Practices,' *Teaching and Teacher Education Journal*, 17: 51–73.

Wang, Q. (2009), 'Retrospects and Prospects of Chinese Basic Foreign Language Education in the Past Thirty Years after the Implementation of the Open-door Policy', *Foreign Language Teaching in Schools*, 32 (2): 1–5.

Wedell, M. (2009), *Planning for Educational Change: Putting People and their Contexts First*, London: Continuum.

Wells, G. (1986), 'Conversation and the Reinvention of Knowledge,' in A. Polland (ed.), *Readings for Reflective Teaching*, 235–37, London: Continuum.

Wentling, T. L., J. Park and C. Peiper (2007), 'Learning Gains Associated with Annotation and Communication Software Designed for Large Undergraduate Classes', *Journal of Computer Assisted Learning*, 23 (1): 36–46.

West, B., H. Moore and B. Barry (2015), 'Beyond the Tweet: Using Twitter to Enhance Engagement, Learning, and Success among First-year Students', *Journal of Marketing Education*, 37 (3): 160–70.

Westbrook, J., N. Durrani, R. Brown, D. Orr, J. Pryor, J. Boddy and F. Salvi (2013), 'Pedagogy, Curriculum, Teaching Practices and Teacher Education in Developing Countries', Final Report. *Education Rigorous Literature Review*. Department for International Development.

Wolf-Wendel, L., K. Ward and J. Kinzie (2009), 'A Tangled Web of Terms: The Overlap and Unique Contribution of Involvement, Engagement, and Integration to Understanding College Student Success', *Journal of College Student Development*, 50 (4): 407–28.

Wong, J. K-K. (2004), 'Are the Learning Styles of Asian International Students Culturally or Contextually Based?' *International Education Journal*, 4 (4): 154–66.

Wong, R. (2011), 'Why Education is Key Leveller in Singapore', *AsiaOne*, 8 March. Available online: http://news.asiaone.com/News/AsiaOne+News/Singapore/Story/A1Story20110308-266982.html (accessed 4 April 2016).

Wong, Y. L. R. (2010), *Developing Literacy in the English Classroom: Engaging Primary Pupils*, Singapore: Pearson Prentice Hall.

Wright, T. (2010), 'Second Language Teacher Education: Review of Recent Research on Practice', *Language Teaching*, 43 (3): 259–96.

Wright, T. and M. Beaumont, M., eds. (2015), *Experiences of Second Language Teacher Education*, Basingstoke: Palgrave.

Wright, T. and R. Bolitho (1993), 'Language Awareness: A Missing Link in Language Teacher Education?' *ELT Journal*, 47 (4): 292–304.

Yang, C. (2016), 'Changes to PSLE grading: What could be in store?' *The Straits Times*. 3 April. Available online: http://www.straitstimes.com/singapore/education/changes-to-psle-grading-what-could-be-in-store?xtor=CS3-18 (accessed 4 April 2016).

Yates, R. and D. Muchisky (2003), 'On Re-conceptualizing Teacher Education', *TESOL Quarterly*, 37 (1): 135–47.

Yeasmin, N., A. K Azad and J. Ferdoush (2011), 'Teaching Language through Literature: Designing Appropriate Classroom Activities', *ASA University Review*, 5 (2): 283–97.

Yetkin Özdemir, İ. E. (2011), 'Self-Regulated Learning from a Sociocultural Perspective', *Education and Science*, 36 (160): 298–308.

Zeichner, K. (2010), 'Rethinking the Connections between Campus Courses and Field Experiences in College and University-based Teacher Education Programs', *Journal of Teacher Education*, 89 (11): 89–99.

Zepke, N. (2013), 'Threshold Concepts and Student Engagement: Revisiting Pedagogical Content Knowledge', *Active Learning in Higher Education*, 14 (2): 97–107.

Zhang, F. and J. Zhan (2014), 'The Knowledge Base of Non-native English Speaking Teachers: Perspectives of Teachers and Administrators', *Language and Education*, 28 (6): 568–82.

Zhang, L. (2006), 'Preferred Teaching Styles and Modes of Thinking among University Students in Mainland China', *Thinking Skills and Creativity*, 1 (2): 95–107.

Zhang, Z., W. H. Hu and O. McNamara (2015), 'Undergraduate Student Engagement at a Chinese University: A Case Study', *Educational Assessment, Evaluation and Accountability*, 27 (2): 105–27.

Zhu, C. and N. Engels (2014), 'Organizational Culture and Instructional Innovations in Higher Education: Perceptions and Reactions of Teachers and Students', *Educational Management Administration Leadership*, 42 (1): 136–58.

# Index